Advance Praise for *to the*

"*to the moon and back* is a wild and ho.̤ ̤ .̤ .̤ .̤ that makes sense of complex and sometimes painful experiences with heart, grit, and courage. Lisa's energy, infectious positivity, and transparency about her own life journey and all its twists and turns will inspire any woman who's looking for the light at the end of the tunnel."
—**Kelly McNelis**, founder of Women For One, author of *Your Messy Brilliance*

"Lisa Kohn writes with an honesty that will grip you immediately and take you on her harrowing, expansive journey. You won't be able to help yourself. You'll be compelled to read her fascinating story—which will entertain, discomfort, and broaden you—and you'll be better for it. She is a fierce, true spirit, who finds her way past anything childhood threw at her—including fanatical cults, confusing love, and life in the dangerous East Village—and makes us see that healing and finding your own ground is always possible."
—**Tama Kieves**, *USA Today* featured visionary career catalyst and best-selling author of *Thriving through Uncertainty*

"Lisa Kohn shows us in her powerful memoir that it is possible to find peace and contentment despite having a rocky, unstable, and often confusing childhood."
—**Madeleine Black**, author of *Unbroken*

"One person's crazy cult is another one's sanctuary. When you are a child from a broken home and that person is your mother (and you're so deep into being a Moonie that you are best friends with the leader's kids), and your father is a party-hearty hippie bartender, a lifetime of confusion, and more, is sure to follow. Kohn's long and twisted journey to make sense of it all will have you quickly thinking, 'There but for the grace of God go I' and marveling at the resilience of the human spirit."
—**Jo Maeder**, author of the bestselling memoir *When I Married My Mother*

"Moving and inspiring! Lisa courageously details how she collected mere threads of childhood normalcy to weave a life strengthened by resiliency and love."
—**Cara Bradley**, author of *On The Verge*

"A teacher and leadership consultant takes readers into the crevices of a cult...The austere tone of the introductory passage doesn't quite represent the vivacity with which Kohn writes about her struggle breaking out of the mold in which her parents trapped her...But this is not just an inside-the-cult book; this is the story of a woman who attempted everything in her power to get out of it...If writing is an evacuation tool to process and understand abuse, Kohn has done an excellent job of producing a text that oozes with honesty and truth."

—*Kirkus Reviews*

"Lisa Kohn offers a personal perspective about life and love within the Unification Church. It's a heartfelt examination of what it's like to be kid growing up in a 'cult.' And about difficulties with family, friends, and adolescence that are often complicated and exacerbated by groups called cults due to their dramas and dynamics. Often when former members from such groups write about their personal journey and recovery it can potentially enlighten everyone who reads it. Accounts like Lisa Kohn's are a necessary ingredient for our collective education because they give us an inside view that only an ex-member can provide."

—**Rick Ross,** Executive Director
Cult Education Institute

to the moon and back

to the moon and back

a childhood under the influence

lisa kohn

 Heliotrope Books
New York

ISBN: 978-1-942762-44-7
Library of Congress Control Number: 2018932967

Cover Design by Jayme Johnson/Worthy Marketing Group
Cover Photographs by Lisa Kohn
Designed and typeset by Naomi Rosenblatt with AJ&J Design

For those who have been in, are in, and are out.

For those whose suffering has felt un-survivable.

And for my kids—being your mom healed my soul

and heals me every day.

I love you most.

a note from the author

Memory is a weird thing. My brother—and only constant in my childhood—often jokingly says I got this completely wrong. (He also says I was too easy on everyone.) That being said, this is a work of nonfiction, and all of the events and experiences described in this book are true and faithfully rendered to the best of my ability. I have recreated all dialogue from memory, and many names and identifying details have been changed to protect the privacy of others.

foreword

When I was a kid in the 1970s, Moonies were the scariest thing I knew. Sure, earthquakes were scary, and tidal waves, and nuclear war. But we lived in Connecticut, so earthquakes and tidal waves felt pretty intangible, and nuclear war was abstract too—the bombs and politicians so far away, and unaware of my existence.

Moonies, though...Moonies were real. They were human beings not much older than I, humans who dressed in regular clothes (unlike those baldies in saffron), and who acted nice enough, but were tasked to brainwash young people. They'd approach someone and begin chatting, and next thing you knew that kid had abandoned all family and friends, and was completely resistant to reason. Parents had to hire kidnappers—*kidnappers*, and deprogrammers!—to rescue their children who, even after deprogramming, were never the same again.

Describing Moonies, people used words like *terrifying* and *cult*. "Watch out for Moonies," parents warned. Don't talk to strangers, especially friendly strangers. Be careful in crowds, and cities...We walked through New York (home of the Moonies) like Roman legions crossing Gaul. I need to spell this out, loudly, because many people reading **to the moon and back** might not remember how insidious—how vicious—the Moonies were. Everyone was scared. Not just me.

And so when Lisa Kohn told me eight years ago, at a cocktail party, that she'd been raised as a Moonie, it was all I could do not to shriek. *What about the brainwashing?* I wanted to ask, and *Was the deprogramming as painful as they say?* I longed to poke her so I could see what a Moonie felt like. Because she looked so...normal. Which in Wayne, Pennsylvania, is normal squared.

Then I got to read her book. I read of her parents and their repeated, exceptional failures at parenting. I read of her life in the East Village, in rotting neighborhoods that stank of chickens and urine. I read of her efforts to find, or build, or join a family. Any family, because family she definitely lacked. And you know what? It turns out that much of what I knew about the Moonies was wrong. They weren't that bad—at least when compared to Lisa's alternatives.

I love *to the moon and back*, and I stand in awe at Lisa's strength and courage. She made it back. She survived—not only survived, but built a pretty damn great life. We should all be blessed with such resilience. Read this book. Enjoy it. Learn something.

—Catherine Murdock, 2018
Author of *Dairy Queen* and *The Book of Boy*

prologue

My brother says that we were raised by wolves. I don't always agree with him, but I don't have a more accurate description of our upbringing. A friend of my dad's pointed out that wolves raise their young with more structure than our parents gave us.

At first I had no idea that anything was wrong with my childhood. Yeah, my dad was a hippie bartender who convinced my brother to smoke pot at the age of ten and who offered to sell me to his friends for drugs. (He was kidding.) Yeah, I was running the household when I was eleven—shopping, cooking, cleaning—because at that point both my parents were gone. Yeah, my brother and I were left to fend for ourselves way more than you might say is optimal. And yeah, I grew up in a cult. My mom was a Moonie and therefore so were my brother and I. For those who don't know what that means, the Moonies were members of the Holy Spirit Association for the Unification of World Christianity—simply known as the Unification Church—the cult of all cults in the American age of cults. Church members gave their faith, lives, and worldly possessions to a self-proclaimed messiah from South Korea. Some call it brainwashing. It was my life.

I knew it was weird, but I didn't know it was bad. When it's all you know, it's all you know. You have no grasp that it could, or should, be different. I knew I could tell stories about my parents and people would laugh in disbelief, but I was oblivious to the fact that my stories covered up pain and emotional scars, and that much of what happened to me shouldn't have happened at all.

I didn't realize I was harmed or that I was on a path of harming myself as I got older. I ended up in abusive relationships, anorexia, and "mild" drug addiction (to name a few things), but it didn't register that these were because I ached so much inside. I didn't know that my psyche was bruised. Or that I despised myself.

As a kid you misinterpret the nasty things that happen to and around you, and you somehow believe you're to blame. As a young adult I internalized this more and more. As an older adult, I still can. I can get lost in darkness and desperation. I can feel unworthy or damaged or hopeless. I have my scars and insecurities, my fears that feel like they'll engulf me. I can be washed over with shame.

But they're moments. As I said to my older child once when they struggled against their own demons, the waves of despair become less powerful and hit you less often.

I've learned to face my terrors and to allow myself joy. It wasn't always an easy thing to do. I've learned that it's up to each of us to create the life we desire. We have the ability to lessen the influences around us that we don't want or don't agree with. When we can't lessen them, we have the ability to keep going despite them. Even when we think we don't.

the past

"Someday we'll look back on this
and it will all seem funny."
—Bruce Springsteen

1 · the vigil begins

Mimi, Robbie, and I were curled up in the big flowered wing chair in my grandparents' living room. We were so tiny—Mimi being four feet ten inches at the most, and Robbie and I being eleven and ten and small for our ages—that we easily fit.

"He was phenomenal," Mimi said. She had a smile on her face and a faraway look in her bright blue eyes. "Just amazing."

"Why?" Robbie asked. I'm guessing he was as curious as I was about this wild change in our mother.

"Well, it just makes so much sense. It's like I finally figured out the answers. I never could understand why Jesus had to die. I never could. And Reverend Moon explained that he wasn't supposed to. It just makes so much sense."

"Wow," I said. I didn't understand but longed to agree with her. I wanted to always agree with her. And besides, she vibrated with warmth and elation, and I wanted to keep that Mimi around.

Before that morning in January 1974, Mimi had tried on religions and movements like some women try on clothes. At one time or another she'd embraced Buddhism, Hinduism, born-again Christianity, sensitivity group training, commune living, primal screaming, meditating, chanting "om," and a vow of silence. The night before, Mimi had gone to hear Reverend Sun Myung Moon— the founder of the Unification Church—speak. If she had found her something in the Unification Church, I was determined to be on board.

"It's like I've been trying to fit a square peg in a round hole for so long, trying to understand this…and now someone finally explained it to me," she continued breathlessly, a smile stretched across her face. "I sat there and listened and kept thinking, *I knew it. I knew it. I knew it.*"

I looked at my mother. I hardly recognized her. She was a new woman, or at least a woman with a vision of becoming a new woman, her heart and mind captured by the Church's teachings—a mixture of Judeo-Christian and Eastern philosophies that proclaimed it time to unite all world religions and bring the Kingdom of Heaven to Earth. She bounced with excitement in a way I'd never seen before.

"I'm going back," she said. "And maybe soon we can all see Father."

Father, of course, was Reverend Moon, not Danny.

My parents had split seven years earlier. Danny had moved to New York City, while Mimi, Robbie, and I had settled into an apartment in a run-down section of East Orange, New Jersey.

Mimi and Danny got married the summer they were out of high school because they "had to." My mom was pregnant. She was the straight-A-student daughter of the Millburn, New Jersey town judge and editor of the yearbook. Danny was the beatnik son of socialist intellectuals in the next town over. The type of kid who, in eighth grade when his class studied democracy, brought toy machine guns to school and staged a coup d'état, establishing himself as dictator. My parents had been introduced by a mutual friend and, like positive and negative charges, were immediately attached to each other. Barely eighteen, with a baby on the way and not many options they were willing or able to consider, they ran off to South Carolina to marry without parental permission.

Robbie was their first "mistake." Their second one—me—arrived about a year and a half later, on September 16, 1963. At the time, my parents lived in New Brunswick, New Jersey, where Danny was studying English at Rutgers University. Mimi had withdrawn from Clark University to raise our family. They were supported by all four of my grandparents and had not intended to have another child. I've been told that one night of forgotten intentions (and birth control) was my beginning.

My parents were free spirits. Even in the culture of the early '60s, even among their friends, they stuck out. We lived in the married-student housing on the edge of Rutgers's campus, a large circle of small houses with a communal backyard in the middle. Robbie remembers this backyard vividly, especially the time he and I wanted to play outside but Danny said no because it was raining—only it wasn't. Danny was tripping on LSD.

Danny was fervently antiestablishment and wore the uniform of the times: long, shaggy brown hair; a bushy mustache or beard or both; ragged bell-bottom jeans with a brown leather belt and a huge brass buckle; and a psychedelic shirt. With his stocky, muscular build—he was five feet four inches tall—and dark hair, eyes, and complexion, I've been told he was quite handsome.

We never called them Mommy and Daddy. "I'm not a label," Danny would say when I was old enough to question. "If you call me Father, I'll call you Daughter. If you call me Daddy, I'll call you Daudy. I am a person. Call me by my name." I would talk about my parents, Mimi and Danny, and people would pause. "You said Mommy and Daddy, right?" they'd ask. "No," I'd reply, avoiding their eyes. "Mimi and Danny."

My parents may have been hippies, but I was straightlaced. I didn't curse, even though cursing was all around me. I dressed as primly as I could in pleated skirts, knee-highs, and buckled shoes instead of flowing dresses, bandanas, and beads. I refused to cross the street if the light was red. Following rules gave me a sense of control.

"Shit," Mimi said early one morning as she stumbled over me. "Lisa, what are you doing?" She had been in the bathroom with the door shut, putting on makeup. I had been sitting, as always, right outside, cross-legged on the cold, hard linoleum floor, leaning against the bathroom door, waiting. Not playing or coloring or looking through my picture books. Just waiting.

I wanted the door open, full access, Mimi within view. I wanted her, and if I couldn't have that, I would make sure I knew where she was at all times. When she went down the hall to the laundry room, I stood in our doorway sobbing. Down the hall was too far away.

When Danny moved out, it carved an aching hole in my world.

My four-year-old self was terrified of losing Mimi as well. Our modest basement apartment had two bedrooms, a kitchen, a living room, and a windowless bathroom, all off one main hallway. The windows we did have were up high, level with the ground outside. In this setup, it was hard to lose anything. Nevertheless, I refused to let my mother out of my sight.

Many times she'd go out and come back late to take the babysitter home, leaving us alone for half an hour or so. I'd jump up in the middle of the night, unconsciously aware she wasn't there and, no matter how late it was, drag myself to the phone hanging on the wall in the kitchen and dial the babysitter's house, often waking her parents.

"Is Mimi there?" I'd ask, my voice quivering. "Is she on her way home yet? Do you know where she is? Do you know when she'll be here?"

Robbie used to tease me: "Mimi is going to go away too. Just like Danny, she's going to leave."

My life was a continuous vigil—I was always attuned to her whereabouts and worked hard to keep her nearby and happy. Like many children whose parents split up, I was convinced that Danny no longer lived with us because of something I had done. I didn't know what or how, but I knew this was my fault. I had to make sure I didn't give Mimi a reason to leave too. When she wasn't home I wandered through our small apartment, waiting for her to come back, repeating the singsong mantra I'd made up to calm myself when I was afraid. "Everything's all right tonight," I sang over and over. "Everything's okay today."

The bedroom I shared with Robbie reflected our different ways of dealing with our fractured family. While I was frightened and clung to Mimi, he was filled with anger and fury and took it out on everything we owned. He got a new Matchbox car-racing set and would break it. I got a new doll or game, and he would bash it against the wall. He smashed every toy into little pieces, which he then scattered around our room. He tore every scrap of paper to shreds just to add to the mess. There was not a bare spot on the floor between our two beds and dressers.

"Mimi, would you put us to bed?" was our nightly request, when she was around.

The answer depended on her frustration level. Sometimes she'd say, "Clear a way for me, and I'll come in and give you a kiss." But other nights, the path through the debris was too disturbing, and all we'd hear was "No, I'm not going in your room. Come out here and say good night."

It was Robbie's mess, but the two of us had to clean it three times a year—for our birthdays and before Christmas. Mom and Pop, our maternal grandparents, would bring us stacks of presents, but we weren't allowed to open them if our room wasn't neat. "Please, will you help us?" we'd ask Mimi, and at first, she would. She'd put *Hair* on the record player in the living room, blasting the music so we could hear it while we cleaned the bedroom. I didn't understand all the words—especially to "Sodomy"—but I sang along. The three of us would start in the middle of the floor and work outward, throwing most of the junk away. Eventually Mimi would get sick of our chaos and practically run from the room, leaving us to finish the endless task. Robbie and I would sit and sing and sort through the garbage until very late, but we would get tucked in and kissed good night.

Despite his anger and teasing, Robbie and I gave each other a sense of constancy and permanence. He was my big brother— although only by one year, five months, and fourteen days. Even now I say that he figured that out, and he says that I did. He had thick brown hair that he wore below his ears, hazel-green eyes, and a slight build. Being close in age and a buffer for each other against the craziness, we were inseparable.

Mimi was the poster girl for the alternative lifestyle that I abhorred. Her hair was cropped so short that it looked shaved, and she made many of her own clothes—out of bandanas, tablecloths, and curtains, using leather cords as shoulder straps and embroidering little flowers along the edges. She had three earring holes: two on one side and one on the other. Back then it wasn't popular; it was weird. She threatened to pierce her nose as well.

Such fashion statements didn't work for me. "Lisa, hurry up,"

Mimi urged one evening as we were on our way to a party. I stood in front of the full-length mirror on the closet door in her bedroom, staring at myself. "Bungalow Bill" played in the background. "Getting ready music," Mimi called it. I wanted to sing along with The Beatles but couldn't focus.

"I can't go," I whined. "I can't wear this!" I had put on the best dress clothes I had: a fancy white lace nightgown and a shiny, light green silk bathrobe. *How can I wear these in public?*

"But honey, you look pretty."

I gazed at myself in the mirror. My wavy brown hair fell just below my shoulders. It matched my dark brown eyes. I was eight and, as always, small for my age, my parents being who they were. I looked even younger than I was. *I suppose I look okay—but these are pajamas!*

In the end, Mimi forced me to go. I felt weird and naked.

Naked didn't bother Mimi. As a single mom, she was just able to support us with food stamps and waitressing money. To supplement her income, she modeled in the nude for art classes. (She won the prize for "most unusual profession" for her ten-year high school reunion.)

"Your mother does what?" my friends would ask. I never wanted to answer. Once she took us with her when she went to model, and Robbie stripped down and posed with her. No clothes on, in front of twenty-plus strangers, sitting there as if everything was okay. They asked me to join them, but I hid in the back of the room, not wanting to look at Mimi and Robbie, much less be related to them. For years I kept a portrait of Mimi from one of these sessions in my closet. Why I never got rid of it, I don't know. I was mortified when my friend found it one day.

When I was six, Mimi decided we should follow a macrobiotic diet, which she considered a cleansing and healing way to eat. Part of that healing was a drink made from the kuzu root. Kuzu has no flavor, a musty smell, and a repulsive consistency, like mucous—thick, globby mucous. Kuzu was Mimi's cure for our colds.

"It's gross," Robbie and I would say when one of us had to drink it. "It's disgusting!" When it was forced on both of us, we came up with a plan.

"I won't tell if you won't tell," Robbie whispered as we huddled at the kitchen sink, trying not to breathe in the kuzu odor rising from the rough pottery mugs cupped in our hands. I nodded in agreement, and we dumped the kuzu and watched it ooze down the drain.

For over two years we rarely ate meat and had little if any processed food. Instead our breakfasts, lunches, and dinners consisted of brown rice, beans, and seaweed. By the age of seven I was well versed in the many types of edible seaweed. There was hijiki, which looks like little black worms, as Robbie pointed out. Wakame that typically floats in miso soup, which Mimi made badly. (She later admitted she cooked everything macrobiotic badly.) Nori that comes in thin, dry sheets like green paper. Arame and ogonori, which are served cold, like a salad.

We ate sitting cross-legged on the brown vinyl tablecloth laid out on the tan living room rug. Our apartment had an eat-in kitchen *and* an eat-in living room, decorated with empty Coke cans on every shelf and windowsill and an American flag draped over the couch along the wall—an American flag that we put away when my conservative grandfather came to visit.

"Remember to chew," Mimi would say to us, as we aimed for chewing each mouthful one hundred times. One hundred was the magic number that resulted in the best digestion and also the highest level of spirituality.

At school we suffered through bag lunches. No one would trade their PB&J for my macrobiotic treats. I cringe when I flash back to second grade. Hiding in the corner of the lunchroom at one of the long, sticky, metal tables, the smell of institutional food—food I longed to eat instead of what I had—around me, the sounds of too many kids with too much energy in one small room, doing my best to avoid the stares I got when I pulled out whatever Mimi had packed. Saddled with sprouted grain bread, seaweed, brown rice, and more and different kinds of beans than anyone could imagine, I longed for white bread and baloney. On nights with Lucy, our babysitter, we could escape our dietary hell and enter refined-sugar heaven. She would smuggle in bags of Tootsie Rolls and Hershey's Kisses. We played hide-and-seek, with candy as our prize.

Robbie built up his store of sweets and processed food whenever we spent the weekend with Danny. Danny would buy Robbie two bags of Chips Ahoy chocolate chip cookies and a bottle of root beer for breakfast and hide in his bed until Robbie's food orgy was over. I, on the other hand, wrote so many stories about food that the school guidance counselor called to speak to Mimi. She was worried I was malnourished.

One year Mimi made brownies for my birthday celebration at school. I relished her brownies—a family recipe and much-anticipated treat for every special occasion. I loved to lick the bowl and spoon as the goodies baked in the oven. I delighted in the dense smell of chocolate working its way throughout the apartment. Whenever Mimi made brownies, I knew I was cared for and adored.

This time, Mimi baked while I was asleep. I took my birthday treats with me in the morning and passed them out to my class, skipping from desk to desk, promising everyone—as I always did—that these were the best brownies ever. Like nothing they had tried before.

I sat at my seat, impatient to dive into my own sugary delight, when I looked up and noticed that no one was eating. In fact, some kids crumpled the brownies up in the paper napkins I had given them. A few walked over to the trash and dumped theirs. "Ew," I heard one girl say.

I took a tiny bite of my brownie. It was disgusting. Mimi had decided to make them healthier this year, using carob powder instead of chocolate, whole-wheat flour instead of white, and date sugar instead of refined sugar.

Our apartment was not only sweets-free, it was TV-less. After someone broke in and stole our little set, Mimi cursed. "I hope they drop it and it smashes their toes," she said. Then she refused to replace it. Mom and Pop offered to buy us a new one, but Mimi decided we were better off without it. Like my bizarre lunches, not having a television affected my popularity at school. I had no idea what kids were talking about when they discussed the previous night's shows. Even in high school I would have moments of "Huh?" when my friends mentioned their favorite cartoons and sitcoms from when we were young.

I remember one year when Robbie and I longed to see *Rudolph the Red-Nosed Reindeer*. We begged Mimi to take us to Mom and Pop's to watch, but she said no. We pleaded and cajoled until she suggested we go down to the corner store, to see if we could watch there.

Near the end of our block was a little luncheonette that sold basic necessities—such as Mimi's cigarettes—and served simple meals at the counter. The owners had a TV near the cash register, where they watched soap operas during the afternoon. Robbie and I set off down the street, bundled up against the winter winds, hoping the owners were in a holiday spirit. I crossed my fingers and promised I'd be good if I could see *Rudolph*.

Luckily they said yes. Robbie and I climbed up on the high red stools at the counter, sipped the Cokes placed in front of us, and watched Rudolph save the day.

The stolen TV was not the only time someone tried to take our stuff. Once, when I was about five, I needed to get something from my dresser. I opened the door to my room, tiptoed through the mess, and saw a string hanging from the window. String with a hook on the end!

I looked up and froze. Two faces peered back at me. "Mimi!" I yelled. "There are kids fishing into our room."

She came running to see a couple of boys a few years older than me sitting outside our bedroom windows with poles and hooks, trying to get whatever they could from the trash on the floor. Because we were in a basement apartment, the windows were high up on the wall, yielding a pool of opportunity stocked with the toys Robbie had smashed in his fits of rage.

"What are you doing?" Mimi shouted at them. They glanced at her and went back to their task.

"What the fuck do you think you're doing?" she shouted again. She turned and ran from the room. I rushed after her through the apartment, out our front door, down the hall, out the door of the building, up the steps, and around the corner to the windows. When we got to where the boys were, they laughed, picked up their poles, and left.

We also needed to be saved from some of the men Mimi was involved with. Larry, who lived with us on and off, was the worst.

"Get the kids out of here or I'll kill her!" Larry shouted from somewhere in the small house. Mimi, Larry, Robbie, and I had gone to visit my mother's friend Tess at her home in rural Connecticut. Robbie was eight years old, and I was seven. We huddled together on the brown pullout couch in the middle of the living room, listening to Larry's angry demands. We were terrified for Mimi—not knowing where she was or what was happening.

"Get them out of here!" Larry yelled again. We turned to each other for guidance, our eyes wide with a mix of fear and confusion.

"Larry, no!" Mimi cried.

At that, Robbie and I jumped up and followed the sounds to the spare bedroom. Larry was sitting on top of Mimi on the bed, with a knife to her throat.

"What did we do?" I whispered. Robbie shot me a look, shaking his head fiercely, urging me to be silent. I ignored him, wiping my face, willing the tears not to make it past the corners of my eyes. I somehow knew that to keep Mimi safe I had to not be scared or at the minimum not seem scared. "I don't want to go! What if something happens?"

"Lisa, shut up!" Robbie hissed through clenched teeth. His body was clenched as well, his face white, his muscles tensed with determination to handle the situation.

I didn't know why Larry had erupted. I only knew I felt a rush of relief when Tess ran into the room, grabbed us, and dragged us away. "Just go," she urged. "Go for a while, and let him settle. I'm sure he'll calm down, and it will be fine."

With that she opened the front door, pushed us outside, and pulled the door closed. Robbie and I crept away in the dark, looking for a place to sit. I reached for his hand, and to my surprise he didn't pull away but held mine tightly.

Larry was in our lives for about four years, starting when I was five. He and Mimi were such a contrast walking down the street together. He was broad and tall, well over six feet, and strutted down the road as if he owned the world. She carried an air of defiance mixed with submission in her short frame. He had dark eyes and longish black hair, graying at the temples. She had bright blue eyes and cropped brown hair.

I don't remember what led up to the fight that night. I didn't know then that Larry was violent. It wasn't until I was an adult that I learned that he hit Mimi regularly. One time he beat her so badly she had to have a friend take her to the emergency room. After that she asked him to move out but continued to see him. She couldn't get away from him, so neither could we.

She hid his aggression from us—perhaps from everybody. I did know that Larry petrified me, even before he threatened to kill my mother. We'd be playing cards, and his comments and leers made me want to crawl back inside myself to escape. I hated to be near him and dreaded being alone with him. I was on guard, incessantly vigilant.

That night in Connecticut when Robbie and I snuck back into the house, we found Mimi alone in the bedroom, sitting on the bed. Larry was gone. We knew better than to ask what had happened, and we sat with her in silence until Tess came back. Tess had somehow convinced Larry to leave and had dropped him at the train. Later we realized he had taken our car keys with him and left us stranded.

2 · crazy street

For most of the time we were in East Orange, Danny lived about half an hour away in New York City. He was always in downtown Manhattan. According to Danny there was "no life above Fourteenth Street." For a while he stayed in a loft in Tribeca, where he painted the floor yellow and let us decorate it with blue squiggles and other designs while he made us jelly pancakes for dinner. And later a walk-up apartment on Sixth Street and Avenue D in the East Village, back when no one went east of Avenue A. One summer afternoon we played on the roof of the building—"tar beach"—and got so covered in melted tar that Danny had to bathe us in turpentine.

Robbie visited him more than I did. I was a mommy's girl. When I did go, Danny would take us uptown to Central Park to climb the rocks, or we'd ride the Staten Island Ferry—twenty-five cents round trip was a cheap way to spend an afternoon. When we were lucky, Danny might spring for a cab back to his apartment, but usually we took the subway. It was beastly hot in the summer but worth it because Danny would buy us candy from the vending machines on the platform, and he'd let us ride in the head car so we could look out the window on the door at the front of the train and watch the lights in the tunnels. We'd come out from the subway at Astor Place, near Cooper Union and the huge black cube. Danny had named that block "Crazy Street."

"Sam," Danny would say to Robbie. "Sam, what do you think of the weather?"

"It's all right, Charles," Robbie would answer. "What do you think, Maria?" he'd ask me.

"I don't know, Sam," I'd say. "I just don't know."

Crazy Street made you act crazy, if it knew who you were. That's why we took on aliases.

Somehow Crazy Street always knew who we were. Danny would hold our hands and swing Robbie and me around so that we walked backward and sideways. "Charles," I'd shout, "what are you doing? Why is this happening?"

"I don't know, Maria," he'd reply. "It's Crazy Street. It can't be helped."

When Danny was with Mimi, he'd had many different jobs, from Fuller brush salesman to newspaper reporter. After they split, there were years when he was an in-house journalist at the United Nations. However, he balked at the "establishmentness" of the U.N. and rebelled: he played chess during sessions he was supposed to cover; smoked pot in the Rose Garden; strolled in past the security guards wearing jeans, cowboy boots, long hair, and an earring; and never showed up without getting high first. To this day he proudly tells me that the U.N. asked him to come back every time he left because he was their source of amusement, their court jester. Even then I wondered why that was something to be proud of and how he could smoke dope on U.N. grounds.

Whenever Danny felt himself too sucked into life at the U.N., he'd quit and find a job as a bartender, which, he said, was the easiest way to work as few hours as possible while making as much money as possible. He started at the St. Adrian Company, on Broadway between Great Jones and Bond Streets, and had stints all over lower Manhattan in the hip downtown scene of the 1960s, '70s, and early '80s. According to an article in the *SoHo Weekly News,* he was "probably the best bartender in town."

There's a term for children who grow up on army bases; they're called "army brats." I was a bar brat. I learned at a very young age how to entertain myself as I waited for Danny to finish a shift. Robbie and I used to make large sculptures from the little plastic stirrer straws that came with the mixed drinks.

I also, apparently, learned how to order a drink. I was at a table along the windows at Broome Street, a popular SoHo bar where Danny worked. As on every Sunday afternoon, the place was packed—mostly with locals because back then SoHo was a neighborhood of starving artists, not tourists. I don't remember whom I was with, some of Danny's friends I suppose, waiting for my dad to meet us. I do remember feeling comfortable in my element. All of seven, I told the waitress, "I'll have a Virgin Mary, please."

When the drink came I took a sip and asked for Tabasco and Worcestershire sauce to fix my drink. "Don't ever," I declared to everyone around the table, "order a Virgin Mary from a bartender you don't know."

This would become one of Danny's favorite stories. He was proud that he taught me so well.

Danny liked to disappear for several months at a time to travel and explore. I knew he was living in Morocco when I was in first grade because of the gifts he sent. Robbie got a vividly colored vest, and I got a Moroccan shirt that I wore for my school picture. It was purple with gold thread woven throughout with, of course, one mistake. As Danny explained in the card, everything in Morocco was intentionally made with one mistake because only Allah could do anything perfectly.

Danny came and went without warning, traveling where his spirit—or friends or desire for drugs—led him. He would be in Algeria or San Francisco, until suddenly he was back. Sometimes he'd surprise (and delight) us by showing up at our apartment in East Orange.

When he returned from one trip abroad, he got a motorcycle. Once he and his girlfriend, Karen, Robbie, and I were stopped by the police. Who knew it was illegal to have four people on the back of a motorcycle? We fit because we were small.

"What do you think you're doing?" the officer asked.

"Just getting home," Danny answered. True.

The officer stared hard, the veins in his neck pulsing, his eyes bearing down on Danny. "What are you doing with four people on a motorcycle?"

I tightened my grip around Danny's stomach, held my breath, and felt Robbie brace behind me as well. Danny would talk about the police—how evil they were and how they picked on people like him because of his long hair and ripped jeans.

"Only two people on a motorcycle at a time," the officer said.

I tensed, my heart pounding, until Danny turned to Karen and told her to hop off and take me with her, that he and Robbie would meet us back at Mimi's apartment. As Karen and I headed to a bus stop, I breathed a sigh of relief.

Danny's motorcycle was also a source of pride for us and amusement for my friends. We had the coolest birthday parties, offering rides around the block as entertainment. Of course, there were two people on it for that.

Danny delighted in the freedom of the '60s and embraced the ideals of free love and nudity. Believing that their lack of inhibition would instill the proper values in us, he and his various girlfriends walked around naked when Robbie and I came to visit. I did my best to look the other way.

One summer day, when I was about six or seven, Danny took us to a friend's house in New Jersey where there was a pool. The adults swam naked. Robbie joined in; he said it was freeing and fun. I refused to get out of my bathing suit and, again, did my best to look the other way.

By the time I was eight years old and Robbie was nine, we knew how to get to Broome Street Bar via public transportation and many Saturdays traveled to New York City alone to see Danny. Mimi would drop us off at the station in East Orange, where we boarded the train for Hoboken. In Hoboken we transferred to the PATH train that took us to Ninth Street and Sixth Avenue, then walked through Greenwich Village to meet Danny and wait for him to get off his shift. I loved sitting on a high stool, sipping my Virgin Mary, watching him while he poured drinks, and sticking my foot in the mouth of one of the big wooden lion heads that ran along the front of the bar.

One sunny summer day, when Robbie and I reached the corner of Eighth Street and Sixth Avenue in the midst of the Greenwich Village Art Festival, which jam-packed the already tight streets with easels, artists, and would-be buyers, the light turned red. Robbie grabbed my hand. "Come on. Let's go. There are no cars coming."

"No," I answered.

"Come on, Lisa," Robbie hissed.

"No, the light's red."

"You are so dumb," he spit out and crossed the street.

I watched him walk to the other side of Sixth Avenue and waited for the light to change. I kept my eyes on him as best I could, but by the time I could cross, Robbie was lost in the crowds.

I stepped into the street, making my way through the huge intersection, until I got to the far corner and froze. I didn't know what to do. I had no idea where I was or where to go without Robbie. He had always been in charge.

Wandering down Eighth Street through the throngs of people, sweat dripping down my back, I tried to focus on what I could, or should, do. I stopped at every corner and looked up and down the blocks, searching for something I knew or someone I recognized. I didn't think to ask anyone for help. I knew I had to take care of myself. I knew how to take care of myself. I was pretty good at comforting myself when I was afraid. "Everything's all right tonight," I sang over and over and over in my head. "Everything's okay today."

I have no idea how long I wandered around the Village looking for familiar sights. Finally I recognized a playground on the corner of Mercer and Bleecker Streets. Relief. *I think I know where I am. I think I know what to do.* It would be easy to get to Broome Street from there. Winding those remaining six or so blocks to the bar, a smile began to creep onto my face. I had been scared, lost, and alone but had found my way.

When I reached the bar, it was packed. I pushed through the crowd, anxious to find Danny and tell him about my adventure. I stopped. Instead of my dad, some bald man was pouring drinks.

I stood, staring at the stranger then looking through the sea of faces for anyone I knew, anyone who could help me, anyone who would even notice me. My heart began to pound again, and I started to cry. *What do I do now?*

Eventually, the man saw me and came over. "Twink," he said. (Danny's nickname for me was Twinkle Star.) *Who was this weirdo talking to me?* "Twink," he repeated, "it's me!"

"Danny?"

"Yes." He laughed.

It *was* him. He looked so different.

"Like my hair? I shaved it off a few nights ago." He had been drunk and thought it would be funny. "Where's Robbie?"

I looked up at him, the tears beginning again. "I don't know."

"Fuck!" was all he said, then he moved away to pour a few more drinks. I worked my way through the mass of bodies, found a stool, climbed up, and stuck my foot in the lion's mouth to calm myself down. Then I saw Robbie. He was alone at the other end of the bar, crying. He too hadn't realized the bartender was Danny; all he saw was a strange bald man. And he had lost his little sister in New York City.

Danny's bald head may have frightened me that afternoon, but usually it embarrassed me. I so wanted my parents and my life to be like everyone else's. They so weren't; it so wasn't. Never was that clearer than the night of my fifth grade class play. We were putting on *The Pajama Game*, and while I was only in the chorus, I was excited because both Mimi and Danny would be there. I rarely was with both of them. (Many years later, when I was in my forties, Danny had a stroke. As I sat in the hospital room with him, Mimi, and Robbie, I felt the weirdest sensation wash over me. "Wow," I said to them. "I can only remember a few other times that the four of us were together.")

I know you're not supposed to look at the audience when you're onstage, but I couldn't help myself that night. I searched the faces and found Danny, in the midst of the crowd, right where everyone could see him. With a top hat. *Why would he do this to me? How can he think the other kids won't tease me?* And did I forget to mention that he had gotten into a bar fight a few weeks earlier and his front tooth had been knocked out? And that he had the tooth made into an earring? Well, he had. And he did. So, not only was his head bald and not only did he wear a top hat, but he had a gap in the front of his mouth and a tooth dangling from his right ear. *How will I ever live this down?*

"Danny," Robbie said one day, "you have fun when you smoke pot. Can I try?" While Danny's life of questioning the establishment and "sex, drugs, and rock and roll" horrified me, ten-year-old Robbie felt differently.

"Let me think about it," Danny answered. I guess even he was taken aback by the request and didn't know how to respond. Family legend has it that Danny asked one of his friends, Gary, what he thought of the idea, and Gary thought it would be cool if Robbie got high. So Robbie got high.

The first time Robbie tried pot was miraculously one of the times the four of us were together. We were in an apartment on Christopher Street, where Danny was housesitting for folk musician Chad Mitchell, of the Chad Mitchell Trio, and Mimi was somehow visiting Danny with us.

"Robbie, want some?" Danny asked, as he passed Robbie a joint. I watched from across the room.

"Is that safe?" I asked. "Is it okay for him to smoke?"

Mimi watched as well. She was taken by surprise and silent. She later told me that her only thought was *If I do it, how can I tell him he can't?*

One night a few months later, sitting at the round kitchen table in Danny's new apartment on Ninth Street between First and Second Avenues, Danny gave Robbie the ultimatum. "If you want to get high," he said, "you have to learn how to roll a joint. You have to do the work if you want to play."

Danny handed Robbie his cardboard box of dope and taught him how to shake the box, to separate out the seeds. He handed Robbie a pack of rolling papers and talked him through the process.

"It's the most fun I've had practicing anything," Robbie said one day. "By the time I got it right, I was totally fucked up." Robbie rolled and rolled—that time and others. Once, in fact, he rolled and smoked so much that he out-smoked Danny and his friends. They were done, and Robbie had wanted to get higher, so he kept going. They thought that was really, really cool.

Robbie liked being stoned. In fact, he liked it so much he was eager to try other things. We were at the free Jefferson Airplane concert in Central Park, and Robbie and Danny were sharing a joint. I was snuggled into Danny's lap, trying to avoid the smoke. Robbie noticed people walking around offering "free sunshine."

"Danny, what's that?" he asked.

"LSD," Danny said.

"Can I try that?"

"No." Maybe even Danny had his limits.

Robbie kept smoking pot. A lot. I didn't partake, of course. I was the good girl.

3 · divorce—a family affair

The summer after I finished second grade, Mimi bought a beat-up old green-and-white van from Danny. It had red paint spots all over it where Mimi tried to stop the rust from eating away at the finish, and it was empty in back—just old green carpeting covering the floor and rickety blue wooden cabinets installed along the sides to hold our stuff. It had space for two people in front, a driver and passenger. Robbie and I fought for the coveted place to sit: the engine, which was between the two seats and encased in a black metal cover. We put a cushion on it in the summer because it got hot—engine hot. We were moving to California to live on a commune. I figured I'd change my name to Sunshine.

Mimi needed time to fix up the van for the long drive, so we left our apartment in East Orange and sputtered the nine miles to Millburn, where Mom and Pop lived. We would spend a few weeks with them and then be on our way.

We never made the trip. We didn't make it across the country. We didn't even make it out of state. Mom was diagnosed with lung cancer as we were about to leave, so instead of living in free-loving California, we settled into my grandparents' conventional home in suburban New Jersey.

I was comfortable there. In the summers before we moved in for good, Mimi had left Robbie and me with Mom and Pop while she traveled on her own for a few weeks. That's when she had found our intended commune. I loved those times at Mom and Pop's—they had a sense of structure and normalcy that I craved. I also hated them, since I wasn't with Mimi. Mom would make us cream cheese and jelly sandwiches on glorious Wonder Bread, and we'd picnic on a blanket in the backyard. I'd look at her as we sat there. *If you were dead, Mimi would come.* I'd realize what an awful thing I'd thought.

Mom's cancer forced her into chemotherapy and radiation. Mimi's endless search for truth forced her into vows of silence. She drove Mom to her daily appointments and never said a word. Each morning Robbie and I would come downstairs to get a hug or ask for breakfast and find Mimi in her room—which used to be the dining room—sitting in her purple slipper rocking chair in the corner by the window, reading, with a sign taped on the wall next to her. "Not talking now," or "Today is a not talking day," it would say, with her little hand-drawn flower signature at the bottom. We knew to leave her alone.

I don't know why Mimi needed to find answers or truth or meaning. I just know that the quest drove her, and she lived life and made choices—for her and for us—based on this need. At one point she studied with an Indian man to learn more about Hinduism. She took us to group meals at the ashram where they played strange music and served mushy food with rice. Even though Robbie and I hated the place, we went as often as we could just to be with Mimi. We accepted whatever she found as her, and therefore our, new way.

One night, however, she went to the ashram without us and didn't come back. I woke in the middle of the night and went downstairs for a glass of water. I walked by Mimi's room, looked at the futon on the floor where she slept, and realized she wasn't there.

I ran to get Robbie. As I burst into his room, he sat up in bed and from a complete deep sleep said, "Mimi said to tell you that she's okay."

I didn't believe him and dragged him back downstairs, where she wasn't. I looked out her window, at the darkness and the streetlights flickering. "Where is she?" I asked. "Why isn't she home?"

Robbie had no words that could ease my fear. I knew she was never coming back and was certain she was dead.

To this day I can feel the dread that overtook me as I stood by the window, watching for Mimi to drive down the street. To this day I'm certain my loved ones are dead when they're late coming home. Just this week I could feel the knot in my stomach and my inability to sit still when my child went out for a walk and stayed out "too long." I've learned to acknowledge these certainties as one of my many leftover irrational fears, but they're there.

Mimi showed up early the next morning. She had stayed up so late the night before discussing God and religion with her Indian friend that it made more sense to her to sleep for a few hours and then drive home. It had made sense to her but not to me.

Mom died from the cancer in February. Robbie and I had been sent to a neighbor's house for dinner. It was late before they let us leave. We came home to find the house full of people eating, talking, and laughing.

"Mimi?" I called, as I rushed upstairs to my grandparents' room. "Pop?" I found Mimi laying out Mom's favorite suit—the nubby pink tweed with large brass buttons—and knew my grandmother was gone. That night as Mimi put me to bed, instead of sitting with me until I fell asleep, she lay down next to me and hugged me tight. Soon I heard her sniffing, then sobbing. I held her, feeling her shake.

Throughout Mom's memorial service I sat silently in the front pew of the funeral home, thinking that somehow all those times I'd wished she were dead while she took care of us had killed her. I felt a lump in my throat and a dull void ache inside my heart, but I didn't cry.

After Mom's death, Mimi, Robbie, and I stayed with Pop in Millburn. Mimi took on the role of caring for the house and for him while he supported us. There was more stability than in East Orange, but I wanted my parents to get back together so we could have a real family like other kids. It seemed possible; they were legally separated, but they never divorced. For years, officially ending the marriage was a final step neither one of them could take.

One Saturday morning as Robbie and I sat in the TV room of Pop's house, nestled in our respective antique rocking chairs and lost in cartoons, the mailman came with a letter from Danny. He had been living in Saint Thomas for a year and a half, bartending and hanging out on the beach. We were planning a trip to visit him and hoped he was sending us information. We couldn't wait to see him.

He described his life so invitingly. "Like beautiful pictures painted on my eyeballs," he had written. Robbie tore the letter open, and I read it with him, over his shoulder. It wasn't about the trip. It was about our parents' divorce, which had just become final.

It had been a family affair. Danny's brother, my uncle Jonny, wrote up the divorce papers. Jonny's law school roommate presented them in court. The best friend of Danny's mother was Mimi's witness, and Danny's father paid for everything. Everyone wanted the long-time separation to be final and legal—everyone except Robbie and me.

Why should I have cared? My parents had been apart for so long I had almost no memories of them together. This time I cried.

It's weird. Do kids of divorced parents always find other kids with the same background to hang out with? All I know is I became best friends with a girl who lived on the next street over, Sarah. We spent nearly every waking minute together. I called her "Swipper Swapper." I don't remember why, nor do I remember what she called me, but I know I had a nickname too. We listened endlessly to "Seasons in the Sun," grabbing the needle on the record player and starting the song over again before it finished. We danced the "Locomotion" and made apple pie—from scratch, without a recipe. The filling was always better than the crust. We argued over whose family was weirder—her mom wouldn't let her dad on the steps to their house. In many ways, Mimi and Danny paled in comparison.

We spent our days together. The nights were tougher. "Lisa, stay over," Sarah would say, and I'd agree. But by ten or eleven o'clock that would change. "I'm going home," I'd announce.

"Again?"

"Yes, again." I'd walk through the common backyards in the dark to get home. Now that my parents' divorce was final, everything became even more about Mimi. I loved her so much, and we had a saying to express it: "Roundabout and back again." We left each other notes with stick figures drawn on them, with the arms like circles that twisted around and around the bodies. *Roundabout and back again.* We danced together in the kitchen, singing the words to "I Love You a Bushel and a Peck" from *Guys and Dolls* and bouncing up and down across the floor.

Well, usually. One day I forgot my lunch for my fourth grade school trip. My teacher called Mimi and asked if she and the class could walk up the block to my house and pick it up. I skipped home.

I rang the doorbell, but no one answered. I rang again. After a long pause, the door opened. There was Mimi, standing in front of us in a green velvet bathrobe and a gray towel draped around her body, with another blue towel wrapped around her head. I wanted to sink into the ground to escape. *Why can't she just be normal, just this once?* I took my lunch from her without a word.

I look back on my early childhood now, and in some ways I can see how unstable and insane it was. In some ways I wonder how I made it through so whole. My mother says it was like I had a steel rod as a backbone, even when I was young. That nothing could fully knock me over.

In some ways, however, it was also idyllic, because what stands out most sharply to me is how much I loved and needed my mother. Maybe the same as every child does. Maybe more. Who knows? Who cares? And back then, no matter what else, I was with her.

4 · talking with the messiah

As excited as she was after Reverend Moon's speech in February 1974, it took months for Mimi to take the next steps. Finally, in the middle of June, Unification Church members convinced her to take a ride with them up to Barrytown—the Church property in Duchess County, New York—for a weekend workshop to learn more about the teachings. She left early Friday morning, promising she'd be back Sunday in time for dinner.

Late Sunday afternoon as Robbie and I played baseball on the front lawn, we heard a honk as a truck pulled into our driveway. The driver got out, walked around to the back, and rolled up the rear panel to reveal the interior. It was empty except for Mimi and a few other people huddled in a corner.

"Mimi!" we yelled and ran toward her.

She was all smiles. She hopped down onto the driveway and grabbed Robbie and me for a hug. "Let's go inside."

"How was it?" Robbie asked.

"Was it amazing again?" I seconded.

"Oh yes," she said, while laughing. "Oh yes." We headed into the house and snuggled up in the flowered wing chair.

"Tell us, tell us," Robbie and I begged. "Tell us about it."

"It was great. I understand so much now. But…"

"What?"

"But I have to go back. I need to go up for a week. Is that okay?"

I hated to let her go, but of course we said yes. There was no way to deny Mimi whatever had her so captivated, whatever she thought was so wonderful. More than anything, I wanted her to be happy. We sat for a little while longer, and she held us tight. Then she gathered a few more things, told Pop she was leaving (which did not go over well), climbed into the truck, and drove away.

Mimi spent twenty of the next thirty days at Barrytown, traveling up and back, and up and back. Whenever she came home she wasn't able to stay. It was as if there was a magnetic pull that drew her there, a compulsion she wouldn't, or couldn't, resist.

Each time we saw her, she was a little different. A little softer. A little easier. At first she stopped swearing. I liked that. She became a bit stricter with us, giving us more regular bedtimes and making us talk politely to grown-ups. I liked that too. She showed up one time looking like a regular mom, having abandoned her homemade tablecloth-and-bandana clothing. She even wore a bra! I really, really liked that. Mimi smiled more, laughed more, and stopped the "not talking" days. I liked all of that.

"It makes so much sense," she kept repeating. "The members, the brothers and sisters, all have their feet on the ground and their heads in Heaven. They're doing such practical things and living for God. It just makes so much sense."

I tried to understand *what* made such sense. Apparently, Jesus himself had appeared to Reverend Sun Myung Moon, (whom Mimi now called "Father"), in a vision. It had been Easter, and Father, who was only fifteen at the time, was up in the Korean mountains praying. Jesus asked Father to continue the work that Jesus had started—to establish God's Kingdom of Heaven on Earth and bring God's peace to humankind.

Over the years, Mimi had taught us how special Jesus was. It astounded me that Father had spoken to him. I tried to imagine what that must be like—to talk to Jesus and be that close to God. How amazing that must feel! How amazing Father must be. I became consumed with the need to see Father myself. To experience his greatness. I longed to be a part of whatever Mimi had found and to share it with her.

Mimi decided to take Robbie and me with her to Barrytown for the weekend. The two-hour car ride felt like forever; I couldn't sit still. I wanted to meet the brothers and sisters—to actually see the place. I had no real understanding of what it was all about but knew that

Mimi loved it, that she was happy, and that therefore it was good. I planned on loving it as well.

Mimi pulled our rusty van up to the steps in front of the main building. A Christian Brothers boarding school before the Church had bought it, the large brick structure featured many windows and entrances, as well as statues of Christian saints. Two Church members sat at the top of the steps, looking clean-cut and well shaven. At that point I didn't realize that all Church members—males and females— had to maintain a wholesome appearance. I couldn't help but notice their broad smiles. "Hi," one said. "Welcome to Barrytown. It's great to finally meet you. I'm John Newman, and he's Wayne Stark. Just remember us as 'John Wayne.'"

We parked our van, unloaded our bags, and found our way to a big gym that was filled with Family members. (Church members referred to themselves as "Family members" and "brothers and sisters" because they were starting God's new family on Earth.) Everyone was sitting on the floor—men on one side of the room and women on the other—facing the front, waiting.

As we took our places, a buzz passed through the gym. People pushed forward and sat up straighter. Father appeared in the doorway and stood there for a minute, then strode to the front of the room and began to speak, with his interpreter at his side. Father spoke for hours. I snuggled up to Mimi, my legs tucked under me and my feet starting to go numb, and tried to figure out what was going on.

I had no real understanding of the Church—the place it held in American culture and society. At that time, as the hippie era drew to a close, many American young people were looking for a sense of higher purpose and community, just like Mimi. Countless religious movements and cults—often described as the "opiate of the 70s" by American media—had sprung up to provide something, or someone, to follow. The Unification Church was one of those. Thousands had joined the Unification Church, drawn to its teachings.

These teachings, the Divine Principle, were a combination of the simple and complex. They mapped out history in a way that made God's love for man and man's responsibility toward God blatantly obvious. In my years in the Church, I was taught endlessly that God created man in His image as male and female, as His children, in order that man (and woman) would mature to perfection and exist with God. Man's sole purpose, in many ways, was to bring God joy and to do this by following God's commandments and laws. To "be fruitful, multiply, and take dominion." I was taught that Adam and Eve were to grow to be adults, marry, and have children—thus becoming the True Parents of mankind so that their descendants could live in God's Kingdom of Heaven on Earth.

However, as we all knew because it was drilled into us over the years, man did not follow God's laws. This is where the evils of the world began. (It is also the beginning of the Church's rules—the rights and wrongs—that I would build my life around and allow to define me, until they all but destroyed me.) This is known, in Church teachings, as the Fall of Man. In the Bible it says that Adam and Eve ate fruit from the Tree of Knowledge of Good and Evil. Father explained in the Divine Principle that Adam and Eve had sex before they were supposed to. They had the first premarital sex, which is the cause of human suffering and pain. The reason we are born with sin—our Original Sin—is because Lucifer (God's archangel) seduced Eve, and Eve then seduced Adam. I think this is part of the reason Mimi stopped swearing and started wearing bras.

Father taught that since the Fall of Man, God has worked to bring mankind back to Him, only God couldn't do it alone. He needed our help. In order for the Kingdom of Heaven to come, mankind had to fulfill its responsibility, bear its burden, and play its part. (This is where it gets tough, and the guilt creeps in.)

Time and time again, mankind has let God down. Adam and Eve failed. Cain and Abel failed. Noah and his sons failed. Abraham failed. The list of people who were too weak or too selfish to live for God is endless, so endless and overwhelming that the pull to sacrifice everything for God is strong and undeniable. So undeniable and so ingrained in me—indelibly tattooed on the grooves of my brain and the inside of my heart—that years later, when I returned to these teachings to research this book, they resonated within me.

The absolute pinnacle of the Divine Principle, the slam dunk that forever glues members (and definitely Mimi, Robbie, and me at the time) to Father and the Church, is that God wanted to save mankind, so He sent Jesus as the Messiah. However, as Jesus himself explained to Father, even Jesus wasn't able to ease God's pain because he wasn't able to fulfill his entire mission.

The plan was for Jesus to marry and raise a family—to establish himself and his wife as the True Parents of mankind, to erase Original Sin from humanity. But he was killed, and God was left wanting more. Wanting salvation for His children. Wanting, needing, the Messiah to come again. Through a series of numerological calculations and historical references, the Divine Principle culminates with an awesome and thorough explanation of how the Second Coming of the Messiah occurred around 1930 (give or take ten to twenty years). It also explains how this Messiah, whom mankind has been waiting for, could only be from Korea.

As far as I remember, Father never officially proclaimed himself the Messiah or the Second Coming, but he was born in Korea in 1920. He married Mother (Mrs. Moon—Hak Ja Han), and, according to Church beliefs, their marriage established them as the True Parents of mankind, the parents who would bring God's Kingdom to Earth. From this Holy Marriage stems the many arranged marriages and mass weddings of Church members—called Blessings. These Blessings erase Original Sin from members and their future children. These Blessings bring the Kingdom of Heaven closer to fruition.

These were the beliefs that wrapped themselves like creeping vines around my mind as I grew up—during my most formative preadolescent and adolescent years—always clasping tighter and holding my life, my soul, and my sense of self together. I was immersed in Principle from the moment Mimi brought us to Barrytown, and from then on I breathed it, drank it, ate it, talked it, and learned it in all that I did, like amniotic fluid surrounds and sustains a fetus. I attended countless workshops and endless lectures—Lecture 1, The Principle of Creation; Lecture 2, The Fall of Man; Lecture 3, Consummation of Human History; and so on—and Sunday services, children's services, prayer vigils, and innumerable other moments of education and dissemination. Principle seeped into my consciousness, my blood, and my very being and flavored who I was, like blue-colored water seeps up into yellow carnations and turns them green. No wonder my psyche today has remnant scars from how the Church carved itself into my brain.

This was the doctrine, and the sense of belonging, that brought in so many members. Back in the 1970s, the Church offered a communal life and an all-encompassing Family of brothers and sisters, with hugs, songs, chants, traditions, and an inclusive identity. There was no reason to look outside for anything, and members threw themselves into the movement—relinquishing their lives, personal power, and worldly possessions.

A departure from, and perhaps reaction to, the free-love attitude of the '60s and the culture of sex, drugs, and rock and roll, Moonies had a more conservative appearance and demeanor. It was understood that the Fall of Man had been due to promiscuity and selfishness, and Church members were therefore steadfastly chaste, conventional, and celibate. I can still hear Church leaders warning sisters that their hair was too alluring. Or criticizing brothers who had visible stubble. Father never had visible stubble.

Members were, of course, always smiling. The infamous Moonie smile. Mass media called my Church a cult and declared that members smiled because they were brainwashed, citing that the Church drew fire from distraught parents because of its authoritarian structure, extreme practices of indoctrination, and insistence on severing close family ties.

The public, in general, didn't understand the movement and was, at times, terrified by it. The media tried to investigate and explain. Berkeley Rice, writing in *The New York Times Magazine* in May 1976, described the Moonie commune's appeal: not only were there no drugs, drinks, or sex, but there also were no problems, choices, or decisions to be made. No decisions to be made was an absolute pull. She went on to report how my brothers and sisters had their days prescribed for them from the moment they were woken, often before dawn, to their last group songs and prayers after midnight, and how they didn't have to deliberate or take responsibility (other than their ultimate responsibility to save the world for God) and could contentedly follow orders. She spotlighted the glassy, spaced-out look on Moonies' faces that worried the public and engendered claims that the Church drugged its members, but she attributed that look, and the Moonie smile, not to drugs but to a natural high on absolute faith and commitment to their messiah.

Moonies knew they smiled because they were lucky to live for God and because they were surrounded by endless love from their brothers and sisters. There were many reasons to always smile. Tears were shed only for God and God's suffering.

We would soon learn this and become part of it. We would discover that crucial in Church life was fundraising—going door-to-door selling American-flag pins or standing on street corners selling carnations and roses. And witnessing—bringing in new converts by "love-bombing" potential recruits, showering them with attention, affection, and friendship. This was something I experienced and thrived on. Once surrounded with this love and bubbling happiness, new members dropped out of school, left their families and their jobs, and devoted their entire lives to the Church, to God, and to True Parents.

The '70s were a time of turmoil in new religious and spirituality movements. Other cults flourished as well. Hare Krishna swarmed through airports in their salmon-colored flowing robes and shaved heads, selling orange flowers and chanting Indian mantras. Jim Jones and the Peoples Temple moved to northern Guyana, where nine hundred and thirteen men, women, and children participated in a 1978 mass suicide by drinking cyanide-laced Kool-Aid. It was an era of mental and spiritual war, of battle for people's minds. Deprogrammers like Ted Patrick, hired by concerned families to rescue members from their respective cults, also thrived. Parents of Moonies paid Ted to kidnap their children—sometimes grabbing them off the street and throwing them, bound and gagged, into the back of a van—and keep them captive until they recanted their newfound beliefs. Cult members were held against their will and subjected to mental, emotional, and sometimes physical pressure in order to undo the hold of the cult on their minds and lives. Parents fought in courtrooms for custody over their adult children, claiming their kids were caught in a state of mental submission and enslavement. Members brought kidnapping charges against their parents and refused to meet with them off Church property.

People, especially children and teenagers, were told to stay away from anyone who approached them asking for money or trying to engage them in conversation, lest they should join one of these new groups and become brainwashed. Young children were warned that "the Moonies will get you if you stay out late at night." Moonies, on the other hand, were warned about deprogrammers. They were cautioned to never let themselves be vulnerable and to never be alone, or they would be kidnapped. Fear reigned on all sides.

We didn't know any of this doctrine, any of the history, any of the controversy on the July weekend Mimi decided to bring us with her to Barrytown. We didn't know it, and it wouldn't have mattered if we did. Robbie and I loved the positive energy that pulsed throughout the building. We loved breakfast early in the morning in the massive dining hall, so many tables of smiling faces and joyous "Good morning, kids!" thrown at us. And the endless supply of pancakes and syrup. We loved the games that were played after lunch—soccer and dodge ball on the big fields that surrounded the building. We loved gathering with the brothers and sisters in a large circle at the end of the day, holding hands and singing "We Shall Overcome" or "The Answer Is in the Hearts of Men" (to the tune of "Blowing in the Wind").

We loved it all. There were hundreds—or so it seemed—of young people who were enthusiastic and fun. The Church was growing in America, and every week more and more newly minted, fresh-faced members in their early twenties were bussed up to Barrytown for workshops on Principle. They were inspired by the doctrine and the promise of Heaven on Earth—and by Robbie and me, who were young and not yet tarnished by the world. There weren't many children in the American Church back then, and we were a delight to them and a reason to have hope. Mimi would tell everyone that she had a son and a daughter, and since we were "hippie" children and Robbie wore his hair long—down to his shoulders and curly—

and I had just gotten my hair cropped close to my face, everyone thought he was the girl and therefore I was the boy. That part I hated. Other than that, Family members were the answers to my prayers. They showered us with the attention and affection I craved. My heart sang.

Most of all, Robbie and I loved who Mimi had become. We loved the smile on her face, the sense of peace and calm that enveloped her. "I know the way now," she would say to us, late at night as we cuddled together in our special room on the first weekend in Barrytown. On that trip the three of us stayed in the same room—we didn't know that it would be the only time ever, on Church soil, that we'd share a room. On future visits to Barrytown we slept in the large dormitories, females in one, males in another. I was with Mimi in a bunk bed in the sisters' area. Robbie fended for himself on the brothers' floor.

That came later, but for now all we knew was whatever had made this change in Mimi must have been good. We followed her wholeheartedly into the Church, and in retrospect, I found structure and rigid rules I could wrap myself around—and within—to feel safer. Despite how insane and wrong it might have looked from the outside.

Mimi, Robbie, and I spent a great deal of time at Church centers that summer. As a family, we were hooked. We'd been love-bombed and wanted only to be surrounded by our brothers and sisters and live for God. Every weekend we weren't at Barrytown, the three of us would visit the Center on East Seventy-First Street in New York City for Sunday services, or Belvedere, a Church estate in Tarrytown, New York, where Father would lecture on Sunday mornings at six a.m. We left Millburn before sunrise to get the best seats. I loved the early morning, warmed by the feeling of closeness to God and the heat of the engine underneath me.

Father spoke in an empty garage on the Belvedere property, standing on a small stage set in the front of the room with his interpreter at his side. There was a blackboard behind them, in case Father wanted to explain his point further with illustration or to thump it with his fist for emphasis. Ornate chairs for True Family were arranged to the left of the stage. Father spoke of God's need for us and of the glory and beauty that would be ours in the Kingdom of Heaven on Earth. He warned us of the evils of the world, detailing how cunning Satan would be as he fought for our souls. He talked of the love that would develop between husbands and wives who were following him and God. He said their adoration for each other would be so great and selfless that they could, and would, "sit next to each other on adjacent toilet seats while they used the bathroom" with ease and joy. (Just like the "Love Toilet," a toilet-for-two parody from *Saturday Night Live,* but Father was not kidding.) He instructed us to always work harder and sacrifice more, to accomplish greater and greater things for God. That became my new mantra: "Work harder. Sacrifice more. Accomplish greater and greater things for God and True Parents."

Brothers would crowd in, sitting cross-legged or on their heels on the hard, cold concrete floor on the left side of the building, right in front of Father; sisters crushed in on the right. Mimi (whom I had started to call Mother since joining the Church, as it wasn't right or respectful to call her by her name) and I would grab spaces as far forward as we could on the sisters' side. Robbie squeezed in with the brothers. I didn't care if I was tired or if my legs started to go numb as I curled up on the floor because I was with the Messiah. I was close to God.

I can't begin to describe how intoxicating that feeling was, being around Father. Beyond special. Beyond lucky. Beyond chosen. Perhaps a combination of undeserving and graced. Not holy, but physically within inches of holiness. No wonder we removed our shoes when we entered a room where Father was or would be and bowed to him as we came in or left. I would have done anything for Father, followed him anywhere.

Every now and then Father would ask new members to introduce themselves to him and to the crowd of Family members. One Sunday morning I did. I can't believe it, when I think of it now. I was only ten and incredibly shy, yet I had the guts to introduce myself to Father!

Mother had moved to the back of the room to be with some

friends, leaving me up near the stage without her. The sisters next to me rubbed my back and tickled my feet as we waited for Father to speak. I leaned into them and their love and felt a sense of contentment that was wonderful and becoming less and less foreign.

When Father asked for introductions, I took a deep breath and stood. And shook. *I'm shaking. I am talking to the Messiah. Of course I'm shaking.* Father smiled upon seeing me, perhaps because I was young and little. I smiled back, unsure and aware of how unworthy I was to be standing in front of him. Feelings coursed through me—gratitude that I could be blessed with knowing about the Messiah, shame that I was so underserving and tainted from my life before the Church, and fear that I would somehow mess everything up. That I would let God down. I knew God wanted and needed more from me than I knew how to give.

Through his interpreter Father asked me my name. I'm not sure my reply was audible. *How does one act around the Messiah?* I was trying to figure that out. I knew I wasn't good or pure enough to talk with him. I felt and heard my voice quaver. I didn't want anything to quaver. I wanted to appear strong. I wanted to be strong. God and Father needed warriors to bring the Kingdom of Heaven to Earth. He asked who my spiritual mother was—your spiritual parent is the person who brought you into the Church. I replied that it was my own mother. We talked for a few more minutes, I can't remember about what, and I sat down, my heart pounding as if I'd sprinted a mile or more. It was good to feel the floor beneath me. I hoped I hadn't made too much of a fool of myself, that I hadn't said anything too stupid.

Even though we lived in Millburn with Pop for the bulk of the week, my heart and life revolved around the Church. I lived for our early Sunday morning drive into New York City or to Belvedere. With the quiet of the new morning and the sun rising, I felt excitement and purpose pulse through me. I was on the way back to where I belonged.

Father was scheduled to speak at Madison Square Garden in September 1974. New York City was plastered with posters of

Father and the promise that "September 18th Could Be Your Re-Birthday." Mimi and I tried to hang posters in the local businesses in Millburn, but when we asked the shop owners, they looked at us as if we were lunatics and shook their heads no. I wonder what they thought of the town judge's daughter following Reverend Moon.

I spent many Sundays walking up and down Fifth Avenue with my brothers and sisters, handing out pamphlets and inviting people to attend Father's speech, enraptured with the thought of bringing his message to the city of New York. The pamphlets proclaimed the evils of the world and the glory of God, with cartoons that depicted crime and sexually transmitted diseases—things I didn't understand but knew were bad. I also knew it was essential that people realized that the Messiah had come and that God needed the world to change.

We'd preach to crowds, or to anyone who would listen, standing next to the giant lions on the steps outside the main branch of the New York Public Library on Fifth Avenue and Forty-Second Street or along the edges of Central Park. We'd march to Times Square, then a den of iniquity filled with sex shops and XXX-rated movies, and I'd shout through a bullhorn about the evils of pornography, comparing New York City to Sodom and Gomorrah. I must have been a weird mixture of cute and pathetic, my tiny ten-year-old self preaching about God. I'd join hands with my brothers and sisters and sing or pray and invite people back to Seventy-First Street to hear a lecture or, even better, up to Barrytown for a weekend workshop to experience the power of life in the Church. I was on a mission to save the world.

One Sunday just before my eleventh birthday, Mother turned to me with a broad smile. "Peach-pie," she said, her eyes dancing. "I have a birthday surprise for you!" We were on our way to Seventy-First Street for the day.

"What, Mother?"

"You'll see when we get to Church."

I didn't want to wait. "Tell me! Tell me now, please?"

"You have to wait. You'll see."

With that I knew the conversation was over. Mother ended

conversations more authoritatively since we'd become Moonies. I guess it was part of her new parental muscle. I settled into my seat—Robbie had the engine that day—and looked out the window at the cars streaming by, trying to imagine what my surprise could be.

As soon as we stepped through the large glass doors of Seventy-First Street, I turned to Mother. I hadn't mentioned anything on the rest of our ride but couldn't wait any longer. I needed to know. "Mother, tell me now. We're here. Tell me now!"

She smiled and grabbed my hands, pulling me close. I didn't care that we were in the middle of the lobby with brothers and sisters around us. The announcements on the loudspeaker in Japanese for phone calls for various members didn't register. I focused on my heart beating, my thoughts racing. I instinctively knew that whatever I was getting was going to be good. "Happy Birthday, Peach-pie. You're turning eleven now. You're old enough to make your own choice to officially join the Church."

"*Really?*"

"Yes, you'll be eleven. I already let Robbie join, because he's older. It's your turn now." Even though, in Mother's reasoning, I wasn't old enough to pierce my ears, I was old enough to choose to become a Moonie. I didn't realize the irony at the time.

This was better than new clothes, better than a pile of books, and better than the special ice-cream cake I had imagined. The Church offices were on the second floor. I flew up the stairs and burst through the door. "Mother says I can join! Mother says I can join!"

The typing and various conversations stopped, and the brothers and sisters sitting behind the desks smiled. I heard their voices echoing and bouncing. "That's wonderful!" "Congratulations!" "I'm so excited for you!"

Kyoko, a Japanese sister who loved to hug me and brush my hair, pulled open the top drawer of her desk and took out a membership form and a pen. "Here you go, Lisa," she said, her smile taking over her entire face. "Come join us!"

I grinned at her pronunciation of my name, grabbed the pen and paper, and, my hand shaking, began to fill in the boxes. Name. Birth date. Address. *It's becoming real. It's becoming real.*

"Thanks Kyoko!" I said as I rushed through the form and practically threw everything back at her. She laughed and handed me my official membership card that she had typed up. *With my name.*

And the date. And The Holy Spirit Association for the Unification of World Christianity (the official name of the Unification Church) printed on it. I stared at the words hard, willing myself to believe what had happened.

I grabbed my new card, held it tightly, and turned to the door. Kensho, one of my favorite Japanese brothers, who always had a hug or a small folded origami crane for me, pulled me in for a squeeze. "Welcome, Lisa!" he said, beaming. (I still smile when I remember the Japanese members struggling with my name because it started with "l".) "Welcome littlest, special sister!"

I smiled up at Kensho, rushed through the door, and bounded down the stairs to show Mother and anyone else around. "Look, Mother!" I shouted, waving my card about. "Look!"

5 · true children

"Mike, you go next," Hyo Jin ordered. Hyo Jin was True Parents' eldest son. The True Children had recently come over from Korea. Hyo Jin and two of his sisters, In Jin and Un Jin—the second and third oldest daughters—were about Robbie's and my age. Again, there weren't many children in the Church in America, so we were the only kids they had to play with.

Mike, who was one of Hyo Jin's bodyguards, climbed into the trunk of the car and James and Steve, two brothers who hung out with Hyo Jin whenever they could, closed it. "All set," we heard Mike say, we being James and Steve, Robbie, Hyo Jin, and me. We climbed back into the car, with Hyo Jin behind the wheel. He was twelve.

Hyo Jin started the car and drove about the Barrytown grounds. This was today's game—to have everyone take turns locked in the trunk while he drove around. For some reason, maybe because I was a girl, I was excused.

When Hyo Jin bored of that adventure, we headed down to the parking lot to ride motorcycles. *The motorcycle!* I had ridden behind Hyo Jin many times, but today he had promised I could ride by myself.

In Jin and Un Jin were waiting for us when we got there, and I headed off with them to sit in the shade under a tree. We played cat's cradle. It's what they wanted to do, and I followed their lead. They were the children of the Messiah. Even their name—True Children—clarified the hierarchy. There were the True Children. They were True. How much more special and important could someone be? Then there were Blessed Children—children of couples who were Blessed in marriage by Father. Again, the name—Blessed Children—

said it all. And then there were the rest of us. Regular, sinful children. Of course I always followed their lead.

"In Jin, you go first," Hyo Jin said.

"Okay, Hyo Jin Oppa." *Oppa* is a Korean honorific used for older brothers.

In Jin rode. Un Jin rode. Robbie rode. Some of the brothers rode. Finally it was my turn.

I studied the motorcycle. It was a bit big for me—and scary. Hyo Jin showed me what to do—how to twist the handgrip toward me to make it go and away from me to brake. That was pretty much all I wanted to hear. I didn't know if I could even take that in. My mouth was dry, and my hands shook.

Hyo Jin stepped back, and I gave the bike gas as slowly as I could.

"Give it more, Lisa, or it'll fall over," James shouted.

I did. It revved faster. Too fast.

"You got it," Robbie called out. I did. *This is good...I think.* I did a turn around the parking lot. I heard birds in the distance, but this required too much focus. *I kinda like this.* Another turn. *Okay, that's enough.* I slowed the bike as Hyo Jin had taught me to, brought it to a stop, and hopped off. It was heavy. I was sweaty.

"Let's eat," Hyo Jin said, and he took off. We headed after him, but I looked over at Robbie. We never knew what to do when Hyo Jin mentioned lunch. Did we follow him and the girls? They ate special food in a separate dining room, often with Father. Did we excuse ourselves and walk to the regular dining room, to eat the same food as the other Family members?

This time, once we got to the main building, Hyo Jin turned to the three brothers. "You guys can go grab lunch," he said. Then to Robbie and me, "Come with us."

"Yeah," In Jin said, clutching my arm. "Come with us."

We walked down the hall with them. I was exhilarated to be singled out, but what if Father was there? Hyo Jin opened the door to the dining room and went in. Robbie followed. I went next with the girls, holding my breath. Before I saw him, I heard him and the conversation about who-knows-what in rapid, loud, emphatic Korean.

"*Appa*, Dad," Hyo Jin and the girls said.

Father responded, then looked at Robbie and me and smiled.

"*Abojei*, Father," we said in unison as we bowed.

We followed Hyo Jin and the girls to the end of the table far from Father, pulled out chairs, and sat down. The room wasn't very distinctive, but Father's presence made it memorable. It had windows along one wall and framed pictures of True Family along the other. There was a long wooden table, with simple carved wooden chairs on each side. What also made it memorable was the food. Father and his Korean leaders, I'm sure, had sushi and other delicacies. Japanese sisters swarmed us with serving dishes of bulgogi, kimchi—and Big Macs. Such a contrast to my past meals of brown rice, beans, and seaweed. True Family liked Big Macs.

Lunch was quick. I'm sure Hyo Jin wanted to get back out to play. As much as I wanted to be around Father, as much as I was honored to be in the same room with him, especially at the same table, the pressure overwhelmed me. I couldn't eat.

Hyo Jin finished, so we did as well. Hyo Jin, In Jin, and Un Jin said goodbye to their father, and Robbie and I bowed again and followed True Children out. We took off, screaming, down the hallway. Father couldn't hear us, with the door to the dining room shut, and any Family members we passed just stepped to the side, smiled, and bowed their heads.

Although the True Children were inherently sinless (they were the first children born without sin, being born to the first True Parents of all mankind) and closer to God, they were, in many ways, just regular kids. Regular kids in irregular surroundings. They weren't allowed friends who weren't in the Church and were usually with Family members who were twice or three times their age. They went everywhere with bodyguards and other brothers and sisters who catered to their every whim and adored them. Revered them. Served them. Hoarded pictures of them. Let them tease them. And throw rocks at them. What adult would allow children under their charge to throw stones at them, repeatedly, if there wasn't the fear or certainty that God must have wanted that to happen since the children who threw the stones were without sin? The True Children were thrilled to be friends with Robbie and me, with whom they could just play.

Family members may have adored True Children most, but they doted on Robbie and me as well.

"Lisa," Kazuko, one of the Japanese sisters who cooked at Barrytown, said with a beaming smile as I walked through the room where she was preparing a celebration meal. "Look at this." She wiped her hands on her apron, put one hand into a deep bowl, and held up a finger with something round and white stuck to it.

"What's that?" I asked.

"A tentacle." She looked at my shocked expression and laughed. "An octopus tentacle. Come here. I'll put it on your finger. And this is shark cartilage. We put this in the soup."

Hyo Jin's wildness consumed us whenever we snuck out of Father's speeches to play with him or when he'd walk into the Barrytown lecture rooms where we sat with other members studying Principle and pull us out. We raced through the twisty halls of the building playing hide and seek and escaping from the bodyguards. We rode horses hard over the grounds of the estate, played basketball in the gymnasium where Father spoke, and jumped off the loft in the Barrytown barn. The two-hundred-and-fifty-acre estate was our private playground.

Family members felt that the True Children could do no wrong and therefore let them (and us when we were with them) get away with anything and everything. Once, we lit a fire on the grounds near the barn and I stuck my foot in the blaze, catching my shoe on fire, watching it burn. None of the adults said a thing. We could do whatever we wanted. No one stopped us.

Barrytown was where I did my first twenty-four-hour fast, a common way to purify oneself for God in the Church. Near the end of my fast, I was helping out in the large industrial kitchen, baking a cake for the next day's lunch. It was a good way to make the last hours until midnight pass and to be of service to the members who worked so hard.

I sat on a stool at the long metal cooking table, listened to the kitchen sisters talking rapidly in Japanese, and inhaled the aroma of leftover curry. I must have been on autopilot, because as I swirled the mixing spoon around the bowl, I put my finger to my mouth to lick off the batter I had splattered.

I froze.

It was as if sirens went off. *I've ruined it! How can I be so dumb?* I had fasted to get closer to God, to make up for the ways I let God down. Not finishing my fast proved how undeserving I was.

Even then I was self-vigilant with a vengeance, thinking that one slight lick of cake batter ruined nearly twenty-four hours of purification. This self-monitoring and self-hatred intensified as I grew older.

6 · memorizing my mother

As if at warp speed, the Church became the center of my universe—the sun around which I revolved and to which I clung for warmth and light. In retrospect, maybe there was a hole in my life that the Church filled. Or maybe it was the hole in Mother's life—or psyche—and I took it on. Whatever the reason, I was consumed. Preaching and proselytizing for Father was paramount. Family members were the only people I wanted to be with. Seventy-First Street, Belvedere, and Barrytown were the only places I wanted to be. There was no room for Danny. Whereas I barely visited him before the Church, now I had no desire to see him. Even Robbie chose the Church over Danny. All we cared about was our lives as Moonies. During our days at home in Millburn, we bided time in school and with friends who had mattered to us until we could get back to what mattered to us now.

Mother especially immersed herself in this new world. At first she was with us throughout the week, and things went on as usual—except for the fact that we now subscribed to a religion that was perceived by non-Family members as bizarre.

"What do you believe?" my friend Donna asked me.

She's Catholic. Sarah doesn't get it. That's okay. Donna will love to hear about Father being the Second Coming of Jesus…only I have to be careful not to actually say he's the Messiah. I'd try and explain.

"What?" she'd ask again. "That's weird. Are you sure?"

Whenever I shared our new affiliation—which I did as often as possible, and not just with Donna but with everyone since the whole idea was to bring the entire world to Principle—my classmates stared at me, intensely. Or rolled their eyes. Or told me I was crazy and strange.

Adults were no more sympathetic. They questioned the Church and were afraid of Father specifically and of Moonies in general. They compared Father to Hitler, to Mussolini, and to Charles Manson. They were petrified of being brainwashed or of having their children brainwashed. I knew that everyone outside the Church was living for Satan and needed to be saved.

With my unwavering conviction and dedication, I didn't notice as Mother headed into New York City a few days during the week to volunteer at Seventy-First Street. At first she was back in time to cook us dinner. Then she went in more and more, taking the first commuter train in the morning and coming home on the last train at night. We were left on our own to fix our meals, as well as get to school and put ourselves to bed. That was fine. Mother still came home to sleep. And it was for Father and for God.

Then she started staying over some nights. And then more. Finally, in January 1975, at a rare time when Mother was around and about six months after my first trip to Barrytown, she sat us down in the same flowered wing chair in the living room. That must have been our special serious conversation chair. It was a cold winter day. I snuggled up with her.

"Sweeties," she began, as she held us close. She paused for a long time. I sat there, feeling for her as best I could, wondering what was next.

"Sweeties, I'm not sure how long I can keep this up—taking the six a.m. train out and not getting back 'til after one."

"I know, Mother," I spit out. I needed her to know I didn't question her at all. "It's too hard."

"And I need to be there. I need to help. I'm being called to be there as much as I can…"

"I wondered what was taking you so long to figure that out," Robbie offered, his voice so subdued I almost couldn't hear him. Mother squeezed us tighter.

"What should I do?" she asked. "What do you two think I should do?"

"Go, Mother." My voice couldn't have been quieter, and I realized I sounded like I *didn't* want her to go. I didn't want her to go. That's how sinful I was; I didn't want her to go. But I couldn't sound that way. "Go, Mother!" I tried again. "Go to where you have to be."

"You're doing it for God," Robbie added. "We know you're doing it for God."

After that I suppose Robbie and I promised we'd be good and assured her that we'd be okay. I imagine we may have talked about logistics, and school, and Pop, and how we'd get to visit her. I don't remember. Everything was a blur. I sat on her lap willing myself not to cry and memorizing the feel of her next to me, the warmth of her body, her laughter, and her smile. It was God's will for her, and I wasn't going to stop her from doing what she needed to do—no matter what. I was prepared and eager to sacrifice and work for God in any way I could, even if it meant giving up my mother.

7 · left in charge

After Mother moved out everything became my responsibility. Pop had, in many ways, shut down when Mom died, and his inability to function worsened when Mother left. At the age of eleven I was the responsible one. I cooked and cleaned. I learned how to do laundry and iron. I handled the food shopping, walking to and from Dave's, the supermarket three-quarters of a mile away in town. Sometimes Pop picked me up, and sometimes, if I bought something he deemed too expensive—like the canned ham when I wanted to bake a Virginia ham like my great-grandmother did—he brought me back to return it and apologize to the store manager. I used a kid's cookbook and prepared a lot of sloppy joes, hot dog casserole, and Shake 'n Bake chicken for dinner. Tuesday was my favorite night because Pop took Robbie and me out to Syd's, a local restaurant, and I didn't have to cook.

Despite caring for Pop and Robbie, I was a normal sixth grader, albeit one who prayed a lot. "Heavenly Father, I'm sorry" were the first words out of my mouth if I missed Mother too much, or I made a mistake at school, or dinner was late or didn't come out right (something Pop often pointed out). "I'll do better" were always my next words. I talked to God constantly, begging Him not to leave me while promising to lessen His pain and suffering. I didn't know how to do that but figured I had to find a way. I walked down the block to school every day, praying or singing Church songs, and came back for my home-cooked lunch of Chef Boyardee ravioli with a can of corn thrown in for extra flavor and nutrition. (Robbie was in junior high school, so he ate the cafeteria food. I didn't have to make his lunch.) I played clarinet in the band and had a leading role, Sarah Brown, in our class play, *Guys and Dolls*. I was even a missionary on the gymnasium stage, imploring sinners to "follow the fold and stray no more." My theater life mirrored my real life. It was Divine Providence!

Fueled by my love to learn and need to overachieve, I did well in school. Really well. "Lisa," my teacher Ms. Friedman said one day, "you have earned too many A-plus-pluses. I don't know what to do with you!" She made up a new grade: A–WD: "A–With Distinction." I earned too many of those as well.

For whatever reason, Ms. Friedman singled me out. We were both Virgos, and she taught me the beauty of our exactness and need for order. She recognized my budding perfectionism and fanned the flames. She took me to see *Anything Goes* at the Paper Mill Playhouse and out to dinner. She gave me hugs and wrote me special cards and notes. I began to call her "Mom." I wonder if she realized what was going on at home. I didn't tell her. I somehow knew it wasn't okay that Mother had moved out and left me in charge. I didn't tell anyone.

When the truth of my involvement in the Church set me apart, Ms. Friedman protected me from the other kids. And from myself. In fifth grade I had been almost normal—hanging out with friends and having crushes on cute boys. I had asked every boy to dance with me one night at a school party in the gym. In sixth grade I wanted to convert my classmates, not date them, and to share the truth as revealed by Father. My classmates, on the other hand, wanted nothing to do with me. To them my Church was a cult, Reverend Moon was to be reviled, and Moonies were to be pitied and feared.

I should have realized this when I decided to bring in a newspaper clipping about Father's speech at Madison Square Garden for my current-events sharing. In retrospect, maybe that clipping wasn't the greatest idea. Standing in front of the blackboard, facing the class, I straightened the headband that held back my long brown hair and smoothed my pleated skirt and buttoned-up cardigan. (I wore skirts to school after joining the Church. They were holier than pants.) I beamed with pride as I held up the article with a huge picture of Father kicking and waving his arms in the air for emphasis, something he did to get across God's words. "This is Reverend Moon," I started.

"He spoke last week at Madison Square Garden."

Murmurs spread through the classroom, and a couple of kids shook their heads knowingly. I suppose their parents had told them what to think.

"He's a great man," I continued. "He's been chosen by God, sent here by God, to save us."

"Lisa," Ms. Friedman interrupted, "what are the facts in the article?"

"Well, they say he spoke last week for hours. That there was an overflow crowd—all twenty thousand seats were filled. It was standing room only, and thousands of people waited outside, trying to get in. And that he spoke about Jesus, God, Satan, and America."

I didn't mention that too many tickets had been given out for the free event, and people had been turned away at the door. Mother, Robbie, and I hadn't gotten in. We'd rented a bus to take our friends and neighbors, anyone who had agreed to go with us, but the Garden was full by the time we got there. I also didn't mention that midway through the speech the Garden was nearly empty. People left in droves.

Even with the details I skipped, hands shot up through the classroom. It was time for "questions and discussion," and I turned to pick Scott, the boy who sat next to me.

Ms. Friedman had another idea. "That's very interesting, Lisa. Thank you. Now we'll head right into math." She wasn't going to let anyone discuss it. I guess she knew the sorts of things they were likely to say.

Ms. Friedman might have stepped in to become my mom, but Mother was gone. There was no one to talk to each day after school. No one to make me lunch, or dinner, or brownies. No one to give me a break from the endless household chores. No one to tuck me in at night. No one to hold me if I cried.

I didn't cry. I learned not to because Mother never did, not that I ever saw. Later, when I was an adult and asked about it, she told me that Church leaders had instructed her to never let us see her cry, never to show any doubt. She also said that she broke down when she first decided to leave us—or in her view, realized she had to leave. She had been praying in one of the Barrytown chapels. She opened her mouth to ask, "Heavenly Father, please guide me," but instead what came out was, "Heavenly Father, please take care of my kids." When she heard what she had said, she sobbed. Her involuntary words convinced her that God wanted her to move to the Church full time.

I also never cried because I was told repeatedly that I was fortunate to have Mother leave. I knew I *should* feel that way. There is a notion in the Church of paying indemnity—people paying for the sins of their ancestors and clearing their descendants from paying for their sins. An individual sacrifices for the sake of the family, the family sacrifices for the sake of the community, the community sacrifices for the sake of the nation, and the nation sacrifices for the sake of the world.

"You are lucky to be able to do this," Family members said over and over. "You are blessed to give up living with your mother. God and True Parents are so grateful."

"It is your gift to God to pay such indemnity," Mr. Nakamura, the Japanese brother who led the New York Church, said. "You are so wonderful and special."

I did my best to feel lucky and grateful. I told everyone I was. I knew I wasn't special.

My life was pretty simple. And then again not so simple. I had my weekday routine in Millburn—keeping the house and clothes clean and us fed, completing homework assignments for school, and excelling in all that was put in front of me. But the Church held my heart. My weekends were for God, seeing Mother, and spending time with Family members. Being where I belonged. I no longer wanted to see Danny at all. I had never been comfortable with his lifestyle, and now I knew it was not just disconcerting but Satanic.

Robbie and I took the train from Millburn to Hoboken, then the PATH train into New York City, and then the bus uptown to visit Mother almost every weekend. It was a relief to step away from my responsibilities and be a child again. I was delirious to see her. She was, ironically, helping run the International Family Association (the

IFA)—the Church program for members who had their own families and children and who therefore couldn't move into the Church full time—like she had. Maybe they didn't have grandparents to take their kids.

Sometimes we got to stay with her at the Center on Seventy-First Street. If there was extra space on the floor in the sisters' bedroom where Mother slept, I could sleep there. Robbie, of course, stayed with the brothers in a different part of the building.

The Center was in an Upper East Side townhouse, surrounded by embassies. It had marble staircases running up the left side of the building, and every room that wasn't used as an office was turned into a dormitory, with bunk beds stuffed in to fit as many people as possible. So many brothers and sisters were crammed in, living there, that they were well over the legal limit. Once, when inspectors were coming to investigate, the members tried to hide the evidence. They took down the third level of the bunk beds and stuffed as many pairs of shoes as they could into the elevator, which worked until the inspectors opened the elevator doors and hundreds of shoes tumbled out.

When there wasn't room for us at Seventy-First Street, we stayed with the Cooks, a family who lived near the Center. They had a studio apartment for the four of them, the mom and three kids. The apartment was nearly empty, with next to no furniture, and covered in wall-to-wall beige carpet. We slept on the floor. One of the boys, Marc, taught me to rock myself to sleep, rolling back and forth in my sleeping bag on the nights when I would lie awake, overcome with jealousy that their whole family was together and with guilt that I felt jealous at all.

I loved visiting the Center, being surrounded by Family members who always had smiles and hugs for me. I felt God pulsing around me and delighted in learning more truth. I was thrilled to stay late on Sunday nights to watch the Christian movies they showed, such as *The Robe*. I enjoyed the communal meals in the basement dining room—the curried chicken and Japanese specialties that the kitchen sisters prepared, especially the little dried fish that squirmed like they were alive when you sprinkled them over warm rice. I was determined to do all I could to help spread God's word and reasoned that my usefulness and contributions were greater at Seventy-First Street than in Millburn. I wanted to live at the Center, not leave every Sunday evening to head back home with Robbie.

Once, I was scheduled for a class trip to the Guggenheim Museum on a Monday morning and begged Mother to let me sleep over on Sunday night. I didn't know where the museum was, but I was pretty sure it would be close.

"Mother," I pleaded, "let me stay. Please, can I be with you tonight?"

"No, Peach-pie. You have to go."

"Please!" I reached for her hand, holding it, and her, tight.

"No, Lisa."

"Please, please, please? I don't want to leave." I tried hard not to cry. I knew she wouldn't want me to cry.

"No. I said no."

She sent me home.

The next morning I boarded the school bus bound for New York City. Sarah sat next to me. I told her how I had wanted to stay with Mother the night before. We pulled up to the Guggenheim on Fifth Avenue, only eighteen blocks from Seventy-First Street. Sarah held my hand. I never cried.

I didn't realize it at the time, but Pop had become depressed when Mom died. His depression deepened when Mother moved out. (According to legal papers that were filed, the court had declared that she abandoned us.) Maybe that was why he let me shoulder the household responsibilities and also why he became distant and harsh. Not that I recognized his absence back then. It was only when, years later, I would see baby pictures of me with him or read notes he'd sent me before Mom got sick that I would realize how much he must have loved us—and shown it—when we were little. I can't help but contrast that with how he treated us after Mother left. Never a hug. Or a word of praise. Just criticizing my (bad) cooking skills. Not the expressions of love that I saw in the old photos and read in the old notes.

He fell behind in his work for his clients, letting their cases lapse, and was then removed from his judgeship and disbarred. As his depression deepened, the local police circled our block and cruised our street, on a suicide watch. I had no idea about any of this. I was immersed in the beginning of junior high school, the Church, the laundry, and cooking tuna casserole surprise for dinner.

One day Robbie and I were called down to the principal's office. One of Pop's close friends had come to take us out of school. When we got home, Pop was gone. He had failed to appear before a state bar association ethics committee, and there was a chance he would be arrested. Rather than being jailed, he was admitted to the psych ward of the local hospital.

Robbie and I were shuffled around for a few weeks while everyone decided what to do with us. Danny was living in the East Village in New York City. He didn't know what was going on because we never told him. Mother, who at that point lived in a Center in Queens, refused to come take care of us when our cousin told her what had happened.

My memories of this time are weird and fragmented. On the first night, we were taken to dinner at a house down the street—Pop's doctor, who had had him admitted. I didn't know that family. We stayed for a while with Pop's close friends who lived on the other side of town. I knew and was comfortable with them. Next Pop's brother and sister-in-law came up from Florida to stay with us. Robbie and I still "reminisce" about the night they sat us down in the living room and insulted and condemned both our parents. Finally, someone contacted Danny, and he showed up to get us.

The day we came back with Danny to pick up our clothes and some twin bed sheets, Sarah stopped by. "Lisa, what happened?" she asked.

I explained as best as I could. "Wow," was all she said.

"Yeah," I replied.

What else was there to say? We sat in silence on my bed, looking around my bedroom that was painted a warm peach color, grasping that my life was changing and who knew when, or if, we'd see each other again. She had been a mainstay of my last few years.

"Wow," she said again. "Wow. You win, you know. Your family really is weirder." I looked at her. Again, what else was there to say?

It was the beginning of seventh grade—just over a year after Mother first took us to Barrytown and introduced us to the Church. Since the moment we'd crowded into the gym to hear Father speak, my life had been intense, but I'd had God, and I'd known what I had to do. Now I was afraid of what would happen next.

8 · just not enough drugs

It was reassuring to have a parent show up to rescue us. I was relieved to get away from the insults hurled by Pop's brother and his wife. It was liberating to be taken out of school during this turmoil. Freed from the endless shopping, cooking, and cleaning that had overwhelmed me in Millburn, I felt like a huge boulder had been lifted off my shoulders. But I didn't want to live with Danny.

His apartment was on Ninth Street between First and Second Avenues. It was a railroad apartment, with each room connected right through to the next. A few years earlier, when he first moved in, Danny knocked down the walls so that it was one long, narrow room. He'd put up a loft bed at one end.

Robbie slept on a couch, and I slept on a foam mattress on the opposite end of the apartment. There was a shower in the kitchen area, next to the one sink and across from the refrigerator and stove. If you weren't careful, if you didn't pull the curtain closed tight enough, you could splash the appliances as you showered. The toilet was in a small space under the loft bed. The best part of the apartment, as far as Robbie and I were concerned, were the two working fireplaces where we experimented with burning trash, newspaper, milk cartons, and whatever else we could find. For Danny, the best part was the fact that we were on the first floor of the building. His cats had immediate access to a communal backyard through the always-open window behind the couch, and Danny could have his first cup of coffee and a cigarette out there on nice days.

For a few weeks Danny let us hang out. We slept late. We wandered through the city streets. We visited playgrounds, like the one on Bleecker and Mercer, which had directed me to Broome Street the day I had been lost, and hung out at the fountain in Washington

Square Park. Danny refused to have us cook or clean since we (I) did it alone in Millburn.

By the middle of November, however, we had to go back to school. Danny found the only local junior high school—I.S. 70—that was supposedly tolerable. Because it was out of our zone, the principal refused to let us in. Danny, who always fought "the establishment" and rules, pushed back. He announced that if we couldn't get in there, he would keep us out of school indefinitely. The principal relented and we were enrolled—Robbie in eighth grade and me in seventh.

We got up early each morning—before Danny, who still bartended at night—ate our breakfasts, packed our lunches, and headed across town. I refused to ride the subway, because it frightened me, so we made the longer trek on connecting buses up Avenue A and across Fourteenth Street. At the end of each day we rushed home and holed up on the couch—Robbie's bed—watching TV, waiting for Danny to make dinner or heating up leftovers he set out for us on nights he had to work.

It was hard for Danny, Robbie, and me to live together. Robbie and I weren't used to living with our father. He wasn't used to living with us. And the apartment was too small.

Late one school night Robbie and I lay in our beds, trying to sleep. Danny and some of his friends were sitting around the kitchen table, which was separated from us by a wooden breakfront Danny had built. They were drinking, laughing, and snorting cocaine. They were loud.

"Please be quiet," I whined from my bed. The noise continued.

"I need to sleep," I said. "You're too loud."

"Go to sleep, Twink," Danny answered.

"I can't fall asleep when you're so loud."

"Lisa, lie still. Leave us alone, and you'll go to sleep."

"I can't sleep. I can't sleep until you're quiet."

"*Fermez la bouche!*" Danny called back. "Stop whining, and shut the fuck up."

"Dannnnny," I cried. "I can't sleep!"

Danny's friends had not been involved in the conversation until this point. Now, Sabu, one of the largest and scariest, who had tattoos stretching up his arm (before it was the norm or cool) and whose name embodied the toughness that was him, stepped into our debate.

"Lisa," he called, "if you really want to sleep, I can help you." He paused, and I waited to hear what was next, eager for his suggestions. "If you don't shut up now," Sabu continued, "I can step on your neck and put you to sleep. You'll sleep all the way until Christmas."

Danny laughed. I shut up.

To this day, Danny tells the story of Sabu with a smile on his face. "It worked, didn't it?" he asks me if we ever talk about it. "You went to sleep."

I didn't want to stay with Danny. Although we'd visited him in New York City since I was little, living there scared me. I was afraid to go out—afraid of the city, the noises, our new life, and of him. Each weekend, whenever possible, we'd head out to Queens to see Mother. That's where I felt most at home.

One night, soon after Danny brought us back with him from New Jersey, something upset him. He threw a mirror at the floor in front of the kitchen fireplace, smashing it in a fit of screaming, cursing rage and frustration. I cowered at the other end of his apartment.

"Twink," he said to me later as I cried, "I can always get another mirror; it doesn't matter if I break it. I can't replace you or Robbie. That's different." I was not soothed. Danny's wild friends, his drinking, his cursing, his drugs—all of this not only scared me, it was ungodly by the Church's puritanical standards. He was a swearing, pot-smoking, bartending hippie. I didn't want to live with that.

Once, as we crossed Second Avenue (as usual, at his insistence, we were jaywalking) Danny asked, "What do you kids want?"

I answered without hesitation. "Please let me live with Mother." I'm sure that hurt his feelings. "We'll see," he replied.

"Danny, I love you, but I don't want to live with you," I explained. "Please let me live with her." I don't remember Robbie answering.

I repeated nearly the same thing to Mother. "Please," I again begged, "please don't make me live with Danny. Please, Mother. Let me live with you. I'll be good."

In the end, my requests had no effect. Mother would not take us back. Her life was defined by her religious fervor, and there was no place in it for young children—at least not her biological children. Church leaders advised her to "stay the course" and gave her thirty dollars to take us out to dinner. Even to this day, I don't get it. Especially now that I'm a mom, I don't get it. But to her it made sense. She explained that living in a Center with so little structure was not the best thing for us. She maintained that our lives would be easier, that we'd be better cared for, with Danny.

Now both my parents regret that they ever left us with the other one. "I didn't realize it was so bad," they both say. What does that mean?

Danny searched for a cheap place that would fit us. Two of his friends who lived a few blocks away, Bill and Gary, found out that their neighbor across the hall was moving out. Danny jumped at the opportunity.

Danny took us to see the apartment one night. It was on Second Avenue between Third and Fourth Streets, around the corner from the Hells Angels' national headquarters on one side and a men's shelter on the other. As we pulled open the old metal door to the building, I was assaulted by the smells: urine from the corner of the foyer where someone had peed, curry leaking out from the cracks in a doorway that led to the kitchen of an Indian restaurant, and stink from the chickens the super raised in the basement. The long hallway was dim and dirty, with cracked tiles on the floor and a lone bulb hanging from the ceiling.

We stepped into the elevator. It didn't smell much better. It creaked its way up—slower than you would have thought was possible—and stopped on a landing between the third and fourth floor—floor "three and a half." Even though our apartment was on the fourth floor, and all the apartments were on whole number floors, the elevator landings (and the communal garbage cans) were on the "half" floors. You had to push a button for your floor and then walk up or down a half flight of steps to get to where you were going.

The apartment was huge. It had one long hallway running from the entrance down to the living and dining rooms, which were spacious and connected and featured windows facing the Second Avenue traffic and noise. There was a decent-sized kitchen off the hallway closer to the front door, plus two bedrooms, a small one and a large one.

On this visit we had an indoor picnic, sitting on metal milk crates with roast beef sandwiches and Cokes from Schacht's, the deli a few blocks up. I looked slowly around, not saying a word—until I couldn't take it any longer. "Danny, it's filthy," I said. "The walls are a weird green color."

"Lower East Side green," Danny corrected me. "And don't worry; we'll paint them."

"There aren't enough bedrooms."

"I'll take the front room as my bedroom," Danny answered. "I'll put up doors." There was a large opening between the two rooms.

"What about the bathroom?"

The bathroom, if you could call it that, was a step up from what we had on Ninth Street, but it horrified me. There was, again, little to no privacy. The toilet and bathtub were behind a door, but it was so old and covered with paint that it didn't close. The sink was across from that door, separated by a small hallway that ran between the kitchen and the dining room. And the white porcelain fixtures weren't white but gray, stained with age and misuse.

"It's gross."

I couldn't know then that the bathroom was in its best shape ever. In the years that followed, I would come to long for the barely closing door—because when it fell off Danny replaced it with a sheet, and then everyone could hear you pee and see you bathe, if they tried. When the wall along the side of the bathtub, along with part of the ceiling, fell down, just missing Robbie while he was taking a shower, Danny put up plastic and left it like that.

Our apartment embarrassed me. It was more than filthy and less than inhabitable. The furniture was whatever Danny could find:

milk crates with glass on top as a coffee table and milk crates with plywood and a foam mattress on top as a couch, with a brown corduroy cover. You had to pick off the cat hair and cigarette ashes when you went to sit down—if it wasn't occupied by one of Danny's friends. Our couch was always a place they could stay. There were holes in the wooden floors that we swept dirt into on those rare occasions we did any sweeping, and the floors were so rough you got splinters if you walked on them barefoot. I'm sure there were mice (or something) because we could hear creatures scratching. Armies of roaches ran out of the kitchen sink and across the counters when we turned on the light at night.

Danny's cats didn't like our new apartment either. They were accustomed to their freedom. They'd never had to use a litter box before; they had gone out the window into the backyard when we were on Ninth Street. In the new apartment they decided to not use the litter box; they went anywhere but there.

Everything exploded the day Danny found cat shit all over a bag of clean laundry in the living room. "Fuck!" Danny screamed. "You little shits!"

I turned to Robbie for guidance. His eyes were wide, staring at Danny, watching him closely. "What do we do?" I whispered. He shook his head at me. I knew to shut up.

"Fuck you and your shit!" Danny blasted again.

Robbie grabbed my hand. "Come on," he hissed, pulling me into Danny's room at the far end of the apartment, where we huddled on the bed.

We heard the cats squeal as Danny grabbed them; we heard his footsteps up the hallway and the squeak of the apartment door; and we heard the thuds as the cats hit against the opposite wall. Danny must have thrown them.

I turned to Robbie again. He willed me to be silent. We heard Danny's footsteps storm back down the hall, and then he screamed at his girlfriend, Rachel. "Get out," he shouted.

"Danny!" she cried. We heard the door slam behind her.

Danny walked into his room and found us on his bed. "Get out of here!" he yelled.

We stared at him.
"Get the fuck out!"
"Where will we go?"
"Out!"
We went across the hall to Bill and Gary's apartment and found Rachel there, collapsed on the couch. None of them knew what to do with us, so we went downstairs to the diner a few blocks away and called Mother on the pay phone to see if we could come out to Queens to stay with her for the night. She said no.

Back then this was just something that happened. Now I look at it in wonder. Even if he was drinking and drugging, how could Danny throw us out, no matter how angry he was about the cats or how frustrated and overwhelmed he felt at having full responsibility for us after many years of not? Even if she was overcome with religious passion, how could Mother refuse to come take care of us or let us come to her? I know there are no answers, and yet I'll always question.

That night we ended up at Rachel's apartment on East Seventh Street, waiting until Danny calmed down and came to take us home. The cats were also collected and allowed into the apartment.

But Danny was done with the cats. Rachel lived on the ground floor and had access to the alleys behind her building. Danny made us put the cats out her window and shut it, leaving them on their own. I wasn't worried about Danny's cats; they were used to being out alone in the city streets. But Robbie and I had brought our cat, Gautzy, from Millburn. She was a suburban house cat.

"Danny, please," I begged. "Please don't put her out."

"They all have to go," he said. "I'm fucking tired of them shitting all over the place."

"Danny, she'll die."

"No."

A week or so later we were at Rachel's apartment again. Looking out the back window, I could swear I saw a cat sitting there, staring. I was sure it was Gautzy, waiting to be let in.

I wasn't comfortable living with Danny, and I wasn't comfortable at school. I.S. 70 was tolerable, but it was still a New York City junior high school. I would walk the halls or climb the stairs and get elbowed in the eye—only to show up at my class to find three other people who had also been elbowed in the eye. Other times, I had to dodge the smoke bombs that were set off in the stairwells.

Besides, I was noticeably different. Church beliefs were outrageously puritanical. I was as well. This fit perfectly with my self-imposed constraints from when I was younger but not with other teenagers.

Church doctrine forbade alcohol, drugs, anything wild—especially premarital sex. Since sex between Adam and Eve, and prior to that Eve and an angel, was the Original Sin and the cause of the Fall of Man from the Garden of Eden, having sex, or even coming close, would all but end my spiritual life. If I fell—if I had sex—I'd be estranged from the Church and all that I knew and loved. I'd disappoint God and True Father and Mother. My mother. She might really leave me, even more than she already had. If I fell, it would prove to everyone that I was as shameful and undeserving as I knew myself to be.

Experimenting with any sort of substance would send me down this path. I'd been told this, and I knew it. That's why, when Catherine, my best friend in seventh grade, offered me a cup of Seven and Seven (7UP mixed with Seagram's Seven Crown blended whiskey) during a class party at school, I wouldn't drink it.

"Here," she said, "have some."

"Uh..." I was at a loss.

"Come on, Lisa! Don't be a jerk."

"I can't," I mumbled, looking away. I had no desire to try it but every desire to keep her as my friend.

While the lives of other kids revolved around listening to "Dark Side of the Moon," cutting class to play pinball in the village or hang out near the fountain in Washington Square Park, and getting someone cute to like them or mess around with them at a party, my life revolved around God. It was the age of the Second Coming of the Messiah, and I was lucky to have found him in Father.

Having spent nearly two years hearing Church teachings over

and over, I knew them as true. My destiny was to one day be Blessed in marriage by Father, and the way to achieve this glorious state was to stay pure, follow the doctrine, and have no doubts. Even if I had doubts, I had to deny them and convince myself that I had none. I had to do whatever I could to save the world, or I would risk losing all that I had.

Toward the end of my seventh grade year, Father was bringing his God Bless America Festival to Yankee Stadium in celebration of the bicentennial. Once again, New York City was plastered with posters of Father. The streets were overflowing with Church members in white jumpsuits, sweeping garbage away—physically cleaning the city, as they hoped to spiritually cleanse the nation.

Family members were determined that the festival would outdraw the disorganized event that had taken place two years earlier at Madison Square Garden. We wanted everyone to hear God's truth. I, being a good dedicated Moonie, determined I'd do all I could to swell the attendance and pinned the big, round button with Father's face on it to my shirt every day when I went to school.

"Why are you wearing that?" kids asked, staring at me. "That's Moon, right?"

"This is Reverend Moon. He's a great man. He has a message for the world from God."

"Yeah, but the Moonies are fucked up, right?"

"Do you want to come hear him speak at Yankee Stadium? He's speaking on June First. It will be amazing!"

"You're not really a Moonie are you?" They looked at me as if I had two heads. "That's fucked up. Don't they brainwash people? Are you brainwashed?"

I smiled at them, showering them with God's love. "Do you want to come and learn what it's all about?"

My life in the Church and my life at home with Danny were irreconcilable. The austere values of my religion clashed with Danny's love affair with drugs.

It was a love affair. Danny adored cocaine. "Blow is wonderful," he cooed. "A one-and-one"—one line of cocaine for each nostril—

"makes you feel like a new man. The only problem is, then the new man wants a one-and-one."

Some of Danny's friends were part of a drug-smuggling ring, bringing back cocaine from South America. Danny dealt marijuana at times. I knew where his box of pot was kept—not hidden but in plain sight and an easy reach on the shelf of the breakfront we had moved from Ninth Street. Danny and his friends snorted cocaine and smoked pot. Robbie now only watched, having stopped when we joined the Church.

Drugs were also the basis for a standing debate between Danny and one of his friends, Tony. The two of them argued over how much coke it would take for Tony to buy me away from Danny. Tony, I hope jokingly, wanted to take me home.

"How about half a gram?" Tony would ask, looking over at me. Danny would shake his head no.

"Three quarters?"

Again, a negative response.

"Okay then, a full gram!"

"Too little." Danny would laugh. "Maybe next time."

I'd watch Tony as he bargained with Danny, then feel his intense dark brown eyes on me, staring, moving up and down. I could sense the heat rising in my face and longed to run from the room but would stay, somehow glued to where I was. Tony would smile and push his greasy black hair back from his forehead. Shivers would run up my spine and arms as I'd look away, curious how much coke it would take for Danny to say yes and what would happen when he did. I always felt a confusing mix of relief and disappointment when the amount Tony offered was never quite enough.

Danny's friend Jerry also gave me that weird feeling. He and his girlfriend, Nicole, had split, but I babysat for their daughter, Megan. Jerry made me squirm when he looked at me. When I was in high school he outright propositioned me to join him and his new girlfriend in the bedroom.

I babysat for Megan throughout high school—spending three nights with her every week, cooking her dinner, putting her to sleep, and passing out on Nicole's bed in the front room of their apartment until Nicole came home in the middle of the night or sometimes in the wee hours of the morning from her waitressing job. She would climb out of a cab and I'd climb in, or she'd have whatever friend gave her a ride take me the seven blocks to my apartment. Sometimes I got home with just enough time to take a shower, dress, and head off to school.

Megan was a sweet kid. Like Robbie and me, she was both enjoyed and tolerated by all the friends. Until one night at Nicole's apartment when the drug of choice was again cocaine. The adults were squatted around the small coffee table in the front room, doing lines. As the amount of cocaine laid out on the mirror dwindled, someone reached for the packet of coke lying on the table to spoon out more. Suddenly Megan came bounding over and bumped into the hand holding the open packet of cocaine, spilling it. Everything exploded. Someone yanked Megan out of the way, while everyone else dropped to the floor, cursing, trying to scrape up whatever they could. I grabbed Megan and held her next to me on a chair across the room.

Christmas was sacred for Danny. Not for any religious reason— Danny was an atheist—but because he loved the gifts and a chance to party. At the same time, he considered Christmas trees sacrilegious, calling them "tree corpses."

Most years he insisted we decorate the large palm tree in the corner of our living room. We would adorn it with tinsel and balls, arguing whether the cardboard angel that I made for Danny when I was little or the star Robbie made of crumpled aluminum foil would go at the top. We'd drape lights around the living room, and Danny would pay homage to the Dewar's Scotch ad he had tacked up on the side of the wooden breakfront. It showed a picture of a man with an ax slung over his shoulder at the foot of a humongous live tree. "That is why we don't have any dead tree corpses here," Danny would announce.

Each year Danny asked me what I wanted for Christmas—and hurried out and bought me something else. "Why should I give you what you ask for?" he explained. "That's no fun."

He liked to disguise his presents, putting them in weird boxes so we would have no idea what we were getting. One year I asked for a clock radio. To my delight, when I unwrapped my present I saw a clock-radio box. *Wow, I got what I wanted!* I opened the box. Danny had bought me a tape recorder instead. I called him my "bubble popper."

Danny went out of his way to throw a big party, inviting anyone and everyone and providing a nonstop supply of champagne from Christmas Eve on in order to ensure a good time. "The more the merrier," he professed, cooking three geese instead of two. I learned from Danny to open my home to anyone—to welcome, invite, and envelop.

One person never came: Mother. No matter where she was, in New York City or farther away, there was always a reason why she could not be with us and should, instead, be at the Church.

9 · this i pledge and swear

Mother moved often, but I tried to see her every weekend. At first she was in Queens, then the Bronx. She cooked for members who lived at Church centers where workshops were held to indoctrinate potential recruits. Robbie and I went to visit and help out however we could, and to attend more lectures. There were always rooms to be cleaned, vegetables to be washed and chopped, brothers and sisters to accompany on errands, and Principle to study and learn. It was always where I wanted to be.

The members delighted in us. "You are so special," they said to me. The sisters hugged me, while now the brothers only smiled. If the root of all evil was promiscuity and unsanctioned carnality, then hugging a member of the opposite sex—even, or maybe especially, a young, budding member—was taboo.

Each Sunday night before we had to go home to Danny, we gathered with our brothers and sisters for the communal Family meeting. Everyone sat in the small living room, which had been cleared of its furniture and stocked as a lecture hall with a large blackboard and folding metal chairs lined up in rows. We prayed to God and True Parents and shared thoughts, inspirations, and conversation about Principle. Then they asked us to perform.

"Robbie, Lisa, sing for us," they cajoled. We shook our heads no.

Mother always stepped in. "Get up, sweeties," she whispered to us. "Share some love." Of course we obeyed, usually singing "To Dream the Impossible Dream," which Robbie sang in his sixth grade school play.

I felt useless, being too young to be a full-time member and accomplish something for God, so I promised to do my best to help True Parents by bringing my brothers and sisters joy. I vowed to make them laugh and feel loved, smiling and playing up my cuteness to the maximum.

Family members' lives were demanding—they woke early and spent each day fulfilling God's will and fighting God's war, witnessing and fundraising, sacrificing their own desires, sleeping in sleeping bags on the floor, doing without nice things, fasting, praying, and paying indemnity for God and to save mankind. I wanted to ease their hardships in any way possible. Members marveled at my apparent willingness to live without Mother, and I swore to everyone that it was nothing, that my situation was painless. I hid my discomfort about Danny, my shame about who he was and what our home was like.

In the summer of 1976, just before my thirteenth birthday, Mother moved down to Washington, D.C. Everyone was preparing for Father's next God Bless America Festival rally at the Washington Monument in September, and Mother was sent to help run the IFA there. It was the farthest Mother had ever been from us. I ached.

With Mother far away we were unable to stay over at a Church center yet found ways to remain connected, going up each Sunday for services and special classes with the other New York IFA kids.

We didn't visit Mother while she was in D.C. She lived in a three-bedroom, one-and-a half-bath, Church-rented house in Virginia, with seventy (yes, seventy!) fellow Moonies. There was no room for us. It was the longest I'd gone without seeing her.

The day of the festival, Robbie and I went with other New York IFA members to hear Father's speech. When we got to the monument and piled off the bus, I looked around, trying to take in the enormity of the event, the throngs who had gathered to hear Father. There were more than fifty thousand people there. I wanted to hear Father speak, but there was something I craved more.

"Carol," I said, turning to the sister who was in charge of the fifteen New York IFA kids. She looked at me as she pulled blankets out of a big black bag to place on the ground. "Can I go look for Mother?"

"Yeah," Robbie joined in. "Can we go find our mother?"

"No kids. Stay here."

"But she must be here," I whined.

"Nope, not today. There's no one to go with you. Stay put for Father's speech."

I wanted to see Mother, to hear her voice and feel her near me, to sit with her through the fireworks at the end of the evening and snuggle in her lap. It had been my thirteenth birthday just two days earlier. All I wanted was a birthday hug. Instead, I wiped my eyes and turned to the stage, ready to listen to True Father. Robbie stood beside me, also silent and resolute. Mother later told us that she spent her entire time at the Washington Monument wandering through the crowds trying to find us.

The day after the rally, a Church leader told Mother to go back to New York. She moved into the new Church headquarters on West Forty-Third Street to again help run the IFA. She also became the housemother for the members who lived there. This was an improvement over D.C. as far as Robbie and I were concerned. We could visit on the weekends, although our main interaction was with the sisters who were assigned to the IFA kids who lived outside the Church. Mother was busy.

I remained driven to prove my worth and win the love and care of my parents (biological and True). Maybe if I followed Principle, was perfect and good, and never disappointed anyone, Mother would love me more and I'd get to be with her more. I never complained, not even the time when I called her and the sister who answered the phone put me on hold—and Mother forget I was there. I waited for forty-five minutes until she remembered, and that was before there was music on a hold line to distract you. She had more important things to take care of and people to attend to than me.

Once, when I was in eighth grade, I couldn't face her. I didn't want to tell her what I had done. We were in one of the sisters' bedrooms at Forty-Third Street. Mother was perched on a bottom bunk, and I sat down on the floor near her. "Mother," I started, and hesitated.

"What Peach-pie?"

"I'm sorry." I looked down at the floor, not wanting to see disappointment in her eyes. "I got a ninety-six on a test. I know I should have gotten a higher grade. I'm sorry." (I wasn't kidding, like I am now when one of my kids gets "only" a ninety-six.)

While Mother lived at Forty-Third Street, our cousin Dale got engaged. Robbie and I were going to the wedding, but Mother wasn't allowed to go. Luann, her Central Figure—the person in charge of her in the Church—forbade her to attend.

Robbie and I needed something to wear. Somehow we were able to buy new clothes. Even to this day, I can't fathom how. Mother never had any money unless she received a gift from Church leaders, and Danny didn't buy clothes for us unless he had to. And he'd never buy dress clothes.

I was electrified to go shopping with Mother, something I hadn't done since she left us in Millburn.

"Mother," I said, as we sat together on the couch in the IFA office at Forty-Third Street. The room was empty except for the three of us. Time alone with Mother. "Do I really only need one dress? What if I need two?"

"You'll only need one, Peach. Don't worry."

Robbie jumped in. "What color suit should I get?"

"What color should I get?" I asked before Mother could answer.

"Hold on," Mother said as she laughed and pulled me even closer to her, then reached for Robbie and pulled him in too. "Hold on. We'll see what they have and take it from there."

Luann walked into the office.

"I'm glad you're here," Mother began. "I'm thinking of taking the kids shopping next Saturday. They need clothes for the wedding."

Luann didn't answer right away. Then: "Next Saturday?"

"Yes, in the afternoon." Mother paused. "If that's okay?"

"Well...no. I don't think so. I think I need you here."

I stared at Luann. She gave no other information. No reason. I could feel my smile fade from my face, although I willed myself not to look, or act, upset.

"But the kids need to go shopping," Mother said.

"That's okay," Luann answered, closing the deal. "I'll take them for you."

Mother, of course, obeyed, and Luann went with us to Macy's, where she bought a blue suit for Robbie and a frilly white dress for me. I tried to enjoy the outing, knowing that I was lucky and that

Mother was doing what she needed to do.

It was wonderful to be near Mother, but we always had to go home at the end of the weekend. Sometimes before we left, Mother would be given money to take us out. We never went alone. She always invited a member who needed some extra nurturing. Invariably the brother or sister would turn to Robbie and me. "What a great mother you have," they would say lovingly. "We feel so cared for by her. You are so lucky."

I don't remember when I started saying Pledge—a weekly ritual in which members vow their devotion to God, True Parents, and the Church. I do remember joining in whenever I stayed over at Forty-Third Street.

Pledge is essential in Church life. Every Sunday, Family members all around the world rise before dawn, dress in their best clothes, assemble in a common room (or alone in front of a picture of True Parents), and rededicate themselves. Each morning that I was lucky enough to say Pledge, surrounded by my brothers and sisters, I was reaffirmed and charged to keep going.

The words echoed within me.

As the center of the cosmos, I will fulfill our Father's Will and the responsibility given me. I will become a dutiful daughter and a child of goodness to attend our Father forever in the ideal world of creation by returning joy and glory to Him.
This I pledge.

I will take upon myself completely the Will of God to give me the whole creation as my inheritance. He has given me His Word, His personality, and His heart, and is reviving me, who had died, making me one with Him and His true child. To do this, our Father has persevered for 6,000 years the sacrificial way of the cross.
This I pledge.

As a true daughter, I will follow our Father's pattern and charge bravely forward into the enemy camp, until I have judged them completely with the weapons with which He has been defeating

the enemy Satan for me throughout the course of history, by sowing sweat for earth, tears for man, and blood for heaven, as a servant but with a father's heart, in order to restore His children and the universe, lost to Satan.
This I pledge.

The individual, family, society, nation, world, and cosmos who are willing to attend our Father, the source of peace, happiness, freedom, and all ideals, will fulfill the ideal world of one heart in one body by restoring their original nature. To do this, I will become a true daughter, returning joy and satisfaction to our Father, and as our Father's representative, I will transfer to the creation peace, happiness, freedom, and all ideals in the world of the heart.
This I pledge.

I am proud of the one Sovereignty, proud of the one people, proud of the one land, proud of the one language and culture centered upon God, proud of becoming the child of the One True Parent, proud of the family who is to inherit one tradition, proud of being a laborer who is working to establish the one world of the heart. I will fight with my life. I will be responsible for accomplishing my duty and mission.
This I pledge and swear. This I pledge and swear. This I pledge and swear.

These words defined my being and passion and gave me hope for a future—my future—when God's Kingdom would be here on Earth and man would live in peace and joy as was intended. Tears came to my eyes each time I bowed before God and True Parents with the sure realization that I had never done enough, that there was always more to do, and that I was blessed to be part of this movement.

I felt even more blessed over the next year when I met an older brother named Hugh.

10 · the ultimate groupie

As freewheeling as Danny was, he didn't want Robbie and me lost in the New York City public high school system. He declared that if Robbie and I didn't pass the entrance exam for Stuyvesant—one of the specialized math and science high schools—or get financial aid from a private school, we would move to Brooklyn. Back then Brooklyn wasn't what it is now, and it was banishment to Siberia in Danny's eyes. Fortunately for him, both Robbie and I made it into Stuy, which was then located on Fifteenth Street between First and Second Avenues, just over ten blocks from our apartment. It was our local high school. Other kids traveled from all five boroughs.

Back then, Stuyvesant was known for its academic rigor. Nowadays it is well known because the late author Frank McCourt taught creative writing there long before he became famous. In Mr. McCourt's bestselling memoir, *Angela's Ashes,* he wrote about how his mother put family first. My mother did too. Only her family was the Church.

Around the same time I started high school, Mother was sent upstate to Barrytown to work in a nursery, where she cared for Blessed Children. Parents would head out on missions around the country and the world, leaving their kids, often as infants, to be raised by Mother and other sisters.

With Mother in upstate New York, we again couldn't visit her on weekends. In her absence, I searched for ways to stay involved. Keeping connected would allow me to fulfill my promise to bring my brothers and sisters joy and love—and minimize my contact with the kids at Stuy who might tempt me to leave Father's path of truth.

High school kids scared me. Each day I walked the halls between classes, studying my fellow students. They seemed so much older.

And from the looks of it, they were into the things I feared: drugs, drinking, and sex.

In choosing friends, I looked for kids who weren't involved in anything Satanic, figuring that would protect me from everything unwanted. I socialized with them a bit but kept my distance and never hung out outside of school. In fact, I became less and less engaged by my Monday-through-Friday life and lived even more for the weekends. I looked for members to whom I could attach myself and continued to go to Sunday services at Forty-Third Street and spend time with other IFA kids or any brothers or sisters who were interested in having me near.

Enter Hugh, a brother enraptured in Father's teachings. Ten years my senior, I was enraptured in him.

Hugh was a soft-spoken Englishman. He was relatively tall, with a thin build and straight brown hair that fell over his eyes (when he wasn't wearing his black beret). He was passionate—about life, about God, about True Parents, about everything. He made me want to be passionate too. I looked up to him as a mentor, or guru. I wanted to be exactly like him and do everything exactly like him, to earn and deserve his love, though at times I wondered if he cared for me because Mother had asked him to do so while she was away.

An artist and zealous musician—he was the guitarist in the Church's rock band, Sunburst, and would jump around the stage and up onto the piano when he played during performances—he inspired me to devote myself more to the clarinet and to learn to play piano. I wanted to create as he did and longed to impress him with some startling accomplishment. Was this a girlhood crush? In retrospect, perhaps, but at the time, I had no idea and would have died from shame if I thought I was attracted to him.

Hugh taught me that rock-and-roll music wasn't always Satanic. I had been raised as a hippie kid, singing Beatles songs and the lyrics from *Hair* and attending free Jefferson Airplane concerts in Central Park, but in the past few years I had all but written off any music that wasn't Church hymns or Korean folk songs.

I spent every weekend with Hugh and a sister named Judy, who worked with him. Father had recently bought the New Yorker

Hotel on West Thirty-Fourth Street and Eighth Avenue, and many members lived there. That's where I went every Friday night, staying until I had to return home on Sunday.

Danny would be bartending at Raoul's, a hip French restaurant on Prince Street in SoHo, when I'd leave, so I'd either drop a note on the kitchen table ("At the New Yorker. Back Sunday.") or call and try and catch him before the dinner rush. "Danny?" I'd start.

"Yeah?" he'd spit back.

"I'm going up to the New Yorker."

"Be home Sunday for dinner," he'd answer and hang up.

Hugh encouraged me to deepen my love for True Parents and my personal connection with God. "Lisa," he said one day as we walked down Thirty-Fourth Street. "Before I found Father I was lost. I prayed for answers, for meaning, and I looked up and saw a 'one way' sign. God told me there was one way, and I found it here."

Now this statement seems a bit grand or cheesy, but back then it was something to aspire to.

"How? How did you get an answer?" I asked.

I prayed for guidance and reassurance of my connection to God. I craved answers. God heard other members more than He heard me. I wanted to be sent a sign as well. They did a seven- or twenty-one minute prayer and received a response. I spent time on my knees—talking to God, promising to do my best, crying to end His suffering, and begging forgiveness for my sins—and got nothing. Mother prayed for a parking space, and there it was. God ignored me.

Staying at the New Yorker allowed me to wake up at four a.m. every Sunday to say Pledge and ride a bus to Belvedere to hear Father. He would speak for hours, and I'd sit Japanese style, with my legs tucked under my body, my feet eventually falling asleep—sometimes with all of me nodding off—surrounded by my sisters, grateful to be there, sure of the truth, and absolute about my future. I knew my destiny: to live for God and True Parents and give anything and everything, including my life—as God's child and warrior.

The New Yorker was rundown—carpets and wallpaper fraying, paint peeling and chipping. We didn't mind. Hugh and Judy had a large suite of rooms in which they worked on their projects. For every Church holiday celebrated at the hotel, they created a huge backdrop for the stage to hang behind the various performing groups who entertained members and True Family during the evening celebration. Visuals of vibrant flowers, phoenixlike birds, and elaborate and colorful designs representing the glory of the East and of Korea covered the tarp. I helped paint the background.

Hugh designed a world map for the fourth floor of the New Yorker, where the main offices were. It was so moving, taking up the entire wall outside the elevators and covered with what seemed like hundreds of tiny lights, one for each Church outpost throughout the world, including the missions in Africa and South America. The first time I saw the map I looked at it for a few minutes, trying to figure out what was weird. Then I realized that while most maps I had seen were drawn with North and South America in the middle, as the epicenter of the world I guess, this map had Korea positioned in the center—at the heart of everything, as it should be.

I helped Hugh during the day, trailing behind him wherever I could. He held my hand as we walked through the hotel halls while no one was around. I felt loved, though a bit confused and guilty. I spent the nights with Judy and her roommate in their small, decrepit bedroom, sleeping on the floor, grateful, as always, to be there.

Following Hugh around morphed into following Sunburst around as well. I became, by my own definition, their #1 fan. Throughout my first years of high school, my self-proclaimed mission was to serve them in whatever way possible, so I hung out when they practiced and traveled with them to different gigs throughout the New York area, up to Barrytown, and as far as Tennessee. I played roadie and gopher, setting up and breaking down equipment for concerts and doing the lowly jobs that no one else would. I memorized who liked coffee, who liked tea, and who wanted hot water with lemon and honey (the sisters who sang).

The members of the band counted on me to help them and trusted me to care for them. As part of the community outreach to bring in members, they played Wednesday nights at the Down Home Inn, a little coffee shop next to the New Yorker. I was there every week, sitting up front, wearing my yellow homemade "Sunburst's #1 Fan"

T-shirt, cheering them on. One night they sang a song that Hugh and another member had written for me, "Lisa." They sang of my devotion, my serving, and my love. Mother came to hear them play it. She, Robbie, and I sat up front, listening, holding hands. My smile could not have been bigger.

During one Church holiday at Belvedere, Sunburst posed for a group promotional shot. I understood why I wasn't asked to be in the picture, but it hurt. Again, I knew I couldn't show it. Instead I played ultimate groupie and asked everyone to autograph the photo for me. I read their inscriptions over and over, hungry for proof of their love. (Thirty years later I still read what they wrote and feel a yearning.)

Each inscription was signed "ITN"—which stood for In Their (True Parents') Name. This was how Family members ended letters, notes, and prayers. Hugh's message was one I reread many times. "Lisa," he wrote, "you've given me more than you can ever imagine. You're the light of my eye." I always wondered what that meant. I always wanted more.

The Church owned a number of properties in Westchester County. East Garden, the beautiful twenty-five-room mansion where True Family lived, was in Irvington. Belvedere was in Tarrytown, the next town over. So was Jacob House, the new Blessed Children nursery where Mother was sent to live in 1978, almost a year after she had gone to Barrytown.

Mother was now close enough to visit every weekend. Eager to see her, Robbie and I grabbed a train up every Friday afternoon and back on Sunday night, or begged a ride home if someone happened to be driving into the city. I helped Mother with the babies in her care, finally feeling like I was contributing. We rose at five a.m. on Sunday to say Pledge, making it to Belvedere in time to hear Father speak.

"You may be right; I may be crazy..." These were the words I heard as the bouncing bed woke me. I was sleeping—on clean, soft sheets!—in the bottom bunk in an extra room at Jacob House. Mother slept on the floor of her room, the walls lined with the cribs for her babies, so there wasn't room for me there. "But I just may be the lunatic you're looking for…" Mother continued singing and bouncing, smiling down at me. I woke—somewhat sullenly, somewhat happy—then remembered I could take a shower in a bathroom that wasn't disgusting, had no roaches, and had a door! I decided to go for all happy. Anyway, I was with Mother. Life was always better when I was with Mother. And I felt safer at Jacob House.

Robbie and I had taken Mother out to dinner the night before—she'd gotten permission to go but, as usual, had no money—and that's where we'd heard the Billy Joel song that was stuck in her head. It was Sunday, and although Father hadn't spoken and I'd gone back to bed after Pledge, Sundays were still full. Robbie and I attended special services with the older Blessed Children who were living with their families in the various Church-owned houses in Tarrytown, and we headed to Belvedere or East Garden after Sunday services if the True Children could play. Many a crisp, sunny fall afternoon was spent in fast-paced soccer games on Belvedere's extensive lawns, and many a gorgeous summer day was spent splashing in the pool in front of the house at East Garden.

I went through the ritual of Pledge. I wouldn't dream of telling anyone that my heart and mind weren't in it. All I could think about was Father's speech at Belvedere that morning. *Will In Jin be there? Will I get to see her?*

Over the years I had become closer to In Jin and Un Jin. In Jin was two years younger than I, while Un Jin was four years my junior. Whenever we saw each other, the three of us were inseparable.

After we got to Belvedere and I moved my way into the garage toward the stage, I thought it through. How to strategically put myself up near the front, to be close to Father, but also near the edge of the row of sisters so I could sneak out if In Jin gave the sign.

I waited with my brothers and sisters for True Family to arrive. We were silent, as always, preparing to receive God's word. *I hope In Jin comes. Is it wrong to hope she comes? I should want to hear Father. But I haven't seen her in weeks.*

Then the hush, and then the ripple of movement and excitement through the crowd. Father was coming. I looked over at True Family's chairs on the side of the stage. *In Jin!* I tried to catch her eye. She smiled and gave me a tiny nod. *Yes!* I inched my way out of the garage, staying as low as possible. I didn't want True Mother, or my mother, to notice.

I waited outside the building, already smiling. I heard her before I saw her. "Hey!"

I turned around. "Hi," I said, smiling more.

In Jin linked her arm in mine. "Let's go."

We stole away from the members, who were huddled, enraptured, at Father's feet. Jim, one of her bodyguards, trailed a few yards behind us—far enough to give us some privacy but close enough to keep In Jin in sight and to act in an instant should something happen. When we were young we shared secrets that were, like us, immature and silly. As we'd gotten older, our inner thoughts and fears grew with us. "You're the only one I can say this to," In Jin started, and proceeded to tell me how she missed True Parents when they were away and about the pressure she sometimes felt as their child. Or she complained about the guards, about never being on her own, about always being watched. I listened.

Our sneaking away did not go unnoticed by True Parents. Eventually Mother's Central Figure asked her to stop us from wandering off; True Children were to sit in their special chairs on the side of the stage.

In Jin was a True Child, and a true friend until many years later when I was no longer allowed near her. But until then, we were together whenever we could be. On Church holidays celebrated at the New Yorker and the Manhattan Center—the old Manhattan Opera House attached to the New Yorker, which Father had also bought—we worked to escape the bodyguards. We dashed through the deserted hallways, rode the elevators (jumping as the elevator descended from the highest floors, to feel the momentary sensation of floating), ran screaming up and down the stairways in the main lobby, and slid down the huge barrier that ran between the two defunct escalators from the lobby to the empty basement that used to house a restaurant and a barber shop in the hotel's heyday. (It was an awesome slide. When the hotel was renovated in the 1990s to accommodate actual guests, little bumps were attached along the barrier to keep anyone from using it as we had.)

At the holiday evening celebrations, I sat on the floor near True Children's special seats in the Manhattan Center theater, waiting for them to be with me no matter how long it took, cheering them on as they performed (the True Children always had to sing, often with Sunburst, as entertainment for members), and joining in the thunderous cheers of "*Abeoji*, Father," "*Mansei*, long live Korea, ten-thousand years" that Korean Church leaders or Father would lead members through at the end of the evening. I swam in their pool at East Garden, conscious to be on my best behavior in case True Parents were around and painfully aware of the contrast between their lives and home and mine.

In Jin had a huge heart and would check on me when we were together to make sure I was okay. "Lisa, my sweet little friend," she'd say as she put her arms around me. I'd lean into her, to soak her up, yet also pull away. *Who am I to be her friend? I don't deserve this.* There was no way I was good enough. And if she knew where and how I lived and what my father was like, while hers was the Messiah, chosen by God.

Once when I was visiting In Jin at East Garden, she called me to her room. I carefully crept up the stairs, sinking into the rich, deep carpet, and along the quiet hallways lined with gilded mirrors and opulent furniture. True Parents could be anywhere; I needed to blend in where I could never blend in. To be neither noticed nor noticeable. I stealthily rushed to In Jin's room, slipped inside, and stared at the beauty and blueness that surrounded me. A canopy bed with a lush cover, both of the bluest sky-blue. A beautiful white desk. A deep blue plush rug. Girlie touches everywhere. I thought of my apartment, of my bedroom, and felt heat rise in my face.

"Lisa, I have something for you," In Jin whispered, smiling, as she closed the door behind us and walked to her closet. I stood there, my mouth open and eyes wide, taking in the beautiful dresses. "Here, I want you to have this," she continued, and pulled out a simple green dress that she had worn to a few celebrations but had outgrown. (Even though I was two years older, she was bigger.)

I didn't know what to do. "Thanks," I mumbled, and reached for it. I couldn't decide whether I felt more touched or honored or embarrassed. I wondered if she wanted to share with me or if she pitied me, particularly when she looked at what I had to wear. It was a struggle to find clothes that were nice enough for holidays or when I was around True Family. (I never wore the dress. I felt too sinful and worried that I would somehow tarnish it. But I could never get rid of it either, not even years after I left the Church. It was too holy.)

In Jin and Un Jin were revered by members. They could do no wrong and were rarely, if ever, reprimanded. I had some degree of immunity when with them but was often pulled aside and asked to make sure "the girls" behaved better, especially when children of the original Korean leaders—two cousins, Jae Eun and Soo Jung— joined our group.

I was hanging out with Sunburst one afternoon in their practice room in the New Yorker, when In Jin, Un Jin, and Soo Jung walked through the door. I hadn't known they were coming, and I couldn't have been more elated. Well, almost. Because as much as I was growing to love Soo Jung as well, I was jealous that she got to spend so much time with In Jin. Soo Jung lived near East Garden. She was a Blessed Child. She was Korean. She was with them more.

The girls had come down to the city to practice for the upcoming holiday. They planned on singing "You Light Up My Life," although they stepped up to the microphone and asked Sunburst to play "Cold as Ice" first. As they launched laughingly into the song, the Sunburst members staring at them with awe and adoration, I remembered when they used to sing simple songs like "Swinging on a Star," which was more my speed. I would never sing a Foreigner song. I didn't even know the words!

When they finished practicing and it was time to go—when Sunburst stopped fawning over them—I stepped out into the hallway to say goodbye. In Jin noticed that her bodyguards weren't around. Jim, along with another guard, had driven them into New York City from East Garden, but I guess the girls finished early.

In Jin smiled. "Let's go," she announced, taking off down the hall. Un Jin and Soo Jung followed. I hesitated. I wanted to do what was right, and they were breaking rules decreed by Father. But I also wanted to help them any way I could. As always, that won out. I decided to join in their reprieve, and the four of us slipped into a stairwell to climb to a different floor then headed to the elevators. A few unsupervised minutes was all In Jin and Un Jin wanted. Just a little less pressure. We knew we'd end up back in the lobby or at the duplex suite that True Family used when they stayed at the New Yorker for holidays. We knew we'd get into trouble for sneaking off.

The truth is that I was the best behaved, or perhaps the most reluctant to misbehave. I wore flat shoes and plain clothing while they wore Candies, tight Jordache jeans, and makeup. I avoided pop culture and rock music (except for Sunburst's) while they danced to disco, sang songs like "Play that Funky Music White Boy," and watched *Saturday Night Fever*. I followed all guidelines and rules put out by Church leaders and Mother, both stated and implied, in order to keep myself pure, while they, perhaps because they were pure, pushed to bend the rules and have a more normal American teenage existence.

I would hear it from the bodyguards. "Lisa," they'd instruct, "stop them from running away. It's not safe."

"Okay," I'd reply, trying to twist my head around how I could possibly change In Jin and Un Jin's behavior. They were strong-willed, like their dad, and determined to gain whatever freedom they could, however they could. I felt for them. They had bodyguards drive them to school and take them wherever they went. They weren't allowed to go to the mall, to friend's houses. Nothing. They were always on display. And they were holy. They were the children of the Messiah, and I was sinful and evil in comparison. How could I tell them what to do or lead them a different way?

I became even closer with Soo Jung and Jae Eun. I was with one or both of them from Friday evening when I arrived at Jacob House to Sunday evening when I left. Although, as always, I was aware of the differences between us. It was something you just knew, kind of like knowing—without consciously knowing—you need air to breathe. It just was. They were Blessed Children; I was not. They were special; I was less so. But being around them made me feel graced and chosen by God.

Jae Eun and I became especially tight, I suppose because we were the tame ones in the group. Soo Jung and the girls were much more wild and rebellious. Like all of them, Jae Eun wanted me to be more Korean.

"Lisa, come with me," she said one Sunday after our services. "I have an idea."

"What?"

"You'll see. It'll be great!"

We walked up the road to her family's small house. Small, but of course I was envious that she lived with her parents and ashamed that I harbored such feelings. Once we were inside, standing on the lush carpet and surrounded by the ornately carved Korean furniture and pictures of True Parents, I felt my face heat up. Coveting was breaking one of the Ten Commandments. I coveted anyway.

"Come here," Jae Eun said, and she dragged me down the short hallway to the room she shared with her sister. "Put on this tiny hanbok." (A hanbok is a traditional Korean dress.) I jumped at the chance and struggled to get it on and tied correctly. It was white with pink accents, a bit small, and very elaborate. Jae Eun put on her hanbok as well. It was a multitude of colors. We posed in front of the mirror with our arms around each other.

"Let's go outside and take a picture," Jae Eun said. I have that picture still. I was beaming. They weren't the only ones who wanted me to be more Korean.

As close as we were, Jae Eun and I also developed a unique, competitive relationship. One of the children in Mother's care was a sweet baby boy named Kenritsu. By the time Kenritsu reached toddlerhood, Jae Eun and I were rivals for his affection. Each of us would work to make him love us more than the other one. We'd ply him with treats, special hugs, and undivided attention and call to him to see which of us he'd go to first. One day I spent hours walking in circles at Jacob House—up the back staircase, across the halls, and down the front staircase—with him in my arms because he was sick and that's all he wanted. I may have been tired, but I was also pleased that I'd been of value and that I had one up on Jae Eun.

My memories of Jacob House are, in many ways, idyllic, but soon my contact with Blessed Children, and with Mother, would come into question.

11 · banished

I rang the Jacob House doorbell. It still felt weird to ring the doorbell rather than to walk right in. "Do you think we'll see Mother today?" I asked Robbie. Spending time with Mother, even for a few minutes, was all I had thought about during Father's speech. I hated to admit that my attention was on something so selfish, but it was.

The door opened and Mary Jo, one of the sisters who cared for the Jacob House babies, grinned when she saw it was us. "Hey kids! How are you?"

"Great," Robbie answered. "Is our mom here? Can we say hi to her for a few minutes?" I wasn't paying attention to their conversation. I was trying to see inside. I missed seeing inside and being inside. I missed Kenritsu. I missed all the children. I missed Mother.

"Sorry," Mary Jo said, looking guilt-ridden. "She's busy with the babies and can't come down. She told me to tell you that she loves you, and maybe she can see you for a few minutes next Sunday."

"Okay. Uh, thanks." Robbie turned to me. It seemed like he took as long as he could to say anything else, as if by postponing his next sentence we stood a chance that Mother would miraculously find time. "Come on, Lisa, let's get on the buses back to the city."

Earlier that year, the Church hierarchy had decided that the growing number of older Korean Blessed Children in the New York area needed more specific guidance and training to keep them away from the evils of American society and the awful influences of American teenagers (such as Robbie and me) in their schools. They were told to spend their summer in a special twenty-one-day workshop at Jacob House for further study of Principle and reinforcement of their connection and commitment. Robbie and I were lucky enough to be allowed to join them.

The workshop did not turn out well. Someone wrongfully suspected that Robbie had a crush on Jae Eun and determined that it was therefore no longer safe for us to be around the Blessed Children. In order to keep Robbie and me away, the Korean woman who ran Jacob House, Jae Eun's aunt, decreed that the only outsiders permitted inside the building were the parents of the Blessed Children who lived there. Unrelated Church members were no longer allowed to visit. Unrelated to the children. It didn't matter that Robbie and I were related to Mother. We couldn't stay at Jacob House on the weekends anymore. We weren't even allowed through the front door.

We went back to staying at the New Yorker on Saturday nights in order to take the chartered buses up to Tarrytown in the morning to attend Father's speeches. The drivers parked in the Jacob House driveway, so we always ended up standing outside the building before we left to go home. And we always asked if we could see Mother, if she could come out for a few minutes.

We were restricted, but I needed my life, and especially my weekends, to be about the Church. I therefore increased my time at the New Yorker, again following Hugh and Sunburst around every spare minute I had. I also spent more time at Belvedere itself, hanging out after Father's speeches with True Family's bodyguards who lived there.

I had become friends with practically all the bodyguards. In fact, with my smiling face and cheerful resolve to bring every Family member as much love and happiness as possible, I became a favorite.

"Connor," I asked one of the brothers one Sunday, "where is that picture of me that you have? The one of me outside the garage, after Father's speech. You said you'd get me a copy for my mom."

"Soon," he answered. "Soon."

The next Sunday I asked the same question and received the identical answer.

A few weeks later, Connor approached me as I helped put away the folding chairs that had been set up to hold the overflow of members that spilled into the driveway during Father's speech. "Lisa," he called, "here's the picture. Sorry it took so long, but all the brothers wanted a copy." I could feel my heart sing, knowing that I'd fulfilled my promise to bring joy and sunshine to my Family.

I was close to many of the brothers who lived at Belvedere, but there were two who, like Hugh, were pivotal in my teen years: Brian and Reggie. Reggie was one of Father's bodyguards and drivers, and Brian helped take care of the Belvedere grounds.

"Lisa, let's grab breakfast," Brian would whisper to me. Father's speech would be over, and people would be wandering about the grounds. I always nodded yes. I was delighted for a trip to the diner and even more so to have Brian to myself.

He was in his mid- to late-twenties, compared to my mid-teens. He was short, stocky, and very cute, with light brown hair and blue eyes. He had a way about him that drew you to him. At least I was drawn. Even in my innocence—I would have sworn that all I felt for him was sisterly love and affection—I reveled in his attention. He was the Sunday school teacher for the Blessed Children services. The one to guide us toward right and away from wrong as we matured. He was also tight with Jae Eun and therefore became another person over whom she and I competed. I was exhilarated to be the one he chose to have breakfast with on a Sunday morning.

As with all Family members, I trusted Brian completely. In retrospect, maybe that trust wasn't well placed. He liked to push limits and test boundaries. Deep inside, I knew that it was a bit off that we were close and that he played up the rivalry between Jae Eun and me, but I didn't care. I was determined to correct his straying ways and bring out his best behavior and, no matter how I might try to fight it or deny it, felt myself turn willingly to him whenever he focused my way.

On another trip to the diner, Brian started to put his arm around me as we walked up the pathway to the door. I pulled away, wanting distance between us and looking at him with disdain.

"Lisa," he said, laughing. "Come on."

"Brian, no."

He smiled bigger. "It's my birthday, come on." He put his arm around me again. "Besides, it will warm us up."

I stepped away from him. "It's not right. No."

"Just this once, as a birthday present?" He pushed himself closer to me, his eyes begging.

Wrong as I knew it would be, I ached to say yes.

"Please?" he asked again, laughing harder.

I caved. It felt good—and innocent. *Brian is my brother. He won't lead me astray.*

Reggie was one of the few black members—the only black brother at Belvedere. Like Brian, he was somewhat short and stocky, good-looking, and well built. And like Brian, he was bent on testing limits. The two of them would often joke about the times they went out for beers. "Guys, you need to stop," I'd correct them, appalled. "It's wrong!" They'd laugh.

Reggie also tried to put his arm around me whenever he could. I always said no, even though it felt good. A bit scary, but tantalizingly good.

Robbie and I weren't allowed into Jacob House for nearly a year. Then, just as suddenly and randomly as the decree came down, it was lifted. By the following spring staying with Mother was no longer off-limits. I was grateful for this change, especially the weekend of the Matching, when my help was essential.

Father was planning a huge Blessing in the not so distant future, an enormous mass wedding—the biggest one ever—and couples needed to be Matched. Father routinely decided who would marry whom in the Church. He would sit at the front of a room with men on one side and women on the other and point from man to woman to Match them as a couple based on their spiritual beings that only he could see.

In May 1979, Father declared a Matching weekend in New York City and invited members from all over the area, and beyond, to come to the New Yorker so that he could determine their future spouses. Mother and many of the other sisters at Jacob House were instructed to attend the ceremony. I stepped in to take care of the kids in their charge so they could go.

I came up to Jacob House after school that Friday afternoon and kissed Mother goodbye as she left. I helped the sisters who remained at Jacob House—those who had too few years in the Church to be eligible for the Matching. There were so many children to watch and so few sisters to watch them.

I felt useful, important, and thrilled. I kept picturing Mother sitting with the thousands of other Family members, waiting to hear who was meant to be her husband. I tried to imagine the scene and what Mother must be experiencing, the elation she must be feeling. I tried to envision what it would be like for me, years from then, when I would have the chance to be Matched. I was overjoyed because I was about to get a stepfather. A father who believed in Principle.

I knew the importance and glory of the Blessing. It was the centerpiece of Church teachings. Marrying someone chosen for you by Father is the culmination of Church life. It's the moment when the Original Sin you are born with—caused by the Fall of Man, by Adam and Eve having premarital sex—is erased. Through the Blessing, couples and all their descendants are removed from the lineage of sinful humanity and entered into God's pure lineage. I was eager to even remotely be a part of this process, to perhaps be a bit less tainted because of Mother's imminent Blessing.

Unfortuntely, the normal Matching process didn't work with Mother. Instead of pointing from my mother to the brother who was meant for her, Father asked her to stand, and he explained to the crowd that she had already been married and had two children. We wouldn't be freed of anything by her Blessing. We would still be impure. Father looked for someone who would be willing to shoulder the burden of two children, especially children who were sinful. Luckily a brother named Phil volunteered.

When the newly Matched Jacob House sisters returned Sunday evening, they went out for a celebration dinner at a local Chinese restaurant—without their new fiancés. The brothers who were Matched to them, my mother's fiancé included, had gone back to their missions, and it was unknown when they would be together again. They'd only had a few minutes to get to know each other after the Matching. Yet it was still cause to celebrate.

I sat at that dinner, grateful for Phil's willingness to join our family. I was delighted for my mother and ecstatic for all of us. I went home to New York City that night full of hope.

One day as I helped Mother in the kitchen at Jacob House, she looked over at me and I knew something was wrong. We were standing side by side at the wooden counter, chopping carrots for the soup she was making for dinner. (There was a short time when she was taken away from caring for the babies and told to cook for the staff instead.) She stopped chopping. She opened her mouth to say something, and I instinctively cringed.

"Lisa, you're so filled with anger. You need to let it out."

I didn't know what she meant. "I'm not angry."

She put down her knife and turned to me. "Pea, you are mad at me."

"No, I'm not. I'm not angry." My voice was soft and shaky. My mind raced, looking for the reason she had chosen to bring this up now, desperate for an answer to guide me.

"Lisa, this is silly. Just get it out. Yell or something, but stop acting like a pain."

I knew that what I said next would be important and that each denial was upsetting her more, but I couldn't figure out what she thought I was angry about. I was certain that the emotion I felt was not anger. I began to cry. "I'm not angry, Mother. I'm not."

"Peach-pie, you are furious with me for leaving," she spit out. "Now you make my life miserable whenever we're together."

I stared at her then went back to the carrots. I could feel tears running down my cheeks. I had no idea what she was talking about. Not only did I not feel angry, but I knew that being angry at her, and specifically angry at her for leaving, would be wrong. I was lucky to live without her, even under the Satanic influence of Danny. I had been told I was lucky so many times, and I knew it. I had thanked God on my knees in prayer for this opportunity. Yet Mother was telling me that I mistreated her. "Mother," I cried, "I'm not angry. I don't know what you mean."

"Lisa, stop it!"

With that she decided to send me away. She talked to Church leaders—she went all the way to the Church president, Nick—and got permission for me to travel to Seattle with him and the International One World Crusade (IOWC), a group within the Church that went from city to city proselytizing and looking for new members. I don't know how the trip was paid for—of course Mother had no money and Danny would *never* pay for me to travel with the Church. It was the summer between my sophomore and junior years at Stuyvesant.

I don't think I realized Mother was getting rid of me for the summer; I saw this as an opportunity to finally, really do something productive for God and True Parents. I was elated to learn that I'd fly to Denver, where Phil lived, to meet the IOWC. This would give me a chance to get to know my future stepfather. I hoped Mother hadn't said anything about how unhappy she was with me and how miserable I was making her. I wanted him to think highly of me and to be awed by my commitment and sacrifices for God. I didn't want him to think I was ungrateful or to learn too much about my home life with Danny.

Phil met me at the airport and took me back to the Denver Center. There I was, far away from home for the first time by myself yet surrounded by things and people that were familiar. My heart beamed knowing that I could go anywhere in the world and be with my brothers and sisters and their intoxicating love and lives.

During my second night in Denver, Phil took me into the local mountains. It was pitch-black and silent. "Look up," Phil said.

I followed his gaze and saw the sky magically filled with stars. "Wow," I whispered. It was like someone had taken a white marker and littered the black sky with millions of little dots. I had never seen anything like it before, city kid that I was. It was such proof of the wonder of God and True Parents. I was filled with such purpose.

The next day the IOWC joined us at the Denver Center, and I was put on a team of members with whom I was to witness all summer. We crowded into vans that would drive us through the Rocky Mountains and Yellowstone and Grand Teton National Parks on the way to Seattle. It was a spectacular trip through gorgeous parts of the country. We were on a tight schedule and traveled full days, but I stared reverently out the windows as we drove, taking in the stunning mountain views. We managed to stay at Yellowstone a few minutes longer than necessary to see Old Faithful erupt. Sometimes I think they did that just for me.

We arrived in Seattle and settled into a small yellow house at the top of a hill, with too many brothers in one bedroom in sleeping bags covering the floor and too many sisters in another. Living with so many devoted Family members was all I ever wanted, and I endeared myself to everyone. I was an anomaly to them and a pure inspiration—being young and spending my summer fighting God's battle to save mankind. I soon became their cute little sister, a favorite.

Our lives revolved around bringing in converts. We'd wake at the crack of dawn for prayers and roll up our sleeping bags so there was space to walk across the floor. After a quick breakfast of cereal or toast, we'd climb into vans—as always, well beyond the legal limit—to head downtown. My team's witnessing station was around the Space Needle. Our van driver would drop us off early at the park entrance, with peanut butter and jelly sandwiches in hand for lunch, so that we could catch people on their way to work.

"Excuse me," I'd say to those walking by. "Do you have the time?"

The idea was to get someone to stop long enough to engage them in conversation. We wanted to find the ones who were seeking, lost, looking for more meaning.

Hoping to find someone, anyone, I'd approach people sitting on blankets on the grass. "Hi," I'd say, smiling. "What are you doing? Are you from around here?" Anything to get them to listen. I'm not sure what they thought when a tiny kid came up to them and preached about God. I was nearly sixteen but looked years younger.

We'd work all morning, wandering through the park, and stop for lunch when our team leader gave us the okay. After lunch it was back on our feet, searching for the people who wanted to hear about Father. The goal was to bring potential converts to the Center for a lecture on Principle and to get them to a weekend workshop away in the woods outside the city. I was able to bring someone once, a college student named Chris.

I look back and wonder what interested Chris. He attended the workshops and went away with us for the weekend. He picked me up in front of the Center and took me for long rides, discussing God, religion, and spirituality. But he didn't seem engrossed in the teachings. He debated and challenged me to think on my own, something I wasn't accustomed to and didn't feel comfortable doing. I wanted to convince him, to convert him, to bring him in.

The summer wore on, and I worked as hard as possible. I missed Mother and wondered if she would still fight with me about my anger. I wrote to Brian and Hugh, bragging of my escapades, and also to Robbie, who was working at Belvedere. Mother hadn't needed to get rid of him, although she refused to see him more than once that summer, even though he was just down the block from her.

I thought about In Jin, Un Jin, Soo Jung, and Jae Eun, but reaching out to them didn't seem like a good idea. They would never live a normal Family member life, witnessing and working for God, so they wouldn't understand my summer. I didn't write to Danny once.

My final days in Seattle were spent at a weekend workshop, doing my best to encourage new attendees to realize the truth of Principle and join (or at the minimum to stay for more workshops and convincing). Each Saturday night during a workshop, Nick asked someone to testify—to share their story up to and since joining the Church. I waited that last Saturday, silently hoping that he would ask me. I wouldn't admit it—it was wrong—but it would be nice to be the center of attention, to have everyone tell me how special and wonderful I was.

He called on a brother from the area. I felt my heart drop but put a smile on my face. I focused on loving this brother, and my Family members, as much as I could.

On Monday Nick took me to lunch at the top of the Space Needle to celebrate my summer. "I'm sorry about Saturday night," he started as we sat there, the restaurant slowly spinning so that we could see the entirety of Seattle. "I wanted to ask you to testify, but we needed someone that everyone could identify with. Your story would be inspiring to Family members but not to everyone else."

"I know," I answered, shrugging. "It's no big deal."

It was time to go home. Back to the apartment and life with Danny that I dreaded. Back also to my junior year at Stuyvesant and the worldly ways of my classmates. Ways that I would soon learn maybe weren't so bad.

12 · little paper airplanes

Mother and I sat on the wooden bench by the Jacob House back door. I was curled up on her lap, hugging her goodbye at the end of a weekend. I didn't mind being small. It meant she could envelop me in this way. She was tiny, but at that point, I was tinier. And even if I wasn't, I would crush myself onto her as long as she'd let me.

In the midst of that hug, as if out of nowhere, I realized I would never live with her again. Until then I had said to myself, *Maybe next year. Maybe then she'll take us with her. Maybe then someone will let us live in a Center...any Center.* That Sunday it somehow dawned on me that there was no next year. I was heading into my last years of high school and would be living with Danny and visiting Mother until college.

Reverberating with this realization, I began my junior year at Stuy. School started off as it had before. I kept my friends at a distance, threw myself into classes but not the social scene, and centered my life on the things and people that mattered: God, True Parents, True Children, and the Church.

Until a tiny paper airplane landed on my desk during English class...

I looked up, unsure of where the plane had come from and what it meant, then unfolded it. "Hi Cutie," was written on the inside. I swallowed hard and looked up again, hoping this was a mistake, but someone I'd never noticed before was looking back at me, smiling. His name was Stuart.

As soon as class ended I gathered my books, stuffed them into my gray JanSport backpack, and got up to leave, throwing my backpack over my right shoulder. My plan was to ignore the note, avoid Stuart, and get out the door before anything else could happen.

But he was too quick. "Hey!" He was standing next to me.

"Hey," I said, looking around for help. "Uh, I've got to get to history." I started toward the door.

"I'll walk you," he said, as he got in stride alongside of me. I headed toward the stairwell, listening to Stuart and answering his questions. What did I think of the book we were reading? What books did I like? Where did I live?

We got to my class, and I breathed a sigh of relief and fumbled with my backpack as I stood in the doorway. "Uh, I gotta go."

"See you tomorrow," he said, still beaming. I couldn't help but notice his smile.

After that, Stuart went out of his way to be with me. He was waiting for me when I got to English, and when the bell rang for the next period, he jumped to the door to walk me to history. I started running into him in the hallways, certain that I hadn't ever run into him before. This was attention I'd never experienced. Not knowing how to handle it, I decided to convert him.

I told Stuart about the Church and my inability—and therefore lack of desire—to date him. He hung around me anyway. I talked of the glory of my religious beliefs and my chance to save the world. He still didn't leave me alone. I preached of God and True Parents. He was not deterred. Our relationship proceeded.

Stuart was intense. He had piercing brown eyes and a personality to match. He had short dark hair and was strong, with a lean, wiry build, a member of the wrestling and football teams. He was intelligent—reading, searching, questioning, and always challenging my beliefs and convictions.

I began to hang around with him and his friends—and their girlfriends. They accepted me into their group, albeit with sideward glances and numerous questions for Stuart. "What are you doing with her?" they'd ask him. "Are you two going out...or what?" They noticed we weren't physical and that I didn't kiss him and wouldn't even hold his hand. We were some sort of a couple, but exactly what wasn't clear.

While I still spent most of my weekends with Mother or at the

Church, I sometimes found myself home on Friday nights, wandering Greenwich Village with Stuart and his friends. We'd have souvlaki and gyros at the Greek restaurants on Mercer Street, sitting at long tables in the back. I delighted in the normalcy of hanging out and being part of a group, while grappling with, or choosing to ignore, the questions inside of me. *What am I doing? What am I thinking? What am I doing?*

They'd walk me home, waiting as Stuart and I said our awkward goodbyes. I'd then sink against the dirty wall of the elevator as it creaked its way to floor three and a half, pinching my nose closed to avoid the stench of the hallway, ignoring the contradiction of my words and actions, grateful that I was heading to the safety of the Church in the morning.

For the next few months, Stuart courted me. I tried to bring him to God and True Parents, while allowing us to get closer. We'd talk on the phone at night for hours, and I'd picture his mother, with whom he fought, and his older brothers, who beat him. We'd ride the subway to the beach on days off from school, laughing as his friend Charlie would hold himself horizontally up on the posts in the center of the subway cars, keeping parallel to the floor. I learned to do wall sits to strengthen my legs and watched as he ran in rubber sweat suits to lose weight before a wrestling match.

I listened as the girls talked about their relationships and their plans to stay together with their boyfriends after high school—they were almost all seniors—wondering what together meant for Stuart and me. We were emotionally intertwined, but we weren't together. We'd engage in torturous conversations on the school stairways as to why I wouldn't date him, why I couldn't get involved, and what we should do.

"Lisa," he'd say, as we sat there, not touching. "I love you."

"Stuart, I can't," I'd reply, while longing to reach out and hold his hand or graze my fingers along his face.

He'd stare at me with such passion that my insides would churn, and I'd ache with conflicting desire and fear. Then he'd get up and walk away. I'd sit there, eyes closed, leaning against the wall, spinning with emotions I didn't understand, until I could summon up my resolve and head to class.

Our friend Jenny put it this way: "He wants you so much because he can't have you. You're unattainable. That's what keeps him craving more."

I was torn. I knew I was hurting him by refusing to become physically involved and hurting myself (at least the Moonie part of me) by allowing our emotional relationship to grow. I couldn't believe I was separating a Moonie and non-Moonie part of me. There had never been a non-Moonie part of me before—not since joining the Church. I detested the situation I was in and myself for being part of it. But I didn't stop.

Stuart and I stayed caught up in this limbo for the school year. Sometimes we tried to ignore the gulf between us. Sometimes we discussed our differences endlessly, each of us trying to convince the other to change. Luckily the summer was coming and with it, a chance to get away.

Between my junior and senior years, Danny sent me to a music camp at Hartwick College in Oneonta, New York. I still don't believe he spent the money, but in retrospect I suppose he loathed our involvement in the Church and hated that I had spent my past few summers in its service. He must have been determined to not let it happen again and was willing to pay for that.

I wanted to get better at clarinet and learn to play piano, but it was my first time away from home that wasn't with Family members. As Mother drove me to camp, I felt the pit in my stomach grow. *What have I done? Why didn't I stay inside the Church again? Why did I let Danny send me here?*

I found myself in new territory. My roommate talked about sneaking out of our dorm to meet boys and drink in the woods. I listened with horror. I wanted to blend in, to be part of the normal crowd, but knew that this was all sinful.

I was also thrown into turmoil by a few close friendships I developed with campers who happened to be bisexual and gay.

"Shrimpboat," my friend Melissa, who was also from New York City, called out to me. Shrimpboat was her nickname for me. I don't know why. I do know that I loved having a special pet name. I felt cared for and adored. "Shrimpboat, wait up," she called again. She was about ten feet behind me. I stopped. "Why did you leave Kim's room?" Kim was also from New York City. She attended the High School of Performing Arts, like many of the kids did.

"I don't know," I answered. How could I tell her? How could I explain my discomfort? Melissa had told Kim that everyone at camp was spreading rumors—that Kim and Cindy, a counselor, had spent the night together in Cindy's room. Melissa and Kim had seemed fine with it, but I didn't know what to think. Or do. I didn't know which confused me more: that everyone was spreading rumors or that the rumors might be true.

Alternate sexual preferences were foreign to me, and my understanding of right and wrong was beginning to blur. Based on my religion's teachings, my friends' sexual tendencies were immoral, but they didn't seem as evil and misguided as the Church made them out to be. They were some of the kindest, funniest, most loving people I had ever met—I, who had grown up in a religion that was supposedly about love for others.

I wrote to Mother for guidance. "Help," I pleaded. "Tell me what to do. My friends are wonderful. They care about me. How can that be bad?"

"Their choices are evil, and so are they," she replied. "Stay away from them, or, better yet, save them. It's your spiritual duty. But be careful. Just being with them will pull you away from God and closer to Satan. You could fall and die a spiritual death."

Her answers didn't make sense, and they didn't feel right. There was an openness and warmth in these people and our friendships that I was drawn to, but because of Mother's instructions, I tried to keep my distance. Still, I couldn't reprimand them as Mother suggested. I just couldn't. Besides, as if out of nowhere, I didn't want to do things anymore just because she told me to. I'm not sure why. Maybe my conversations with Stuart, and with Chris in Seattle the summer before, were pushing me toward questioning. Or closer to establishing opinions and choices of my own. Maybe being away from the Church for the first time gave me space to find my voice and thoughts. All I know is that I wanted—at least a little bit—to do what was right for me. Whatever that was.

More than anything, I wanted to help my friends resist sin. I longed to scream at them, "You're making a mistake! Can't you see?" I wanted them to step away from their lifestyle and to take them to a workshop, to bring them to Father. I decided to pray for them.

I prayed for them because they were lost, but I began to realize how lost I was as well. All these deep, probing conversations I was having with people—people who were outside the Church—were causing me to question. "Why am I in this Church?" I found myself writing in my journal. "How am I in this Church? Am I at some point going to give everything up and move in? When?" I knew I could never leave, but thoughts of leaving went through my head. Thoughts of suicide went through my head. Knowing I was bad. Wanting to be good. Getting close—too close—to people who didn't know Principle. I felt myself cracking.

My confusion crescendoed as the summer drew to a close. I went to the end-of-camp party. I danced with boys for the first time in my life. In fact, I danced for the first time in my life, unless you count the school dance in the gym in fifth grade. I danced fast to disco songs; I was so little and light that nearly any guy could fling me around the floor and across his body so we looked as if we knew what we were doing. I danced slowly too—held tight against guys I'd learned to care for in some way. I had a great time, sprinkled with intense shame. I was pretty sure I was coming from pure places with innocent feelings, or I hoped I was. And I knew that Family members, and more importantly Mother and Church leaders, would frown on what I was doing.

The next day Mother came to pick me up with Brian, who was driving a tour bus for the Church and had offered her a ride. It was a gorgeous summer morning. The sun blazed, and I soaked it into my skin as I stood outside my dorm waiting for them, my bags piled next to me. I reflected on the summer—my thoughts and questions, my confusion. I reflected on the night before—the fun I'd had, the people I'd grown to love and would miss. Other than Stuart, these were the first non-members that I'd let deep into my heart and life since joining the Church.

My smile grew as the bus pulled up, the door opened, and Mother and Brian climbed down. I felt my heart lighten and jump a beat. Overcome, I ran to Mother and gave her a huge hug hello. I wanted to do the same with Brian but didn't. I couldn't. I had spent the summer getting close to my new friends and had danced with them and gotten physically, albeit not sexually, intimate. I had hugged them goodbye, male and female, at the end of camp. However, by Church teachings hugging a member of the opposite sex would lead me to sin. Perhaps especially with Brian.

"Hi," I said stepping forward, my impulse to embrace him growing to a physcial ache. He looked good, and it felt good to see him. Still, I hesitated. I cared about Brian, and as far as I could tell my feelings were sisterly. He would gladly hug me hello, but that was a path to evil. Besides, Mother was right next to us.

"Hi," he replied, with the hugest smile. "Welcome home."

With that simple exchange, that thwarted greeting, I felt a seismic shift within me. At that moment, standing in the sunshine on the side of the road with the strong desire to hug Brian and the knowledge that it would be sinful, coupled with the Church's label of bad for my friends with alternate sexual preferences and the experiences I had had—and loved—up until that point, I felt my certainty snap. Before this summer there had been no doubt as to my future or the strength of my conviction. I had always known what I wanted in the long run. I was always going to live my life in the Church. That morning, however, all the questions that had been simmering in my mind came to a boil, and part of me began to wonder if a life in the Church was something I possibly couldn't, or wouldn't, pursue. All of me was horrified by that thought.

13 · the prodigal daughter

I returned to life in Tarrytown to find that things had gotten worse.

As soon as Brian pulled the bus into Belvedere, I jumped off and ran up the hill to Holy Rock—a huge boulder just behind the main house that Father had consecrated. I had to pray, to find God, to repent for the doubt that had entered my mind.

I knelt, my head pressed against the cool stone, tears streaming down my face. "Heavenly Father," I begged, "please help me. I'm so lost. I don't know anymore. Please tell me what to do." I felt the warmth of the sun on my neck and back, like God's love pouring down on me. I prayed harder.

Mother stepped up behind me and knelt down as well. "Lisa," she said, "we have to talk."

"What?"

"While you were away," she started and then hesitated. "While you were away," she began again, "Father announced that True Children can only be with Blessed Children."

"What?" I tried to grasp what she was saying, my cheeks still wet.

"True Children can only be with Blessed Children." She watched me as her news sunk in.

"What?" I gasped. "Why?"

"I don't know. I really don't know. Father said that it's essential to protect them from Satanic influences. I was told just before you came home."

"But," I began, and paused. "But, then I can't be with In Jin-nim and Un Jin-nim." (Adding -nim to the end of a name is a show of respect and adoration in Korean culture, to make the name honorific.)

"I know, Peach-pie. I know."

She put her arms out to hold me, and I fell into them. I sat there with her, in silence. *Why did Father do this? What does it mean? Does someone somehow know of my uncertainty and questions? Does someone know I've strayed? How can I handle not seeing In Jin? Maybe I really am bad.* I could no longer be with the girls, and I didn't know why. I was cut off from my truest, closest friend. A friend I worshipped and adored. It must be God's will, but I didn't understand.

Years later I discovered that the final decree was a result of Jae Eun's personal trauma (and continued jealousy of me). Unbeknownst to everyone, Brian, *my* Brian, had seduced her. Yes, she was underage. Yes, she was a Blessed Child. And yes, it was sinful on many levels by Church doctrine. Nonetheless, he did. To protect herself, and to punish me for being close to him and keep me away from him, she told everyone that I had crushes on the brothers at Belvedere, especially Brian. She announced that I wanted to become involved with them, to have sex with them. Again, especially with Brian. Because of this, Father decided that his children would only be allowed to be with Blessed Children. Blessed Children, who were purer, like Jae Eun. Father was afraid I was a dangerous influence. Father, *the Messiah*, thought I was evil and made the decree to keep me away.

Despite Father's decree, or perhaps because of it, I plunged into my senior year of high school. Robbie was starting his freshman year at Drew University. It was the first time we'd been apart for longer than a summer, and I felt left behind with Danny. I also felt left behind at school, as many of my (and Stuart's) friends had gone off to college. Looking for new people to hang out with, I spied two girls whom I somewhat knew, Julie and An, sitting on a car on First Avenue eating lunch. (As our high school campus was the New York City streets, we sat on the cars parked outside school.) I had seen them around but never talked to them, even though An was in my homeroom. They were socially out of my league—part of the in-crowd. They wore the standard uniform of carpenter pants and three-quarter sleeve concert T-shirts, and overalls on "overall Thursdays." And they made it look good. They went to, and threw, parties. They were cool and were friends with the cool kids, something I had no right to be a part of. Still, I walked up to them. "Hey," I began, pausing to catch a breath, "can I eat with you?" Their nods of yes launched our friendship, and I embarked on a new Stuyvesant experience.

My feelings of safety and comfort in the Church had begun to diminish daily since Father's decree. I felt watched by Church leaders, judged and restricted. At the same time I was terrified that the restrictions wouldn't be enough to keep me safe. I began to feel unsure about what I wanted and what I knew. What I did know was that feeling confused was wrong, and therefore I was sinful. Still, I couldn't pledge my life to the Church with misgiving roaring inside of me, so I decided to step away, just a bit, to experience the outside world and to come back more devout. I convinced myself that I had followed Mother into the Church as a child—never questioning or doubting it, or her, once—and needed distance to make an adult decision to return. And stay. It was the only way to commit wholeheartedly, and question and stray no more.

With this resolve, I began to spend less time at the Church on the weekends. I no longer went to see Mother. I no longer went to see Hugh. I no longer went to Belvedere to hear Father speak. I threw myself into the social scene at school, making up for the three years I'd kept myself separate and different. My friendship with Julie and An (and soon their good friend Debbie) brought me if not into the in-crowd, on the recognized outskirts. I got to know more kids in my high school class and began to call more and more of them friends. As my circle grew, I found that they weren't all evil and scary. It was fun to hang out on a Friday or Saturday night—going to movies or out to dinner, wandering the Village, or doing nothing at someone's house. It was nice to be in my apartment on the nights I didn't hang out, although I was alone, as Danny still bartended weekends. The times I stayed home through Sunday, I liked waking in the morning and taking it easy. I felt guilty for lazing about, guilty for not being with Family members, and guilty for not saying Pledge and bowing to True Parents. But I also enjoyed myself.

Danny delighted in having me around more and went out of his way for me. He and his girlfriend, Alice, a French woman ten years my senior who had cropped blond hair and a tatoo of an eagle on her forearm, who was funky and cool and fun, would take me to fancy brunches at hip downtown restaurants. He spent his bartending tips on fine food, fine alcohol, and fine drugs. And baroque recorders— baroque music had replaced rock and roll in his repertoire. Our apartment was often filled with what sounded like honking geese of different sizes as Danny attempted to play baroque recorders and oboes.

Danny was happy to share the pleasure of fine food with me. We'd take as much time as we wanted with no Church service for me to rush to, they with their mimosas and me delighting in my freshly squeezed orange juice. I may have been experimenting with living outside Church confines, but I still didn't drink. I was underage— although Danny would have let me—and alcohol was sinful. Still, it was good to be with Danny and to feel closer to him.

One cold winter Sunday our restaurant of choice was One Fifth Avenue—on the corner of Fifth Avenue and Eighth Street, a block from Washington Square Park. It was the epitomy of upscale, downtown culture; Robert Mapplethorpe lived in the building's penthouse. That day, as we walked home from brunch, Danny turned to me. "Twink, do you want a new jacket?" he asked.

I was astonished. Danny didn't buy me things, especially not clothes. Bohemian that he was, clothing was never important to him. I had once asked him for new jeans, and he refused, saying that they were too much money and I didn't need them. (To my delight, later that day when I went to my bedroom, I found forty dollars tucked under my pillow. Alice had, as always, stepped in to mother me without Danny knowing it.)

"Sure," I replied, the uncertainty in my mind making my answer sound like a question. "I'd love a new coat." With that, we set off downtown. I had never gone clothes shopping with Danny. In a store along Broadway we found a gray, puffy, bubble down coat that I adored. Danny pulled out a wad of cash—his tips from the night before I'm sure—and bought it for me. "Thank you," I said, in shock. *Maybe he cares? Maybe he's not that bad?*

Each new experience away from the Church felt weird and uncomfortable—but also enticing. Having made almost all new friends, few of them knew about my life as a Moonie. Debbie, however, did. She had once gone with me to hear Sunburst play at the Down Home Inn years earlier, before we were close friends. I guess she wasn't frightened of the Church. She would check up on me during my forays into a more normal life. "How ya doin'?" she'd ask as a group of us hung out on a Saturday afternoon, wandering from her apartment in Chelsea down to the village, then over to Broadway to shop in the vintage clothing stores, Reminiscence and Canal Jeans. "You okay being here?"

"I'm having fun," I'd answer. "Is that wrong? Is this leading me to Hell?"

But I kept going. I spent a weekend at Julie's house in Brooklyn. I told myself I should leave for the safety and surety of the Church, but I didn't. On Sunday morning I didn't wake up to say Pledge—although I did contemplate locking myself in the bathroom to do it. It was, in some ways, easy to play hookey and forget what I knew. It was horrifying that it was easy.

Alcohol and boys didn't interest me, but my friends were into both. Being close to this worried me. What if I experimented too? Desperate, I looked to my counselors from the past for guidance. "Be sure to see Father at least once a month," Brian advised. "Trust your heart and in Father," Hugh encouraged. This was not enough to steady me. I turned to Mother, practically begging her to tell me not to continue—to forbid me to be with these people. For some reason, she refused.

Wanting to avoid the torment of the previous school year, I determined to keep my relationship with Stuart platonic, but late one afternoon, as classes let out, he grabbed me. We made our way to the top of the stairs that led from the Fifteenth Street entrance to the first floor. Students streamed by us on their way home. Standing there so close, leaning against the wooden banister, nearly touching, every particle of my being could feel him—the hardness of his body, the intensity of his passion. We said everything we'd said so many times before, again with no resolution. He looked at me, as he always did, staring deep and hard into my eyes. I longed for him to kiss me but couldn't allow myself to do anything. I needed him to break my impasse—to make a first move so that I could respond.

"Lisa..." he implored.

"What do you want me to say?" I answered. *Please, please kiss me.*

"What are we going to do?"

"You know I can't do anything." *Please, Stuart, please.*

He walked away in disgust. Julie and Debbie ran up to me; they had watched from the hallway on the other side of the glass doors. "We thought you two were going to kiss!"

If only we had.

I turned again to Brian. He was, perhaps, the most rebellious member I knew, but he was still in the Church, and I was still emotionally attached to him. Despite everything he said and did, he managed to find a way to stay. Hell, he had been Matched to a Korean sister, and they were to be married, like my mother and Phil, as soon as Father planned the next mass ceremony. Brian professed his love for his fiancée (although he had never met her—they'd been Matched by photos) and newfound devotion and gratitude to Father for putting the two of them together. Also, he cared for me and didn't want me to lose my way. That I was sure about. *He'll help me. He'll help me figure this out.*

I headed up to Tarrytown for the weekend to see Mother and spend time with Brian. Saturday night he and I took the train back into the city, walking over to the Down Home Inn to hear Sunburst play. They had returned from a few months in California.

It was great to be with Brian and surrounded by brothers and sisters, so many of whom I knew and loved. I hadn't realized how much I had missed it. I was absorbed, as always, in Sunburst's music and in the glow of attention that emanated from Hugh (who was also engaged via photo to a Korean sister) and the rest of the band. I sat in my front-row seat, enveloped in heartwarmingly familiar places, people, and emotions. I was still cut off from In Jin. I ached for her—to see her and talk to her and laugh with her—but this was home. I realized there was no way I could leave. It was what I knew, and it felt so right. It was where I belonged.

Hugh called me aside during a set break. I ran up to him, and he squeezed my hand. I longed to tell him all that had been going on but instead just soaked in his love, keeping my hand in his as long as I could. I reveled in all there was for me in the Church—knowing I was in a safe place with people who would protect and care for me—and remembered my love of God and True Parents. "I'll Never Leave You Anymore." I whispered the title of a Church holy song to myself—and to God—under my breath. "I'm so glad to come home."

I had known the story of the Prodigal Son since my first days at Barrytown; it was perhaps the most popular skit during entertainment nights. Every workshop some group would act out the story of the father whose youngest son took his inheritance, squandered it in wild living, and then returned, asking to be forgiven by his father and hired as a servant. But instead the father welcomed his son back, killing the fattened calf and celebrating, proclaiming, "What was lost is found." Sitting there in the Down Home Inn, I felt like the Prodigal Son who had returned, a bit ashamed—I had always sworn I'd never stray as that son had—but gloriously grateful to be back.

Brian and I stayed through the performance and caught one of the last trains to Tarrytown. It was heady to be hanging out with a man, an engaged man, who was eleven years my senior. I was high from the evening and the attention and affection I'd received.

As soon as the train doors opened, Brian pulled me onto the platform and down to his pickup truck that was parked on the street. It was late, and there weren't any other cars, or people, around.

"Brian, what?" I said, laughing. "What's the hurry?"

He turned me to face him and was silent for what seemed like a few minutes. "Your eyes," he said and paused again, holding me steadily in his gaze. "Your eyes are so intense. You look right into me. You can see into my heart and soul."

I stood there, aware of the night, the darkness, his hands grasping mine, his fervor, and how close he held me to him, knowing I should pull away but somehow unable to, tingling. Not sure what I was feeling but certain I was feeling something.

He looked at me for a long time, as I waited, breathless, wanting more—and not wanting more. "Be careful," he said. "Hugh is in love with you. You should keep away from him."

"*What?*" I asked, my bewilderment most likely showing on my face.

Brian said nothing. He let go of my hand to open the truck door so that I could climb in, then shut the door behind me. He went around to the other side, got behind the wheel, and started the engine.

I sat still for a few minutes as we drove up the hill away from the station. Until I couldn't take it anymore. "Brian, what are you talking about?" I couldn't handle—I didn't understand—what was going on.

"Nothing. Never mind." He drove me back to Jacob House in silence.

I woke the next morning even more confused by what Brian had said to me and the way he had looked at me. What had he meant by his comment about Hugh? I went through the motions during Pledge, standing and bowing as I was supposed to, but my heart and mind raced through the events of the night before. *Have I done something wrong? Does Brian sense something off in me or my behavior? Is there something in my relationship with Hugh that is sinful and dangerous?* Reciting Pledge was second nature, and I could follow along without missing a beat.

As we headed off to Belvedere, I determined to grab Brian after Father's speech so that he could explain, but even though I raced out of the tent as soon as Father finished, Brian was nowhere. I asked a few people if they knew where he was but couldn't draw attention to the fact that I was looking for him. Ever since Jae Eun told everyone that I was in love with Brian, I was watched. People were searching for proof of my infatuation.

I went to school on Monday with renewed resolve to keep my distance from Stuart and watch my overall behavior. Seeing Brian, even with him acting weird, and being in the safe confines of the

Church had reminded me of everything I risked, all that was mine to lose, if I succumbed to the Satanic influences around—and maybe in—me.

I had to be careful. I enjoyed my friends. Their love and acceptance felt, at times, more unconditional than my life in the Church. There was less judgment for what I did and how I did it, and no puritanical standard of behavior to live up to. There were no people who were inherently more pure and special than I was. Who were True and Blessed while I was not. But I had to keep myself separate. My promise to God was that I wouldn't leave, that I wouldn't stray. The only way to do this was to steer away from anything tainted and to avoid getting even remotely involved with boys. To remember who I was.

I shut down my feelings for Stuart and kept myself aloof. We had more impassioned conversations, but my heart was no longer in them. I told him again and again that whatever we had had, it was gone. I was done.

Stuart and I were over. This was good. I reasoned I had learned how to avoid becoming involved with a boy and assumed I was safe. I would no longer have to worry about sinning or abandoning God, nor feel torn and tormented. I was out of harm's way.

With this false sense of security, I continued my foray into teenage life, spending every weekend at home with my friends. Having just been up to Tarrytown to hear Father speak, I knew I could avoid temptation.

Julie and I became inseparable. Since Danny worked weekend nights and I was alone in the apartment, I spent from Friday night until Monday morning at her house in Brooklyn—taking the D train to Newkirk Plaza and walking the few blocks to her home. I was there so often I began to call her mother "Mom." Sometimes we took the F train out to Forest Hills, in Queens, to have a late-night meal at the T-Bone Diner and then walk the forty-five minutes down Continental Avenue to An's apartment. These were delicious times. We talked about school and college (we were all applying) and boys— even if I wouldn't date a boy, I was learning to talk about them. We went to the movies. Julie loved Woody Allen and got me hooked as well. We started with *Stardust Memories* and worked our way backward from there. We wandered through the Village, stopping for hot chocolate or onion soup at Le Figaro Café on Bleecker Street, or sitting by the fountain in Washington Square Park. We had no money. We just hung out.

Julie's house became my sanctuary when things got out of control at home. One night, as Danny was making dinner, he went to get ice cubes from the tray in the freezer, only to discover there weren't any. I had, of course, been the last one to use ice cubes, and I had, of course, forgotten his repeated instructions to fill up the tray when I emptied it.

Danny stormed down the hall, empty tray in hand, looking for me. I was in Robbie's room, sitting at the desk doing my homework. With Robbie away, I sometimes worked in his room. It helped me miss him less. When Danny found me there, he threw the plastic tray to the floor. It bounced and skidded to a stop. "What the fuck were you thinking?" he yelled. "There's no ice."

I looked up from my books and down at the ice cube tray on the dusty floor. I froze. "Danny, I'm sorry," I stammered, not sure of what to say and scared I'd say the wrong thing and enrage him further. "I forgot."

"Forgot? You always forget. You're so goddamn fucking selfish!"

I jumped up and eased myself away from him, toward the window. I would have gone toward the door, to try and get out, but he blocked my way. The cold air seeping through the hole in the glass pane hit my back. I shivered. From the cold? From fear? From both? I'm not sure. I could feel my heart pounding and my neck tightening. I looked straight at Danny and then down to the floor to avoid his gaze. "I'm sorry. I'll remember next time."

"Next time," he hissed, grabbing my shoulders and shaking me hard. "Next time!" With that he stormed out of the room and down the hall, leaving me trembling and crying. I grabbed my coat and keys, made my way downstairs to a pay phone, called Julie, and retreated to her house. I thought of the time, all those years ago when we'd first moved in with Danny, when he threw the mirror in front of the fireplace, smashing it. He had promised to never do the same to me. I was glad to have someplace to go.

I was determined to stay away from boys, but there were many other things I could learn about. Julie took me out to Long Island one Saturday for a party at the house of someone she knew from camp. Everyone was drinking—except me. But my past resolve to stay away from alcohol was weakening. I was intrigued.

People hung out by the pool—some swimming, some lying on chaises talking, a few couples making out on the far side of the backyard. "Pulling Mussels From a Shell" played on the boom box. It was hot, and I was thirsty. Heading inside to the kitchen to get something to drink, I opened the fridge and saw beers on the shelf. All of a sudden, I wanted one. Well, simply to taste one. My friends drank. Brian and Reggie drank. I sometimes felt weird for not drinking and wanted to be less different. I wanted to see what it was like.

I reasoned I could have one sip with impunity, so I grabbed a beer and an opener, looking around the kitchen to see if anyone would notice. I don't know why I worried about getting caught. They didn't mind if I drank, and there weren't any parents around—or any Family members.

I knew if I hesitated I wouldn't go through with it. Rushing, not wanting anyone to come into the kitchen and see my awkwardness, I opened the beer. Foam poured out over my hand. *What do you do with the foam?* I took a sip and grimaced as the bitter taste hit my tongue. I hated it and hated myself for drinking it. *What was I thinking? Why did I do that?*

I dropped the opener on the counter, dumped the beer down the sink, threw the bottle in the garbage, rinsed the foam from my hand, and rushed back outside. I felt God staring down at me, with tears in His eyes and anger on His face. His disappointment was palpable. I felt it wash over me like the beer foam, hitting my heart, pouring over my body, and coating me with a sticky sense of unworthiness. *What have I done? What am I doing? Do I deserve all the decrees that have been placed on me? Am I truly evil?* I swore to stay away from alcohol.

Only I didn't. I went to parties—parties with rock music, not the Church ballads I was used to. With drinking and dancing— fast dancing to "Saturday Night's Alright for Fighting" and slow dancing, which meant being closer to a guy than I was ever allowed. One night I danced and drank and wound up in a sleeping bag on the floor next to a boy named Josh. He reached for my hand, and I didn't pull it away. We lay there talking, with him tracing his fingers along my wrist. *What am I doing?* I enjoyed the attention.

By Monday morning I was a wreck. How would I act when we were in English class? What would I do? I always perched on the windowsill in Mr. McCourt's overflowing classroom, and Josh sat right beneath, in front of me. "Hey Josh," I could start, "about Saturday night...don't bother liking me, okay? I can't get involved with anyone." That would be stupid.

I was a mess. Wanting more and not wanting more. Trying things and shameful about trying things. At this point Danny decided to step in and offer me guidance, guidance that was different from the advice most parents give their teenage children. "Go out," he instructed. "Get drunk. Get a boyfriend. Have an unhappy love affair." (He claims he didn't say this one.) "Fail a few courses." These experiences, he professed, would enrich my life. His advice was weird and his restrictions few, but he did forbid me to do certain things. "Don't ever," he stressed, "shoot up smack in the middle of Second Avenue. If you want to shoot up, come upstairs out of traffic."

This didn't soothe me. I turned again to Brian.

He had been sent away from Belvedere to an abandoned motel off the highway in the middle of nowhere in the Poconos. It was the new Church workshop center. I didn't know that he was there because of his relationship with Jae Eun (despite his engagement to and professed love for his fiancée in Korea). I had no idea that I was looking for help and guidance from someone who was lost.

Along with the potential new recruits, I took the big Church bus from the New Yorker to the Center for the weekend. I crashed on the floor in the sisters' room, cried my way through the lectures, and spent much of my time praying and doing my best to remember Principle. My conviction felt shakier than it had ever been, and I wanted to find the way back to absolute certainty, safety, and dedication.

Much of my time was also spent trying to get a few minutes with Brian. It seemed as if he went out of his way to not be alone with me. I now wanted the hug I turned down when I came back from music camp, the arm draped around my shoulders that he offered many times, the look into my eyes (and soul) that riveted and shook me. I wanted to be told I was special and beautiful. But Brian stayed away.

On Saturday night I grabbed him and begged him to talk with me for a few minutes. "Brian," I started, sitting at the round table at the edge of the main lecture room, "I need your help."

"Lisa, I've got nothing to give. Give it to Father. He's your only hope."

I leaned nearer to him. I longed for his closeness and didn't want anyone else to hear what I had to say. "But Brian," I whispered, "I don't know how to anymore. I want to turn to Father, to turn to God, but it doesn't make sense."

"Lisa…" He paused and pulled away from me as a few members walked through the room.

I knew I had to confess to him. To let him know how lost I was. How much danger I was in. "Brian, it's starting to make more sense on the outside." I hesitated. I could feel tears in my eyes and throat and tried to calm my breathing. "It's starting to feel better there."

"Lisa," he practically shouted, now that we were alone again, "it's not better on the outside. It never is. You'll fall!"

"Brian, don't yell," I mumbled, looking down. "I'm not going to fall…it's just…I don't know. I don't know what to do anymore."

His voice got very quiet. "Don't do anything." He stopped for a very long time. When he started speaking again, his voice was somehow even quieter, yet more insistent. "Look at me." He waited. "Look at me!" He put his hand under my chin and tilted my head up so that I was staring at him. I searched his face for something, I didn't know what. "Look what happened to me." He stopped one last time, as if reluctant to continue. "Trust me, don't do anything."

"What do you mean, look what happened to you?"

"Nothing. Nothing. I meant nothing. Look, I'm not one to counsel you…to counsel anyone. I keep making mistakes. All I can tell you is that you don't want to make a stupid mistake like I did. Father forgives. He understands we're human, but you don't want to. Trust me."

14 · kissing back

I decided to throw Julie a surprise birthday party. Because Adam, a guy within our large circle of friends, had the same birthday as Julie, the party would be for him as well. Alice gave us her apartment for the evening. I moved in a stereo, brought over albums, and pushed the few pieces of living room furniture against the walls.

A nearly empty apartment on East Thirteenth Street with no one over the age of eighteen present on a Friday night was a gold mine in the eyes of much of the senior class. By the time I showed up with the guests of honor, the party was in full swing, the lights were off, the punch was finished, and someone was refilling the plastic bowl with a can of pineapple juice and a bottle of rum.

I'll never forget that party. Or the uneven mix of pineapple juice and rum. Over the last few months my experimentation with alcohol had grown, having a sip of something here, a beer there. On that night, however, I indulged in the potent punch, as well as the huge jug of white wine passed around the dance floor. I overindulged.

With the rum and wine taking over my reflexes, I didn't recoil when Adam kissed me. We were sitting on the side of the dance floor while "I Wanna Be Sedated" pulsed around us. How apt. Adam leaned over toward me and put his lips to mine. I didn't pull away. In fact, I kissed him back—even though I had never noticed him like that before.

As incoherent as I might have been, I still heard the voices screaming from far away in my head. *What are you doing?* This wasn't sex, but it was against everything I had been taught, everything I believed, everything I'd steadfastly held on to throughout my relationship with Stuart. The date is ingrained: April 3, 1981.

On Monday at school, Adam barely talked to me. For me our kiss had been momentous. Earth-shattering. Groundbreaking. It wasn't to him. I vacillated between horror at what I had finally done and humiliation over the fact that the first guy I kissed didn't seem to notice it—or me.

Until he did.

A few weeks after the party, a group of people, Adam included, decided to go see *Excalibur*. I did my best to keep my mind off him, but he focused his attention on me. As we hung out after the movie, he and I joked. He was cute. I somehow convinced him to give me a small gold ring he wore on his pinky. I put it on my middle finger and kept it. I still have it.

The next day Adam invited me out on our first real date: breakfast in the Village. We sat across from each other in a booth in the little corner diner on Eighth Street and Waverly Place, perched on the vinyl red benches, eating eggs and toast and talking about I don't know what. Then he walked me home. It was a warm Monday morning; we were off from school for spring break.

As we headed down Second Avenue, nearing my apartment building, fear shot through me. *Okay, when I kissed him I was drunk, practically unconscious, and completely unaware. What will I do now?*

Adam reached for my hand, and the world began to circle entirely and only around the sensations that ignited. It felt good. Tingles up and down my spine. It also felt really, really bad.

We reached the door to my building and stood in silence as traffic—both people and cars—streamed by us. I didn't notice. I was trying to figure out what to say and what to do. I was certain Adam could hear my heart hammering in my chest. "Thanks for breakfast," I managed. "Uh, I have to go."

"Yeah. See you soon." With that Adam leaned over and kissed me. Again I kissed him back, only this time it was a conscious choice. The feeling of his lips on mine—soft but pressing. The wave in the pit of my stomach. The relaxation and tension coursing through me at the same time. I turned and rushed to open the door, fumbling the keys and stumbling through.

The rest of the week was a blur. I didn't see him again, although we talked on the phone nearly every day. I couldn't believe what I was doing and that I was enjoying it, when I wasn't vividly imagining the Hell I was damning myself to and the horror I would have to face when someone found out.

Adam and I started dating and became a steady couple at school. I embarked on a path I had sworn I would never walk, searching for each next step, aware of land mines that threatened to explode my life. Still, I moved deeper into the relationship. I was also having fun: Holding his hand was fun. Kissing him was fun. Having him wait for me after class was fun. Hanging out with him at the end of the day was fun. I tried to ignore the rest. I entered the secret society of dating and joined my classmates in something they'd known about for a while, but I had been ignorant to. I began to feel more and more like everyone else, more as if I belonged.

Except for Stuart's reaction—a combination of confusion, disgust, and rage. He couldn't understand why I'd refused him, and us, for so long only to start up with someone else. I couldn't understand it either. In some ways it just happened to me, or I simply let it happen. Instead of resisting as I always had, I'd allowed myself to get caught up and carried away.

Besides, Adam was such a contrast to Stuart. Whereas Stuart was intense and serious, Adam was anything but. And he was cool. He ran track and wore inside-out, ripped sweatshirts before it was a trend, and rolled-up bandanas tied around his head holding back his long, curly, brown hair. The bandanas and sweatshirts matched in color—white, blue, orange, green, whatever. He was a clown. In fact, his nickname was Clown; it was embroidered on his track jacket. His comic nature was a contrast to my ultraserious tendencies.

He made fun of me, my friends, his friends, everyone. It was a relief to joke and tease rather than think about the conflict of my life in and out of the Church. In some ways, however, it was obnoxious. Practically every sentence he spoke when he was around me had a synonym for *short* in it—a play on my height. "I'm going to sit down for a short time," he would say. "Take a little break. I need a wee rest. I have a tiny ache in my back. Maybe a small time off my feet will help." He was five feet seven inches, but I was an easy target. He could go on and on and on.

Danny was delighted to see me involved with a boy. I was clueless. Although I'd taken sex education and knew the basic details, I had no idea how one went about dating and making out. I'd seen kissing in movies but not in any real relationships around me—not between my parents, certainly not in the Church, not even with any of my friends at school, who were all unattached at the time. Julie had broken up with her boyfriend of a few years just before we started hanging out. An was single. And Debbie's boyfriend was in Port Jervis, New York. She'd met him when she was a counselor at camp. I never saw them together.

I had witnessed Danny with various girlfriends over the years, but he was never someone I wanted to emulate. I didn't know how far I was required to go beyond kissing—and when. When do I let Adam put his hand up my shirt? Should I? Would I? Or down my pants? I couldn't contemplate that. And actual sex—intercourse—SAIF (Sex As In Fuck) as my friends called it, was beyond my comprehension.

I didn't know what Adam thought, what he wanted, what he expected of me. I was certain he'd been with girls before but didn't know what that entailed. I didn't want to be prudish, although I *was* prudish, but I also didn't want to be easy, whatever that was.

I stumbled along, doing my best to ignore the huge "not supposed to" that loomed inside me yet still confused as to what I should and shouldn't be doing. Then Adam took me home to my apartment for the first time, after we'd gone to see an evening movie. We were in my room, lying on my bed, talking. I reached over and took his hand, and he kissed me. I pulled away to catch my breath and looked around at the light blue walls I had painted just before senior year and out the window at the alley between the buildings. For a moment I felt a sudden calm, a peace, a sense of "I can figure this out."

Danny's footsteps approached from the other end of the apartment, creaking on the floorboards, getting louder and louder. Adam jumped up off the bed and seemed to hurtle across the room. The footsteps stopped abruptly, somewhere around the kitchen. "Good night, Lisa," Danny called. "I'm going to bed. I'll see you in the morning."

Adam looked over at me, a smile starting in his eyes and inching its way until it took over his entire face. My heart sank as I realized that the excuse that my dad wouldn't let me do anything no longer held any weight. I was on my own to figure this sex thing out, and Adam knew it. He walked back over, lay down, and reached for me. I felt myself pull away and also sink into him. We continued to kiss and to hold each other for what felt like hours—perhaps he had picked up on my underlying hesitation. After he left, I lay in my bed, sensing the indentation on the mattress where he had been. With troubled and sweet thoughts, I fell asleep.

Hanging out with Adam evolved into hanging out with Adam and two of his best friends, Pete and Rich. They became my best friends as well. The four of us grew to be a steady thing—many dates with Adam were actually a night out for four. The three of them would keep me company when I babysat for Megan. Pete and Rich sat on the windowsill listening to "Father and Son" playing on the record player, while Adam and I entwined on the daybed. Until Adam would suggest that they leave. Late-night movies coupled with late-night meals at the T-Bone Diner in Forest Hills, where Adam and Pete lived, or the Kiev near my apartment, were for four. I went to the prom with all of them—officially with Adam, but the four of us agreed to head together to the club where our prom was held.

A month or so into our relationship I decided to let Adam know about my involvement in the Church, not realizing that someone had already shared my secret. It was late at night, and we were at Julie's house. A few of us had just come back from Sheepshead Bay in Brooklyn, where we climbed over the fence and hung out on the beach in the dark.

I had to tell Adam the truth about my upbringing. I could no longer pretend that the Church didn't exist. I woke in the middle of the night, unable to sleep, worried that somehow someone would find out that I was dating a boy. I was on constant alert for Family members as we walked through the Village or SoHo. I dreaded the reckoning I would eventually have to face and wanted Adam to know what I was dealing with. The contradiction between what I was doing and what I had grown up believing was tearing me apart. It amazed me that I had kept it from him for so long.

I took a deep breath, closed my eyes, and launched in. "Adam, I have to tell you something."

"What?" He was lying next to me on Julie's bed, lost in his thoughts, looking up at the ceiling.

"I'm a Moonie."

"What?"

"I'm a Moonie. You know—Reverend Moon. The Unification Church. The Moonies."

I lay there in the silence, waiting for far too long. What would he say? How would he react? How would this affect things?

Adam turned to look at me. I wanted nothing more than to get up and walk away, as far away as possible. He looked deep into my eyes. "How can you be," he asked, "when your head isn't shaved!"

That was his answer? I shared my deepest, darkest secret, and he teased me about being a Hare Krishna?

He joked, and yet my confession catapulted us into an intensity of emotions. As much as it was fun to be with Adam—to date him, to hang out as a couple, to slowly feel more comfortable with making out—I couldn't do it just because I was having a good time. My pull from the Church was like a slingshot that hurled us into passion. By the end of senior year, we were entrenched in the throes of first love, and I was consumed with confusion and despair. I was, in many ways, happier and closer to my friends than I'd ever been before, and also damned to Hell and letting God down with my every action.

If I didn't know this well enough on my own, it was told to me repeatedly with great fervor by everyone in the Church. The news of my evil ways—my misguided and dangerous steps toward a life of ruin—had leaked out to many brothers and sisters, and the summer between high school and college became my summer of decision. Mother brought me to a workshop at the New Yorker, practically locked me in a room, and spent countless hours tearing apart my new life. "What are you doing? What are you thinking?" Her questions pelted me, harder and harder.

"I don't know" was always my reply, and the barrage would start.

"You're ruining your life by leaving Father, Lisa. You have to make a choice. You have to decide. You have to stop this."

I didn't know what to say or what to do. I didn't want to face her or to look her in the eyes. I knew I stood to lose my mother again but couldn't stop seeing Adam. I didn't want to. Sitting across from Mother on the hotel-room bed, I could only whimper, "I can't, Mother. I can't." I ached for a hug, for her reassurance, but Mother was tense. Her body was rigid. There was no place for me.

She didn't explicitly mention the possibility of my falling, or sex, but I knew that was what she meant. The funny thing is, my relationship with Adam was innocent. We had never come close to having intercourse. I would never fully remove any clothing, nor let him. Sex? Absolutely not. The air-raid sirens would go off in my head.

Wanting to bring me back into believing, Mother borrowed a car and drove me to Barrytown. I guess she thought that by returning to where it all began, I'd realize what I was risking. Instead I felt trapped—physically trapped in upstate New York and emotionally trapped spending time with her when all I wanted was to be with Adam and our friends. She told me I had to resolve whether I was in or out. The consequences of both petrified me.

At night at home I'd lie on the floor of my bedroom, in the dark, choosing the songs I'd play over and over on my record player. It could be my and Adam's songs: "Keep on Loving You" or "Sometimes When We Touch." Or it could be "Only the Good Die Young." I heard my life played out each time Billy sang, "You know your mother told you all that I could give you was a reputation. She never cared for me. But did she ever say a prayer for me?"

Robbie was back for the summer from his freshman year at Drew. He also tried to save me. "Just decide," he yelled, sitting at the kitchen table. As I sobbed that I couldn't, he got madder. He repeatedly told me that I was ending my life and abandoning God and my pledge to bring the Kingdom of Heaven on Earth. I already knew this but couldn't leave everything and everyone I'd found on the outside.

Family members who felt close to me tried to help. I had numerous heart-to-heart conversations—outside the New Yorker, at diners and delis, and on street corners. They counseled me lovingly and also threatened banishment from all I had known. "Are you in or out?" they demanded. "Yes or no? Do you believe, or are you leaving and letting us and God down?"

One might think that I talked with Danny about my decision. I didn't. I knew what he'd tell me to do. And I hadn't dropped my judgment of his life. I'd spent nearly a decade knowing he was under Satanic influence. That hadn't changed. Even though I felt closer to him as I pulled further away from the Church, and I enjoyed being with him more, I neither respected nor wanted his opinion. Besides, he didn't have meaningful conversations. Not with me.

I did, however, talk to Adam. And Pete. And Julie. And Rich. And An. And Debbie. And all my close friends. Obsessively. Repetitively. Incessantly. Too many conversations became serious—about the choice I had to make. Too many yearbook entries included the question "What will you decide?"

That summer I worked at *The News World*, the Church's New York City paper. I clocked in every morning and spent my time either cataloging pictures for the photography department or answering the phone in Spanish for *Noticias Del Mundo*, the Spanish daily paper. I was surrounded by Family members, brothers and sisters I'd known for over half my life.

In the past, this would have been the most comfortable place for me. Not now. *Has Mother told them? Do they know I have a boyfriend? Do they know what I'm doing?* During every conversation with a member, I was consumed.

Many days Reggie came to take me out to lunch, as he now lived at the New Yorker. We'd walk to the coffee shop at the corner, sit in a booth, and he'd start. "Lisa, what are you doing? What are you doing with him?"

"Let's not. I'm hungry and have to get back to work."

He'd continue, ignoring what I said. "It's a mistake. You're too good for him."

"Reggie, stop. You don't even know Adam."

"I know he's a punk," Reggie would say, leaning forward. "I know he only wants one thing. And I know you can't give it to him. You can't fall. You can't leave."

"I'm not leaving. I'm not." With that I would pick up my sandwich and try to eat, swallowing to force the food down.

Each afternoon I clocked out, headed downtown, and made plans to be with Adam. It was all I wanted; I was more myself and more sure of myself when I spent time with him and our friends. During my years in the Church I had tried to believe that people loved me. Now it somehow felt real. For the first time I felt valued because I was me.

Adam must have thought I was something of value; before the summer ended he asked me to marry him. Maybe he was tired of my dropping his hand and crossing to the other side of the street when we'd walk through Little Italy at night and I'd see someone in the distance with a bucket of flowers to sell. *A member.* My heart would pound, my pace would quicken, my eyes would freeze, and without realizing it, my hand would slip from his. Maybe he wanted to stop my sullen silences. Maybe he wanted to solidify that I was his and we were together.

It was a beautiful summer city night. We were sitting on a park bench at Forest Hills High School, near Adam's apartment in Queens. His mother had made us spaghetti and meatballs for dinner. He suggested we go for a walk, and we ended up near the basketball court at the school.

Sitting there next to Adam, I felt a calmness I hadn't for a while. I hadn't talked with Mother, nor seen her, for a few weeks. For some reason, Robbie was leaving me alone. Adam and I had managed to avoid big issues for a few days. I felt relaxed. I leaned into him, feeling his warmth, until he knelt on the ground before me, looking up into my face. "I don't ever want to lose you," he said. "Every time you go to visit your mom, I'm afraid you won't come back. Please stay with me and marry me."

I didn't answer. I wanted to say yes but knew I should say no. I couldn't say either. I felt my mind swirling, nausea creeping through me, tears starting to run down my cheeks. I loved Adam, more than anything, and wanted to be with him, but we were desperate, feeling as if forces were pushing against us. That wasn't the way I wanted to get married. Besides, we were too young; we were only seventeen. Just like my parents. I'd sworn I'd never do what they did, marrying so young. And I couldn't pull so completely, so definitively away from the Church. I couldn't make that choice.

Adam wasn't the only one to propose to me that summer. One night Robbie convinced me to head up to the New Yorker with him to see Brian and Reggie. At that point I had been avoiding all members, even or especially Brian and Reggie, and would rather have been with Adam as the summer was coming to an end and we would soon be heading off to college. Each minute we had together was precious.

Brian and Reggie hated that I was dating Adam. They assumed we were having sex; Brian kept warning me about pregnancies and kids. They were determined to do whatever they could to bring me back. "Lisa," Brian started, while we hung out in Reggie's small room at the New Yorker, "you have to stop."

"Brian, leave it alone."

"Lisa," he continued as he put his arm around me, a smile on his face, pulling me too close, "he's just a little kid anyway. He's not worth it. What does he know?"

"Brian, stop!" I pushed him away, trying to smile.

Reggie approached me from behind and also put his arms around me. "Lisa, don't be with him."

"Reg, not you too."

"Seriously, Lisa, drop him," Reggie continued. "Be with me. Marry me."

I felt my head, my world, begin to spin. "Reggie, you're engaged!" I spit out.

"No, that's okay. Lose him. Marry me!"

I stepped across the room, uncomfortably laughing. Reggie's fiancée was a Japanese sister to whom he pledged his undying love (even though he'd never met her).

Danny also thought I was having sex. We were walking down Second Avenue, near Eighteenth Street, when he decided to talk with me about it. "Lisa," he began, looking straight ahead, careful not to catch my eye. "You're dating Adam. Maybe we should talk."

"Talk? About what?"

"Well, the most important thing is for you not to get pregnant."

It dawned on me what he had on his mind. "Danny…" I interrupted timidly.

"So I was thinking," he continued talking right over me, "I was thinking I could take you somewhere to get something."

"Danny, there's no need." My voice couldn't have been more subdued.

"It's okay. You don't have to tell me anything. But you have to be careful."

"Danny, there's no need," I stammered. "Can we stop this now?"

Danny was so sure I was having sex that years later he told friends and strangers—with me nearby or not—about how I lost my virginity. "They stopped taking the foam mattress into her room when he stayed over," Danny would say. "That's how I knew. I'd walk to the kitchen, on my way to her room to ask her something, and I'd stop, thinking, 'My daughter is in her room with a guy. The little slut. She's doing it in there,' and walk the other way." He'd laugh.

15 · the bridge

I ended up at Cornell University by default. I had no clarity, or guidance, as I applied to college. At Stuyvesant you were supposed to choose seven schools, some stretch and some safety. My first two picks were easy: Harvard and Yale. In the Church, the only colleges that were highly regarded, that Father spoke about, were Harvard and Yale. I knew I was supposed to go to one of them. I added a few of the other Ivy League Schools to my list—Brown, Cornell, and Penn—and also Williams and Duke. I'd only visited two of these schools: Cornell I'd gone to visit one weekend with Julie, to keep her company, and Yale when another friend had gone up for the day and offered me a ride.

I was rejected (and dejected) from Harvard, Yale, and Brown and got into the other four. I didn't want to go to a city school, so I eliminated Penn. Danny, for some bizarre reason, told me I couldn't go to Duke. And Williams—well, as much as I thought I might like it, Stuart's best friend, Tim, was going there. Because I had refused to date Stuart and had gotten involved with Adam, Tim thought I was lower than the scum of the earth. He also knew about the Church, and Williams was such a tiny school. I reckoned he could—and would—make my life miserable.

I haphazardly picked Cornell. When I decided, Danny said, "That's far away. How will you get there?" I felt myself tense. How would I get there? Suddenly, as always, Alice piped up from across the room. "I can't wait to see Ithaca."

As the summer before college wore on, I couldn't choose between Adam and God. My burning desire was to avoid the decision. My insane hope was that Adam would join the Church so we could be Blessed.

I invited Adam to a lecture at the New Yorker. Because he was uncomfortable going at all, much less alone with me, I invited Pete, Rich, and An as well. None of them were interested in the teachings. They came because they cared for me. Adam ate before we met, in case a meal was served; he didn't want to risk being drugged into submission by eating Church food. That was how afraid everyone—even my boyfriend—was of the people and places of my childhood.

Pete and Rich argued with the lecturers, pointing out flaws in the doctrine, inaccuracies and irregularities, while I cowered in the corner of the room with An comforting me. I wasn't sure what embarrassed me more: showing the Church to the four of them or their outright denial of what I knew as truth.

In the end, the evening at the New Yorker had no effect other than making it blatantly clear that my friends thought Principle was ludicrous and that Adam would never come to accept Father. We could never be Blessed. I had to make my final choice myself.

Adam and I spent countless hours in intense conversations and arguments. We fought about the Church and argued over my inability, or unwillingness, to leave. We debated religion (of which he had basically none), and I tried to explain, convince, and convert him. In desperation, I forced myself to a decision.

I made a condition—a promise to God—that I would see Adam only three times a week for the rest of the summer. Although I longed to spend every minute with him, especially as we were about to go away to school, I felt that this separation, along with prayer and relentless study of Principle, was the only thing that could and would save me. I worked to convince myself, beyond all doubt, of my wrong ways and determined that when we went to college in the fall—with me in upstate New York and Adam in New York City at NYU—our relationship would end. I would break up with him. Even though my new life felt so good, my terror about leaving was too huge. I had to go back.

But as soon as Adam, Danny, and Alice left me at school—Adam had taken the ride up so we'd have a few more hours together—my resolve cracked. I wasn't able or willing to stick with my decision. Adam and I had a saying, "Always come home." It was our promise to each other to weather the storms fighting against us. I hugged Adam goodbye that day, hard, and knew that I always wanted to come home to him. Still. Always. I talked to him every day—ah, the glory of reduced phone charges after eleven p.m.—and became more and more tormented. Although I couldn't make a decision—if I even thought about it, it was excruciating—my actions made it clear what I was choosing. I was, by sins both of omission and commission, leaving the Church.

Being away from home, from everyone and everything I knew, made it somewhat easier. Making new friends probably helped as well. Annie, my roommate, and I bonded, practically within minutes, talking about the boy she left at home and the one I was keeping with me. And some of the cute ones who lived on the floor beneath us. We taped rainbows on the cinderblock walls of our dorm room, plugged in my record player so that we could fall asleep to "Wreck on the Highway" every night, and made our new home a home. We were, in many ways, the epitome of opposites attracting. She was tall to my short. Preppy to my pseudo-punk and thrift-store trash. She wore multiple turtleneck dickies with the collars sticking up, and I wore my Adam-esque inside-out sweatshirts and bandanas of every color. But she was warmhearted and fun to be around, and we became much more than just roommates.

At first I didn't mention my background to her or anyone else and kept up with the freshman scene of frat parties, drinking, and socializing. But as much as I enjoyed standing in line by the beer trucks, holding my red Solo cup and waiting for my Genny Cream Ale, listening to "Super Freak" blaring in the background, these non-Church activities kicked up guilt and shame and my certainty that I was wicked and unworthy. I couldn't keep it to myself, not with such confusion about to explode out of me, so I told Annie.

"I get that more than Judaism" was her response, good Catholic girl that she was. I felt understood.

I also told my friend Fred, whom I'd met my second night at school. I had spent that evening in activities on another part of campus and was on my way back to the U-Halls, what we called the freshman dorms, where I lived, when Fred stopped me. "Do you know how to get to West Campus?" he asked. (West Campus was where the U-Halls were.) "Sure," I answered, not believing he was lost. "Follow me." He did—to West Campus, to my dorm room to meet Annie, to walk by the gorges, to become close friends.

Like me, Fred was self-searching and spiritual. I was drawn to that. He was kind, warm, and caring, and, of course, he was cute, with his reddish-brown hair and impish smile. The first time I told him about the Church, he put his arms around me and held me. I felt safe as we sat there that night, tears streaming down my cheeks.

I did my best to distance myself from the Church—physically, mentally, and spiritually—until a fateful Tuesday morning as I walked through the Straight, Cornell's student union, on the way to class.

I was with Fred and his floor mates—much of my time was spent with him, his roommate, John, their floor mate Harold, and a number of the other guys from the fourth floor of U-Hall 1. John cracked a joke, and as I looked over toward him, I saw the banner hanging from the wall. *Shit. What is CARP doing here?* The College Association for the Research of Principles was the Church's group that recruited on college campuses. They had come here to preach and proselytize. I scanned the members behind the table. A couple of them looked familiar, but there was no one I knew. *I guess I'm safe—but do I look familiar to them?*

My friends saw the banner and table as well. Although CARP tried to hide its affiliation with the Church, people knew.

"Moonies, seriously?" Matt said.

"They make me sick," Marcus added. "Why don't they just leave?"

I tried to ignore their conversation, and I tried to ignore the Moonies. Neither worked. Fred looked at me, wondering how I was doing. The Church members also looked at me, probably wondering why I wasn't on their side of the table, explaining Principle to everyone. But they let me walk by. I avoided them every time I passed through the Straight, eyes focused ahead of me, moving fast.

Even though Fred watched me with concern, I don't think anyone knew what was going on inside me. Not even me. On the surface I was a happy, albeit complicated, college student. It was a façade I worked hard to keep up. But in my head and heart—my very psyche—I was cracking.

At Cornell they joke about people committing suicide by jumping off the bridges. Someone had painted "jumping zones" and "watching zones" on the suspension bridge, and all the freshmen had heard a rumor that you were guaranteed an automatic 4.0 should your roommate jump. Before a stressful exam, Annie and I would teasingly suggest the option to each other, in order to win a good grade. (These days they have nets under the bridges as a deterrent and safety measure.)

Then came the day that that option became real. I was heading back to the dorms from my job at a day-care center off campus. On my way home I took the Stewart Avenue Bridge over Fall Creek Gorge. Halfway across the bridge that afternoon I stopped and stood still, unable to continue. I gazed down the road, toward where I was going, and over the railing to the rocks below. I could hear water splashing and, if I listened for it, birds singing in the distance. I could feel the sun beating down. Frozen there—seeing but not seeing, hearing but not hearing—thoughts of plunging to the bottom of the gorge surged inside my head. I know it sounds clichéd, but the minutes passed in a super slow motion, and I didn't think I could go on—not the rest of the way across the bridge and not with my life, after the choices I had made. Each day was taking me further and further from the Church and all I had known, believed, and loved. Self-condemnation and remorse simmered inside me like a newly active volcano about to erupt. Everything hurt too much and was way too hard. Way too hard. I stared up at the sky, tears in my eyes, desperate to reconnect with the God I'd known through much of my childhood, longing for the sense of purpose and meaning that had sustained me for so long, begging for the all-consuming doubt and anguish within me to be lifted.

High places are known to fill one with an urge to jump, to experience the sensation of falling—called "high-place phenomenon"—but my feelings that day were different. It was almost as if I was empty, with a vacant pit inside me that echoed my torment and despair. I stood there, with the gorge below, and contemplated the fall. How long would it take? What would it be like? It was a beautiful autumn day. The sun was shining, the leaves were turning, and the air was crisp. I was in my freshman year of college, with my future in front of me, but I had no desire to make it to the other side of the bridge.

I couldn't choose a path for the rest of my life. I couldn't. Death was the easy, only, and best way out of the situation. If I was dead, I wouldn't be ashamed of failing and walking away from the Messiah and my responsibility. I wouldn't be another person who wasn't strong enough or good enough, who turned against God and killed God's heart. Or I wouldn't have to leave Adam. This would all be done.

I stood on the bridge for ten or fifteen minutes, looking over the railing, studying the rocks with their jagged edges and the water calmly bubbling, thinking about the immediate release I would experience. I wanted to fall to my physical death to avoid falling—having sex outside of a Blessed marriage—to my spiritual death.

Eventually I turned away and walked back to campus. Why? How? To this day, I don't know. Why did I return to my dorm and act as if nothing had happened? How did I find it in myself to do that? What got me through that moment? Was it what got me through everything leading up to that moment and what would, hopefully, get me through everything else yet to come? I have no idea. People ask me now how I made it through—without cracking, without succumbing, without being far too damaged. Again, I just don't know.

Maybe I didn't jump to my death that day because jumping would have been admitting defeat, and I was too stubborn for that. Maybe there was a part of me that loved life and that somehow saw some possibility and hope, or some chance for peace, even with my turmoil. Maybe there was a will in me to survive. Maybe I was protected by some greater power in the universe. Maybe I do have a steel rod for a spine. Maybe I'm just lucky.

I may have decided not to throw myself over the bridge that day, but I still didn't know how to throw off the shackles of the Church. How to lessen its influence and control of my mind and life. I didn't know how to make a final choice to leave, and I didn't know how to be anything but a Moonie. I didn't know what not being a Moonie meant.

I began talking more about my past and my experiences growing up. No surprise, my life became a series of late-night conversations. Annie and I discussed it endlessly, often with our friend Doug, who lived on the first floor of our dorm and was raised half-Catholic and half-Jewish. Perhaps this made him more open to differences. The two of them got it and me the most, listening without judgment, questioning without condemning, allowing that it might have been—or still could be—good in some ways, and good for me. I also huddled on the floor of various dorm rooms, surrounded by most of the girls on my floor, or gathered in the lounge at the end of the hall with friends and strangers around me and was bombarded with questions. "What did you believe?" people asked. "How could you believe that?" "What do you think now?" "Your mother is still in it? How weird." Everyone had heard the horrors of the Church. They knew that Moonies were brainwashed (and wondered if I had been—or was). They were certain that Father was evil and that the Church was horrendous. They insulted, or laughed at, the Moonies that stationed themselves in the Straight. The Moonies that were there to win converts. The Moonies that looked at me as I walked past their tables rather than joining them in their holy war, as I avoided their stares, wishing I could avoid the Straight completely so I didn't have to feel their silent questions and my shameful answer.

"What do you think now?" was the hardest question for me. I wasn't sure what I thought. I tried to explain how I had loved being in the Church—until I no longer did. How I was mostly sure that the Divine Principle was true, but I just didn't want to believe it anymore. Or at least not follow it. How I was pretty much convinced that Father was the Messiah. I was just choosing to walk away.

I turned again to my usual places for advice and help and wrote to both Hugh, who was out in California again, performing and witnessing, and Brian, who was now in Alaska. Alaska! I remember when he told me he was going. Father had a fishing business there. I kept asking him, "Why? Why Alaska?" It was weird that he'd be sent there. It was far away and remote. As if the motel off the side of the road in the Poconos wasn't enough. Brian had no real answer for me.

I told them of my anguish and of the day on the bridge when I nearly jumped. Hugh responded immediately, telling me to be strong, to be true to myself, and to be with Adam if I wanted to spend the rest of my life with him (and if not, maybe to keep dating him for the experience but to avoid a sexual relationship). Brian wrote pages and pages professing his profound love and burning desire for me— that it was me he had wanted all along. I didn't understand and didn't know what to do with that, especially with him in Alaska. And engaged.

My mind continued to swim. At one moment I was overwhelmed with how much I loved and missed Adam, convinced that the rest of my life would be spent with him. The next moment I was full of desire to be back in the Church, certain that in being with Adam I was giving up my way of life, answers to all questions, and a chance to save the world. And at times I would be frustrated with the long-distance aspect of my relationship, as the tension of our separation brought out Adam's obnoxious nature full-force. If I was going to risk my life by being involved with someone, maybe I'd be better off with someone at school with me. Even though it increased my confusion and guilt, I had my eyes on a few guys around me.

I decided to go see Mother, who was then living in Wilmington, Delaware, teaching at a Church preschool. I hadn't seen her since the summer, when our every conversation was about how dangerous and misguided my actions were.

Our first day together was awkward and stilted. I didn't know how to act or what to say. Through all my turmoil I felt a new, stronger me somehow emerging, but I wasn't sure Mother wanted anything to do with this person. (I don't know how much she had wanted to do with the old me either.) There was a constant lump in my throat, and I had to think through everything I said before opening my mouth.

Then we went to the movies. For some reason we decided to see *Only When I Laugh*, a movie about an alcoholic mother in recovery and her messed-up relationship with her daughter—perhaps not the best choice based on what was going on.

We arrived back at Mother's apartment that evening, both of us rattled. We started talking about, or trying to avoid talking about, Pledge. It was Saturday night, and I was supposed to wake with her at five the next morning to say it. The old me would have.

We sat on the small couch in her living room, not quite touching but not quite a formal distance apart either. "When do you want to get up tomorrow?" Mother asked.

I could sense the care with which she posed her question, the hesitation behind her words, and responded just as tentatively. "I don't know."

"Well," she continued, "what are you thinking you want to do?"

I turned to face her. "Mother," I started, pausing and swallowing hard to gather courage, "are you asking me about Pledge?"

"What do you want to do, Lisa?"

"I haven't said Pledge in months," I stated with as much confidence as I could. Then my voice faltered and fell into a whisper. "I don't know if I can tomorrow. I don't know how I feel about it...I just don't know if I can."

Silence filled the room, running up the very edges of the walls. Finally she spoke. "Okay." Again a long silence. "Okay, I'll get up and say Pledge, and you wake up whenever you wake up."

I didn't know what to say. I turned to look at her, tears coming to my eyes. "Is that okay?"

She paused again, and I waited. "Yes, Peach-pie, I guess it's okay."

"I want you to be happy with me, Mother; it's all I ever wanted."

I found a glimpse of release just before Christmas break. Over the months I had become closer and closer to Fred. He was the guy I thought most about dating instead of Adam.

Fred went with me when Steven Hassan—an ex-Moonie who now deprogrammed members and traveled to college campuses speaking about the deception of the Church—came to Cornell. We sat on fold-up chairs in the small meeting room above Noyes dining hall, listening as Steven warned the audience of the evils and dangers of the Church. Steven explained brainwashing and mind control in diligent detail and pointed out that Moonies would lie, cheat, and steal for Reverend Moon. He warned against speaking to members, counseling that even one quick conversation could lead to psychological immersion into the insane teachings of the Church—teachings that were so bizarre yet so complex that it was virtually impossible to intelligently refute them. He warned that all of this, all of the outward religiosity, was a front for Reverend Moon's endless thirst for money and power and his determination to dominate the world.

I listened to Steven's speech that night, his diatribe against the Church, my body trembling with a vibrant mix of anger and loss. When he finished, I joined the line of people waiting to speak with him. I couldn't leave without confronting him on what I felt—what I knew—were his lies. Yet I could barely stand. It was hot in the room. There wasn't enough air. My straying from the Church had nothing to do with the horrors Steven spoke of. I never felt brainwashed and didn't need to be deprogrammed. (In retrospect, did I?) I resented Steven, hated Steven, for insulting everyone I knew.

By the time I got my turn with him, much of the crowd was gone. That was good. I shared my reaction, my disagreement, my vehement rejection of what he had said, and he looked right at me. "Wow." He nodded. "You've been a Moonie nearly your whole life. I can help you if you want."

"I'm fine!" I spit out. "I'm just fine." I turned and ran.

Fred found me outside the dining hall, sitting alone on a low wall, trying not to cry. He held me and listened for hours as I refuted what Steven had said, explained what I had experienced, and debated what was true and what was right.

After that night our conversations about the Church became more and more frequent—and more and more circular. I incessantly lisa kohn | 141

deliberated what I should do and talked endlessly about my pain. So much so that, late one night as we sat in a lecture hall somewhere on campus where we'd obstensibly gone to study, in the middle of my monologue of confusion, Fred blurted out, "Lisa, get off your pity pot."

I stared at him, shocked, caught mid-sentence. "Everyone has tough times," he continued. "Stop feeling sorry for yourself and move on."

I was stunned. Fred had always been willing to listen and had been supportive. Now he was telling me to shut up, and all I could hear in my head were the endless questions that haunted me. *What if it's the truth and I walk away? What if Father is the Messiah?* I looked at Fred. "But what if it's right?" I whispered. "What if it's right?

We sat in silence for a while. Fred put his arms around me and turned to look straight at me. "What if," he started and waited. "What if it is right, but it's just not right for you?"

Fred's perhaps off-handed comment gave me a crack that I could begin to crawl through, or maybe it widened the crack that had appeared all those years ago when Brian picked me up from music camp. All I know is that in his words I found a glimpse of a way to even comtemplate extricating myself from the Church and its hold on me. "What if it's not right for me?" became my new mantra, replacing "Everything's okay today. Everything's all right tonight," which I'd used to take care of myself through my childhood. I repeated it over and over (and over) during the rest of my first term, as I prepared to go home for Christmas break. "What if it's just not right for me? What if it's just not right for me?" It wasn't much, but it was all I had.

I was heading home to New York City, and I didn't want to be there. School felt like home, and I didn't want to see Adam. My dissatisfaction with how things were between us was growing, although by what I said to him—never complaining and always telling him how much I loved him—and by my plans for break, you would never know.

Adam was coming to my house for Christmas. I had never had a boy to any family gatherings. I was crossing a line. Acknowledging our togetherness and my distance from the Church.

I would be crossing another line by going to the party Adam was throwing on New Year's Eve. There are four main holidays in the Church—Parent's Day, Children's Day, Day of All Things, and God's Day. God's Day is New Year's Day. Every year since we first visited Barrytown, I had spent New Year's Eve and Day in the confines and practices of the Church. Every New Year's Eve I sat with my legs bent underneath me surrounded by many sisters, with brothers on the other side of the room, listening to Father speak. I ushered in every New Year with prayer and shouts of "Abeoji! Mansei!" This year I intended to dance, drink, and party.

Before the holidays, on the night I got back to New York City, Adam and I went to Raoul's to visit Danny. It was my first time there when I was of age, eighteen and legally able to drink. Danny made the most of it. As Adam and I sat at the end of the jam-packed bar, perched on our black leather stools, Danny poured me glass upon glass of very expensive champagne, loudly celebrating, with everyone around, my age and the fact that I drank. Sitting there, allowing my father to usher me into drunken oblivion, I remembered, as I'm sure he did, how when I was younger I complained when he cooked with alcohol. He'd steam mussels in beer, and I'd refuse to eat them until he promised that the alcohol had burnt off. Now I drank his champagne, and as I climbed the circular staircase at the other end of the bar to go pee, holding tight to the railing and feeling the champagne in my brain and my shaking legs, I could see Danny talking with his customers, two-deep at the bar, looking up at me and beaming. My steps away from the Church were, I'm sure, as he perceived them, steps toward freedom and toward him. He'd always hated the Church and my involvment in it. He was thrilled to see me drink.

Then came New Year's. God's Day. In some ways it was easier to be in Forest Hills, in Adam's apartment, than at the New Yorker. I was with my friends from high school and the one I loved. I was encircled by everyone who knew me well, knew my journey, and loved me pretty much no matter what I chose in the end. "Roxanne" blared from the speakers as my friend Roxanne walked into the apartment. I was where I belonged.

But in some ways it was harder, especially when I stayed through New Year's Day to be with Adam instead of heading up to the New Yorker for the God's Day entertainment as I had promised Mother. Adam and I needed to talk. Many of our conversations still focused on the Church and my decision, but they had also begun to circle around a different, but equally difficult, decision.

While Danny was convinced that Adam and I were having sex, we weren't, and it was becoming more and more of an issue. I knew it was something Adam wanted because he told me all the time. He told me again that night, but I was not ready. I didn't know when, or if, I'd ever be ready. Even fooling around at all could freak me out. One minute I'd be fine and the next I'd turn away wracked with guilt. How could I contemplate sex? My whole being shook when I thought about it.

Adam professed patience. But for how long?

According to legend, the statues of Andrew White and Ezra Cornell, the founders of Cornell, would rise from their seats at opposite ends of the Arts Quad and meet in the middle of the Quad to shake hands if a virgin walked between them at exactly midnight. As much as the thought of sex terrified me, the realization that I would make them shake hands humiliated me.

The whole relationship thing confounded me. Not only did I feel horribly innocent, but my life in the Church, and specifically my determination to adore and be adored by every member—brother and sister—set me up as an idiot about relationships. I wanted Adam, and I didn't. I wanted to be involved with other guys, and I didn't. And apparently I flirted beyond belief.

I didn't realize I flirted, and it wasn't my intention. I interacted with every guy I met as I had, and would, with any and every brother in the Church—smiling, endearing myself, and offering as much love and attention as I could muster. Doug yelled at me over and over about how I led guys on and made them think I liked them. I never realized the signals I sent.

I held on to "maybe it's just not right for me" and continued my slow departure from the Church during the second semester of freshman year. In retrospect, it was a departure that took years to complete. If people today ask me when I left the Church, I say I'm not sure, or somewhere between eighteen and twenty. Anything more definite than that would have shattered me. Or shattered me more. While everyone around me at that time could—and would—declare me "in" or "out," I couldn't. I just couldn't.

I found that the only way to decide was to not decide. I did my best to walk away. To ignore it. Although God was all-important to me, I couldn't think of God without thinking of Father's definition of God. And I couldn't think of Father's definition of God without driving myself back to the bridge and the need to end my life. I did my best to not think about whether, or what, I believed. To not think at all.

If anyone asked me the question that had stumped me in the beginning of the year, "What do you believe?" I might answer, "I don't know," or better yet, "Nothing." I chose to take things day by day. I no longer described myself as a Moonie; rather, I had been a Moonie. I thought I was done with it.

With my growing love for life on my own and away from my religious past, I continued to move further from the Church and closer to guys. I was increasingly attracted to Fred. But as close as we became and as much as we wanted to be together, Fred wouldn't date me, because I was with Adam. And I couldn't break up with Adam. He was a known, albeit imperfect, commodity. I had left the Church for him. How could I leave him and live with my decision?

Even when Adam and I agreed we could each see other people, it was not enough for Fred. Again it took a drunken night and an unconscious reaction to someone else's action to propel me out of my endless back and forth over what I should do. I was at a fraternity party with Fred and the guys who lived in his dorm, in particular, Harold. I had always thought Harold was cute and knew he had a girlfriend at home, so I figured he was someone who was safe. I could be friends with him and not have to worry about signals I was inadvertently sending or relationships that would screw me up more.

Until we danced. "Rock Lobster" was playing, and I was having fun. We twisted our way down toward the floor as the B-52s sang "down, down, down," and the next thing I knew Harold was kissing me.

Taken by surprise, I kissed him back, not quite sure what had happened but swept into the moment and eager to move ahead without having to think about it first. Even when I couldn't choose to get involved with someone, I could unwittingly respond. I spent the rest of the night with Harold and avoiding Fred, who sat waiting for me on the frat-house living-room couch.

After that kiss, Harold and I started seeing each other. He was the "get out of jail free card" that broke my impasse. We got closer emotionally, all the while creeping around lest anyone should know what we were doing. We never got close physically. If I wouldn't sleep with Adam, I certainly wouldn't sleep with Harold.

No matter whom I was with, sex frightened me. I knew it was a matter of course for nearly everyone around me, although fortunately for me, not for Annie, a good Catholic girl who protected her—and my—virginity. I had the string from an animal crackers box tied around my right wrist, swearing that I'd keep it on until I lost "it." Annie checked on that string bracelet often.

I wasn't proud that I was seeing Harold, Fred's good friend and dorm mate, while it was Fred who had meant, and still meant, so much to me. But Fred had refused to date me while I had Adam, and Harold had kissed me anyway.

As guilty as I felt, my every thought was to spend all my time with Harold; I wanted to be wanted. But Harold wanted secrecy. He refused to let anyone know that he was cheating on his girlfriend or that he'd gone behind Fred's back. It was clear to our friends that I was Fred's, even though we weren't dating, and therefore whenever we were with other people Harold would ignore me. I got it. What we were doing was wrong.

I'd be in tears at something Harold had done, sobbing on my bed, and Fred would show up at the door to my room to say hi. It was wrong. I would hang out with the guys from their dorm floor, studying for finals in Morrill Hall and sneaking glances at Harold when no one was looking. I'd meet him later in my room, when none of them knew where he was. It was wrong. I needed the summer break to come and this deceit to end.

My belief that a change of venue over the summer would somehow transform my situation and emotional struggles was mistaken. I spent my time at home back with my high school friends, loving every minute of it, and still torn. Adam and I did much better when we were in the same city, yet I wanted to experience something and someone else. I felt like a twelve-year-old, a junior high school girl: completely mixed-up about boys. So what if I was eighteen and the boys I was mixed-up about were old enough to be drafted?

The one mature choice I made that summer was to avoid working at the Church. In fact, I had as little to do with it as possible. Mother was still stationed in Delaware and doing her best to keep our relationship smooth. Robbie was home and had started his own journey away from the Church and was therefore less harsh with me. This space from the pressure of everything I had known and everyone who needed me to stay allowed me to step further away and to become more comfortable with my new life. I began to feel at peace with what I was doing. I began to feel good—until the day I had the best seats ever at Madison Square Garden. The day my mother got married there.

16 · best seats at the garden

I had been to the Garden a number of times before for concerts
and other events and had sat in the highest and cheapest blue seats,
closer to the roof than to the stage. But on my mother's wedding day,
Robbie, our cousin Bobby, and I sat in the red seats, the best ones,
which circled the floor of the arena.

It was July 1, 1982. A beautiful, hot summer day. Just over three
years since Mother had been Matched to Phil and nearly every other
brother and sister I knew had been Matched to someone I didn't
know. Robbie, Bobby, and I sat stiff in our seats that morning and
watched the endless procession of two thousand and seventy-five
women dressed in identical long white lace-and-satin gowns with
lace veils and two thousand and seventy-five men in navy blue suits,
white shirts, and red ties enter the Garden.

This was Father's first Blessing in America. It was the first mass
marriage in America, Father's largest mass marriage ever at that point,
and it was big news, with television cameras positioned everywhere
to capture the bizarre event and broadcast it to curious audiences
across the world. The seats were only partially filled. Even with over
four thousand men and women getting married in one spot on one
day, the friends, families, and loved ones (those who had actually
come and passed through a metal detector—and protestors outside
the Garden carrying signs like "Let Our Children Go" and "Hitler,
Jim Jones, Moon"—in order to attend the ceremony) scarcely filled
the stadium. But the floor was full of couples—a sea of black and
white. Couples who barely knew each other; couples who didn't
speak the same language; couples who were promising themselves to
God and each other "till death do us part."

Somewhere among that never-ending procession of women was

Mother, about to marry Phil. At that point I had met Phil two or three times, and Mother had met him only a few more. Also somewhere in that procession were Hugh, Brian, Reggie, and many of the brothers and sisters I had known for so many years. My life in the Church paraded across the stadium floor as I sat there and watched. As the entire world watched, in amazement and incredulity.

Mother was thrilled about the Blessing; to her it was the ultimate goal of her spiritual life. She had invited the three of us to celebrate with her on this joyful day, but it was anything but joyful for us. "What is she thinking?" Bobby muttered, sitting there in disbelief and anger. Robbie was stone-faced and silent, while I squirmed in my chair, futilely looking for her among the brides, aware that my distance from the Church had been growing—and growing.

I watched Father and Mother face each other on podiums in the middle of the arena. Dressed in long white Korean robes with gold trim and ornate white-and-gold crowns upon their heads, they sprinkled the couples with holy water as the procession wove... and wove...and wove between the two podiums. Mendelssohn's "Wedding March" played softly in the background as the brides and grooms wound their way around the Garden for what seemed like an eternity. It takes hours for over two thousand couples to marry.

I thought back to Mother's Matching and how grateful I was that Phil had agreed to join our family. How delighted I was for Mother and how much I wanted the same thing to happen to me. I had looked forward, in awe, to the day when I would be Matched, when Father would choose my husband-to-be. I had had every intention of being part of a mass wedding and of pledging myself to God, True Parents, and my new husband. Now, watching the ceremony at Madison Square Garden, seeing True Parents standing there, it was all I could do to stay in my seat.

Along with the rest of the world, I watched my mother marry Phil—or pretended to since I had no idea where she was in the crowd of brides and grooms—and willed myself to be happy for her. We met her after the ceremony for a quick hug, kiss, and celebratory lunch. And then I ran away. Away from the Church. Away from Family members who looked at me with questions and accusations.

Away from the feelings. And away from the Garden.

I dove back into my summer, back into my relationship with Adam, and back into my adolescent angst. It may have been painful, but it was better than looking at my choice to desert God and my destiny, my choice to sever myself from all that I had known and loved. My visceral reaction at the Garden—my lack of reverence for Father and Mother, the urgency with which I had had to get out of there, the sick feeling in the pit of my stomach—made it clear to me that I had left the Church. Even if I hadn't realized it up until that point. Even if I couldn't allow myself to realize it then. I had left.

I counted the days until I could go back to school, impatient to return to the place where I now felt most at home.

17 · never too thin

I was excited to return to my sophomore year and to escape connections with the Church. There were too many Family members in New York City who knew me and expected to see me. Besides, Adam had transferred to SUNY-Binghamton, only an hour away. Having him close would be a plus. So too would be living in an off-campus apartment with Annie and four other girls we knew.

Our apartment had four bedrooms for the six of us—two doubles and two singles—a small kitchen, a dining area, a living room, and one bathroom. We divided up rooms based on willingness to share and ability to pay. Annie and I had the smallest and cheapest room, with a bunk bed to fit us. I slept in the top bunk, climbing up to it using a well-positioned trunk as my ladder.

I didn't mind the sleeping arrangement, but I soon became disenchanted with the apartment. We were on the bottom floor of a building that was set up against a hill. (Everything at Cornell was part of a hill. You'd go to a party at night, and it was uphill. You'd come home, and somehow you'd still have to walk uphill.) With next to no light coming in, the apartment felt dismal and secluded.

My relationships with Harold and Fred were equally dismal. Harold returned to school engaged to his Brooklyn girlfriend, so there was no longer anything between us. He avoided me.

Even worse, Fred found out about Harold. I hated that. I don't know how he found out. I don't even know how I found out he found out. I just remember that as soon as Fred knew, everyone else knew, and that core group of friends were no longer my friends. They wouldn't hang out with me or even talk to me. They walked by me on campus and ignored me in class. Because of what I had done—funny that the blame lay entirely on me and not on Harold—

they wanted nothing to do with me. Even though part of me thought I deserved their rejection—I despised myself for how much I had hurt Fred—it left me reeling. I had lost too many people already in leaving the Church. I didn't know how I could handle losing more.

I came back to school determined to continue my search for who I really was, and included in that search was a decision to try what many people around me raved about. It was time to smoke pot. I had been practically the only one in my freshman dorm who didn't, other than Annie, and that was going to change at The Who concert. Annie and I were road-tripping to the Syracuse Carrier Dome with a few guys from our freshman year dorm—Billy, Frank, and Doug. We'd gotten tickets—good floor seats—and were standing in our row, passing a joint. As always, Billy handed it to me to pass it along. Instead I held it. And held it. And held it.

I looked at the joint—innocuous, yet scary and meaningful—smoldering, pinched tightly between my fingers. Taking a deep breath to calm myself, I put it to my lips, feeling an equal force pulling it away. I inhaled and held the smoke in, as I'd seen everyone—my friends, my brother, my father, his friends—do for years.

Not sure what to expect, I waited, feeling my pulse rush. *Is this fear? Excitement? The pot?* My eyes began to tear, and I exhaled.

I became the center of attention, even more than the music. "Lisa!" Frank said. "What are you doing? Guys, look at Lisa!" Annie's face registered shock and disappointment. "Lisa, not you too!" And in my mind: *What will Danny think? "You wonderful little slut," he'll probably say. I'm sure he'll be proud.*

There was another change in my life that Danny probably would have been proud of as well.

I was in Binghamton visiting Adam for the weekend when I decided it was time for the string bracelet to come off. Our relationship was tense and tenuous, and I reasoned that having sex might make things better.

We had talked about it for so long, and Adam had somewhat resigned himself to my saying no, only now I wanted to say yes. I thought it was what we should do and what I needed to do. My past demons—my former rules and strict guidelines—seemed far away.

Adam didn't believe me when I told him I would go through with it. But I did.

It was momentous, even as it wasn't. *I don't feel any different.* The next morning, I waited for punishment to fall from the sky. I walked through the Binghamton student union wondering if anyone could tell, as if there was a huge scarlet letter pinned to my chest. *No. I am the same old Lisa.*

Only I wasn't. Within days my world came crashing down. I was not punished for having sex by God or True Parents, or even my own mother. Rather, I was the force behind my descent into a hellish existence. I needed to suffer for the sin of sleeping with my boyfriend. I didn't articulate this or even comprehend it, but my shame pushed me on a path to slowly kill myself. I hadn't jumped from the bridge the year before, but now I had to pay for my evil, wandering ways.

How? At the beginning of the school year, I had started dieting to lose my freshman five—or ten—and gain some control in my life. After Adam and I had sex, I stopped eating.

I stopped eating, but my world revolved around food. Not what I was going to put in my mouth, but how I could avoid it altogether.

During Christmas break, I went to visit Danny at Raoul's. The restaurant was experimenting with serving brunch, and he was experimenting with working days instead of nights, to hopefully lessen his daily cocaine use. His shift was over, and we were sitting at a table in the garden room—the dining area through the kitchen. Danny was about to order himself something and looked over at me. "Twink, what do you want?"

"I'm okay." I brushed imaginary crumbs off the white tablecloth.

"You haven't eaten lunch. You have to eat."

"Danny, I'm okay." I knew my voice was strained. I hated mealtimes.

Danny got up from the table and walked into the kitchen. When he came back, he carried two plates of food. He placed one in front of me, sat down next to me, and took his first bite. Omelets. The smell of fried onions wafted up toward me. The melted cheese dripped out the sides.

I watched Danny for as long as I could, grabbed my fork, and began to nudge the food around. One by one, I picked up five strawberries—the garnish—and ate them. I pushed the plate away and got up to go.

Danny looked at me, his eyes revealing a mixture of disgust, anger, and frustration. "Eat, Lisa."

"Danny, I'm fine."

"You have to eat something." His words came out like gunfire, and I could see the exasperation and concern on his face. "You have to eat, or you can't go back to school."

"I'm fine. I know what I'm doing." With that I walked away, certain that I needed to be thinner and that I'd already eaten too much that day anyway. *Five strawberries contain a lot of sugar. They're high in calories. I need to be more careful.*

Danny didn't stop me from going back to school, and returning to Ithaca made my relationship with food worse. I monitored everything that went into my mouth and punished myself when I couldn't restrict what I ate. I exercised nonstop—taking aerobics classes, doing Jane Fonda workouts, and going for long jogs around campus. I rushed to the scale every morning, tightening my control if the needle ever budged up and celebrating silently when the pounds fell off.

If breakfast was more than a slice of toast or half a grapefruit, I wouldn't eat lunch. When I did have lunch, it was a small container of Dannon plain yogurt. These meals I could control because my campus meal plan didn't cover breakfast and lunch. Dinner, however, was a challenge, a precipice over which I had to throw myself each night. I spent every afternoon in the library to stay away from my apartment. Annie would most likely be there, and she always asked me to have dinner with her, to watch what I ate.

As evening came, I'd walk down the hill from the library, hoping I wouldn't run into anyone. Being on my own meant fewer questions. I was oblivious to the beauty around me, the view of Cayuga Lake in the distance, the stars in the sky.

Making it safely, alone, to the dining hall that was nearest our apartment, I grabbed a tray and headed toward the obstacles I had to face before I could fall into bed with a flat stomach. My eyes darted around the room to make sure I avoided everyone so that I could eat in peace. At the same time, I steeled myself to overcome the threats around me: The bread table. The ice cream freezer. The entrée line. The smells. I didn't know how to avoid the smells. How to dislike the smells.

I made my way over to the salad bar, grabbed a plate, and piled it with lettuce. Lettuce was safe. Carrots were okay. A bit sweet but okay. Cucumbers were mostly water. Green peppers: I didn't like them, but they were low in calories. I pushed past the avocados—too fattening—past the croutons, past the cheese. As a treat, I poured on some vinegar. I liked vinegar; somehow its acidity made me feel like it was burning calories.

I grabbed a fork and a glass of water—I was good to myself and drank a lot of water—and made my way to the loft dining area, upstairs, away from the smells. I looked around the room, searching for a spot in the corner where I could sit and eat. But every once in a while...

Shit. There was Vicky, a girl in my psych class.

"Hey Lisa," she called. "Come on over."

Trapped. "Uh, sure." I headed to her table and took a seat. And smelled her food, as she stared at my dinner.

"That's all you're eating?"

"I had a huge lunch and something a little while ago at the Straight." I looked away.

"Wow, I wish I had your restraint."

We talked about boys, classes, our professor—who knows what. I moved my food around and took a few bites, waiting just long enough so that I could leave without being too rude. I had to go. I interrupted Vicky in the midst of a story, a sentence even. "Uh, thanks," I said. She stared at me. "I gotta study," I lied. "I'll see you in class."

With that I pushed back my chair, grabbed my tray, and practically ran down the stairs—away from the food, the smells, and the people.

As I fled, it hit me. I had eaten so much. I had too little control. I was disgusting. *I'll do better tomorrow. I won't have green peppers. I won't use vinegar. I'll do better tomorrow.*

I spent my days thinking about food—what to eat, what not to eat, what I had eaten, what I could eat later, what I couldn't eat, when I would eat, what I wanted to eat but wouldn't. All my concerns about the Church, about Adam, and about other guys—all of this was replaced by my love-and-hate affair with food.

The only time I ate was with Adam. I'd visit him in Binghamton, and we'd go out for Chinese food. I'd let myself have a bit of sesame noodles. They were still my favorite. He'd come visit me, and I'd share bites of his PMP (Poor Man's Pizza—French bread with sauce and melted cheese) from the Hot Truck that parked each night at the edge of campus and sold food to starving, drunk college students.

As I continued not to eat, my life continued to fall apart. Full of self-pity (this time I knew it), I clung to everyone and with that, pushed them away. As I needed Adam more and more, he had a harder time being with me. I hated being dependent, but my inner core was gone. He was my lifeline. He was all I had.

I pushed Annie away too. My insides churned as I wondered whether she, or anyone else, cared about me. Whether I had any friends. Whether I deserved to have any friends. I was certain I did not. The treatement I got from Fred's friends—who supposedly used to be my friends—was enough to convince me, if nothing else did. Annie, along with my other roommates, spent her time trying to get me to eat, but I refused. I knew better. It felt good when I didn't eat. I loved noticing my stomach rumbling. The light-headed sense I got when I skipped a meal proved to me that I was stronger, more capable, and more alive.

I was killing myself bit by bit and enjoying it. I hit eighty-two pounds and wanted to go further. With each lost pound, each lower number on the scale, a smile would creep over my face, and my fists would clench with power.

My roommates kept up their harangues until I finally agreed to go to the student health center for help. At the clinic, I was assigned a nurse, Mrs. Bonde. She was to monitor my food intake and teach me about nutrition. I was also assigned a psychology graduate student, Sue, with whom I could talk.

Not eating had begun to affect my body. I no longer got my period. Now that Adam and I were having sex, I was worried about getting pregnant. I went for endless pregnancy tests. Standing at a pay phone, calling for results each time, I could feel my heart in my throat as I prayed to be spared. My parents had gotten married because they had to. Robbie had been a mistake. I had been a mistake. As much as I loved Adam, I did not want to be forced into making such decisions. I couldn't abort a child, and I couldn't not. I couldn't marry Adam, not when things were rocky. Pregnancy would be the ultimate punishment for all that I had done, just as Brian had warned me years before.

Luckily the result was always negative. My body was shutting down from lack of food.

I spent nearly four months in therapy with Sue and working with Mrs. Bonde, struggling—to eat, to not eat, and to talk about anything other than eating. The good news was I didn't think about the Church or about leaving it much.

I didn't talk about it much either—or actually at all. I never brought it up. I was afraid that Sue, like everyone else, would judge the Church and was convinced that her negative perceptions would color everything I said. I didn't want to defend my life and the Church anymore. Avoiding the topic completely, I talked about school— and food. And thought nothing of it. Even as I declared a major in psychology. I had liked Psych 101—with James Maas teaching it, everyone had—and thought that whatever job I eventually got, it would involve working with people, so understanding people would help. I made no attempt to understand myself.

With Mrs. Bonde I discussed the nutritional elements of food and how many calories were necessary in a day. I had no idea anymore. Did I eat enough? Too much? Too little? There was no possibility of eating until I felt full, as I had long since killed my gauge of fullness. Besides, the feeling of that much food in my stomach affected me like nightmares had when I was a kid. I'd break out in a cold sweat, nausea would creep through me, and my heart would pound.

Mrs. Bonde somehow convinced me that it was okay to eat three meals a day and even to have an ice cream cone every now and then. That was as terrifying and tormenting as leaving the Church had been a mere year ago. She called me out when I tried purging. I had heard of sticking your finger down your throat to force yourself to throw up but never got good at it. I couldn't figure out exactly where to put my finger, and besides, it grossed me out. I tried laxatives.

Mrs. Bonde stepped in before purging in any form could become another addiction. She hugged me at the end of each session. That was my favorite part. Sometimes I wanted to never let go of her or for her to never let go of me, but I would pull away. It was the right thing to do.

My journals were about food...and Adam...and food. My conversations were about food. My fights were about food. Even as I stayed in counseling and claimed to be getting better, my image in the mirror disgusted me because of the way my belly stuck out, and I delighted when my pants hung off me and hunger pangs hit. It was proof that I was good at something. I could talk a good talk about being careful and eating, but when left alone I knew it was quite simple. I needed to eat less and lose more. *No matter what we all say, it's good.*

Mother, who never visited me anywhere, came to see me. It was her first time—and only time, unless you count graduation two years later—to visit me while I was at college. (After I graduated, she would go back to Ithaca a number of times to see a Church friend of hers, but she only came to see me twice during my four years there.) She took me out to dinner—I'm sure to get me to eat—then she, Annie, and I sat in the kitchen of our apartment having bowls of ice cream with peanut butter swirled in for dessert. I don't know how I managed that. I do know I cut my usual amount of food for a week to lose the pounds I gained.

As my obsession with food continued, my relationship with Adam deteriorated. It was no longer other people who were coming between us, at least not for me. He very well may have been seeing other people. (Years later, mutual friends told me that he was.) I was caged by my inability to be in relationship, with him or even with myself. Still, I clung to him, centering my life around him and counting on him to help fill the hole within me that I couldn't admit was there.

There were times when things were good, when I felt as if he cared and was willing to hold me and help me, to listen when I talked. He'd visit for the weekend, and life couldn't have been better. We'd hang with Annie or see a movie—easy times with no serious discussions and no fights. Adam would sometimes bring pot and we'd party, although I often ended up curled into an incoherent ball with my head in his lap, certain that the high would never go away. It wasn't my drug. There were times when he seemed not to care at all or to not be willing to deal with me, leaving me alone to work through these things. These things that were all mine.

His phone calls became less frequent, and when he called, our conversations dragged. I had nothing to share. "I miss you," was all I offered one day.

"Are you eating?" was his response.

"I had an appointment with my counselor today."

"Is that what you want, Lisa?"

I tried to explain, and he went silent on the phone. So I stopped. He didn't want to hear what I was going through, and I didn't want, or know, how to explain. *I'm as okay without you as you are without me*, I screamed inside my head when I felt him check out. *I think about you as little as you think about me*, I longed to scream out loud. *I can go without seeing you, happily without seeing you, as easily as you can without seeing me*, I cried internally in defense.

I said none of this, struggling with feeling like I was losing myself for him but desperate to save both myself and the relationship that I'd hung everything on. I clenched my way through our conversations, longing to express my thoughts but not sure what they were and where things stood. Adam would retreat, and in response I'd either frantically chase after him or pull back.

Our apartment fell apart. Perhaps six college-aged women should not live together. We fought constantly. Some of us did not have the money to pay high heating bills, so we'd turn down the thermostat and keep warm with sweaters and extra blankets. Next thing we knew, those who could afford it were resetting the thermostat upward. We'd set it lower. It went back and forth.

Cleaning was also a source of contention. After Valerie left her dishes in the sink without washing them one too many times, others left nasty notes for her on the kitchen table. When the offense continued, dirty dishes were taken out of the sink and left on Valerie's bed.

With about a month to go in the school year and on the lease, Jane moved out. She was willing to pay rent in two places rather than stay in the apartment. With relief I took her vacated room, leaving the one I shared with Annie, whose need for neatness, organization, and order clashed with my slow descent into self-absorption.

Deciding to surprise Adam, I grabbed a ride to Binghamton on a Saturday afternoon. I was thrilled to spend a few unexpected hours with him. Our two-year anniversary had just passed, and I was feeling a bit in control.

I found him in the library and snuck up from behind, eager for his amazement and joy upon seeing me. I remembered how excited and happy he had been a year earlier when I had shown up outside Radio City Music Hall for a Devo concert and to spend the weekend with him. He'd enveloped me in a big hug, with a huge smile on his face. This time he turned to me and said, "Uh, hi."

"Hey. I wanted to see you."

"Lisa, we need to talk." His voice was almost too quiet for me to hear. I knew we were in the library, but Adam had never been one for following rules. I reached for the chair to steady myself. This was not the reception I imagined.

"Let's go outside." He gathered his books. "We can talk better there."

Adam walked in front of me, in total silence, out of the library and across the quad, until we reached a short, squat wall off the edge of a path. He put down his books and turned to me. "So, I guess you didn't get my letter."

"What letter?" I kept my eyes on him, looking for answers.

"I wrote you a letter and mailed it a few days ago. You didn't get it?"

I sat down, in silence, staring at him.

"I can't do this anymore," he started. I felt nausea hit in the pit of my stomach. "I can't keep being with you. It's too hard. It's too much. I need some space."

"But things have been good recently..." I stammered, not knowing if I believed this but certain I had to convince him of it, to hold on to him at all costs.

"Lisa, I love you. I think I want to spend my life with you. I just can't now. I need space. I need not to worry about anyone else but me."

It didn't matter that I had thought these same things before, that I had screamed them in my head whenever I felt his absence—physically, emotionally, and psychically. I didn't want to hear him say this. I had changed my life for Adam and had given up everything for him—the Church, the Family, the Messiah, Mother.

We talked, sitting on the wall overlooking campus. Or he talked, and I listened. It was a beautiful early-May day. I was blind to it. This was supposed to be a sweet couple of hours stolen away with my boyfriend, a break away from the drudgery of preparing for finals.

When it was time for my ride to Ithaca, Adam walked me to the car. I held back my tears, determined not to let him see me cry. "I love you," he whispered, as he hugged me goodbye. "Remember that. Remember. 'Always come home.'" That was what we said to each other—used to say to each other—as we clung together. Now we were apart.

"Yeah. Good luck on finals." I got into the car, not knowing what to do except go back to Cornell and wait for his letter.

The breakup left me reeling. Wasting days until his "Dear Lisa" letter arrived. Reading, over and over again, how much he loved me, how wonderful I was, what great achievements were in front of me, how he probably wanted to spend his life with me, and how he was leaving me.

I did the classics. Sitting by the phone, longing for it to ring while knowing it never would. Reading and rereading letters, cards, and my high school yearbook. Playing our songs. I felt my love turn to hurt, my hurt to pain, my pain to anger, and my anger to hate. It all seemed senseless. If he loved me, why was he breaking up with me? If I had questioned and doubted so much, why was I devastated?

I talked to Mother. She didn't say she was happy for what had happened, but there was hope in her voice. Maybe now I'd go back to her, back to God. Maybe now I'd pray and say Pledge. Maybe I'd realize the wrongness of my path, and with no Adam to lure me farther away, I'd return. She wasn't the only one who thought these things. I thought them as well.

Without Adam to come get me, I wasn't sure how I'd make it home for the summer. Danny rented a car so that Rich could drive up to get me. I felt fatter and fatter.

18 · wanting to be wanted

Within the first few days of being home I heard from Adam. We went to a tiny restaurant in Little Italy for dinner and wandered the streets afterward. I was angry at him but longed for us to be together. It felt normal to be with him and absurd that it felt normal since we were no longer a couple. I wanted him, didn't want him, wanted him to think I didn't want him, and desperately wanted him to want me. At the end of the evening he hesitantly asked me out. How weird to be asked out by someone I had built my life around for over two years. He didn't call me for days.

Finally I called him, and we met again and talked for over an hour, standing outside the doorway of my apartment building. My neighbors brushed past, entering and leaving, but I didn't care. All that mattered, as we stood there in the beating sun surrounded by the sounds of the Second Avenue traffic, was getting Adam back and proving to myself—and maybe to him—that I was lovable, that he loved me, and that we should be together. I could no longer be cool. I cried, hating myself for showing signs of weakness. "I love you," I declared. "Maybe there's a middle ground," I reasoned. "Maybe there's some sort of relationship we can have without suffocation. Think about it."

"Maybe," he answered. "I will."

I went to see *Return of the Jedi* the next night with Pete and Rich. Adam showed up. He sat next to me in the dark and entwined his fingers with mine. The movie was irrelevant.

After the movie, we poured out onto the busy street. Adam nonchalantly turned to Pete and Rich. "Guys," he said, "I'll take Lisa home. We'll see you later." He grabbed my hand and started walking before I could respond to Pete, who looked at me with concern in his eyes.

"Yeah, see ya," I mumbled.

We headed toward my apartment, not talking much. Adam kept his hand in mine. "Can I come up?" he asked when we got to my building. There was no way I was going to say no.

My mind was bursting with questions as we made our way to the elevator. I wasn't going to risk anything by asking any of them. We stood in silence for the slow ride up to floor three and a half and as we walked the last half flight. I opened the door to the apartment and let him pass by, and it registered that Danny and Robbie weren't home. Thank God. I wasn't willing to reveal to anyone what was happening.

I followed Adam down the hall, into my room, and onto my bed. He kissed me, and, as always, I kissed him back. I kept thinking he would leave, that that's all we would do. He was, after all, the one who ended our relationship, the one who wanted to be on his own. But instead we had sex. Casual sex. With someone I loved, but who had broken up with me. Who was still broken up with me. Who had no commitments to me whatsoever.

Adam left that night and promised to call me soon.

He did. The more I saw him, the more I slept with him. And the worse I felt. I knew he was also seeing some Binghamton girl on Long Island. I didn't know if he was sleeping with her as well. As much as I cared, in some ways it didn't matter. I couldn't stop what I was letting happen. Still, I hated myself for begging him to be with me and didn't understand who I was becoming and what I was doing. It had taken me years to have sex with him in the first place, and I'd only been able to take that step because we'd been in love. And now...

Adam couldn't be with me, but he couldn't stay away. Whenever a group of us went out he'd show up and spend the evening half all over me and half ignoring me. He'd invariably want to go home with me. I'd invariably let him.

Then I met my married man.

I got a summer job waitressing at The Cupping Room Café in SoHo.

Rick worked behind the bar.

He was newly married and told me, over and over, how much he believed in monogamy yet how he knew he would eventually cheat on his wife. "Would you sleep with a married man?" he posed, as he poured me another custom-made blueberry vodka daiquiri after my shift. "Have another glass of champagne," he'd offer as I sat at the bar. "I need to see how drunk you have to be before I can seduce you." "Think about it," he'd say on the days we walked out of the bar and up West Broadway together. "Just think about it."

I did. I began to feel more in control as the summer went on and part of what carried me through was this ongoing litany in my head. *Would you sleep with a married man?* Adam would blow me off, and I wouldn't care. I could have an affair with a married man. I couldn't believe I was considering it. Where had my morals gone? Yet it felt good. I'd go out with high school friends and be bored. *Would you sleep with a married man?* I liked knowing that someone wanted me. I'd flirt with men at the restaurant and get close to getting involved, then freak out and run away. But I had *Would you sleep with a married man?* to hold on to.

Then Brian called me. He told me he loved me and that he'd always loved me. That he never stopped thinking of me and that it had been me he wanted all along. That he was glad he was in Alaska and we were more than three thousand miles apart because it had been hard for him to restrain himself in the past, and he didn't think he could now—now that I was free. That he was glad Adam had broken up with me, even if he couldn't have me because he was married. And that he wanted to be with me, to hold me, to make love to me. I was mostly silent on the phone, my mind trying to make sense of what he was saying. "*Really?*" was pretty much the only response I could offer. He called again, a week later, to warn me to get out of his life. To tell me that he was a complete fuckup and that he'd fuck me up if we got any closer.

What was I doing with all of this? What did I feel for Brian? How could I be contemplating getting involved with a married man—two married men! Sex with Rick would merely be sex. Why did it have a hold on me?

I so wanted to be wanted, to have someone find me attractive. I needed someone—maybe anyone—to make me feel good about myself. My emotions and desires surged in ways I couldn't explain and didn't understand, yet I was constantly aware of my inexperience and naïveté.

I had only ever been with one guy, only kissed a few more. Most of the men around me were older, and I was sure I'd be out of my league sexually. That they'd know how innocent and immature I was, and not in a good way. Or that I'd do something stupid or wrong. They were hitting on me, and inside I felt unworthy and ugly, not sure of what they saw that appealed to them and certain that there was nothing there to like.

I'd find a guy attractive and not know what to do about it. Danny had a friend, Will, who was the chef at Raoul's. He was nine years older than me and adorable—just five feet seven with a slight build and dark hair that fell over his brown eyes—and also so downtown and cool, always dressed in black. He'd stop by our apartment to hang out with Danny, and all I could think about was talking to him. But what would I say? I sat in the living room with him and Danny, certain I'd sound stupid or immature if I opened my mouth. He'd walk down the hall to leave at the end of the night, and I'd stand at the door to Robbie's room, thinking of his deep brown eyes and trying to find some interesting way to get him to notice me. "See ya, Will" was all I ever managed. Did he even respond?

I could pretend that my mental affairs with various men were easy for me to contemplate, but the Church was barely two years in my past. I was still haunted. The thought of doing anything with anyone, as much as I claimed to want to, was debilitating. It had been one thing to leave the Church for my love of Adam. It was another to continue to stay away when I realized that Adam and I were wrong.

Food became an issue again. It had never really stopped. I may have started eating at the end of my sophomore year, but I felt fat. Now I worked in a restaurant, with food, four days a week for eight hours—serving food, looking at food, talking about food, and not eating food. I restricted what I ate: perhaps a muffin as I opened the restaurant in the morning, a Granny Smith apple for lunch and another on the way home at the end of my shift (they were crunchy and filled me up), a tomato salad (with avocado if I was splurging) for dinner. No oil, just balsamic vinegar of course.

Every now and again I'd binge. We served tarragon chicken salad at the restaurant. Made with mayonnaise, it was creamy and delicious and fattening. Desperate at times, I'd stuff a croissant with chicken salad and wolf it down, hiding in the wait station. The guilt would hit me like a two-by-four across the head and in the gut. *What are you doing? You're so disgusting.*

It was repulsive how I stuffed food into my mouth, hoping no one would see me. Even more horrible were the urges inside me to not eat. *I'm so fat.* I was scared to diet but longed to be as thin as I had been. I craved the surety and control.

Maybe a change of scenery would help. And if that didn't do it, maybe something more radical.

19 · my drug of choice

As my disastrous sophomore year drew to an end, I had gone to the dean to find out about transferring for a semester. I needed to get away, someplace warm and easy. University of New Mexico or Arizona sounded good.

"Wouldn't you like to go abroad?" she had asked. "Maybe to Europe?"

"I can't," I had answered. "I'm here on financial aid. I can't travel abroad."

Apparently I could. By choosing a program through a New York state college, I was able to keep my aid and scholarships. I ended up at a school in Scotland. University of Stirling sat in a small town of the same name in-between Edinburgh and Glasgow.

Danny and Alice had gone to France during the summer to visit her family, who lived outside of Paris. Danny flew me there to spend some time with them before my semester in Scotland started. *Vive la différence*. Big wooden doors opened up onto courtyards. Bathrooms featured pull toilets and hand showers and in the restaurants, foot holes cut into the ground in front of another hole in the floor that everything went into.

One night I went out, and when I got back it was so late that the hallways in the apartment building were pitch black. I got off the elevator to find my way into the apartment, feeling around for a light switch. I couldn't find any. The only things noticeable were tiny rectangles of light. Little did I know these were light switches. They looked exactly like light-up doorbells you see in the States outside someone's home. Under the mistaken impression that that's what they were, I didn't want to touch them and risk waking anyone up.

I spent most of my time with Alice's younger brother, Jean, and his friends. They took me around Paris and out partying every night. We communicated in a variety of languages. Although I had taken two years of French at Cornell, I had also taken years of Spanish in high school. My mind got them jumbled. Jean spoke English to me; he liked to practice. I somehow thought in Spanish, translated to English, and then translated to French.

I had a little button on my WWII gas-mask bag that I used as a purse. "Why Be Normal?" it read. Jean and his friends were stumped. I wasn't sure if they didn't understand because it was in English, or if they thought it was a silly question.

I didn't think it was silly. I'd been trying to answer that for years.

After my week in Paris, I had a week in London before heading up to Stirling. My program gathered students they were sending to different schools in the U.K. and scheduled a week of sightseeing and touring. Food and self-confidence remained problematic. I either spent my time agonizing over what I had eaten or worrying whether people liked me. My behavior didn't betray my angst. I was probably the loudest in the group.

I called Hugh, who now lived in London with his wife and young children, and had dinner with him. I hadn't seen him in years and hadn't communicated with him since I wrote to him after nearly jumping off the bridge.

It was great to spend time with him, despite my anxiety about being with a Family member now that I had exiled myself. But he was more than just a member. He was someone who had taught me, whom I had worshipped and followed blindly. I wanted him to approve of the new me and wanted to show him how strong, cool, and wild I was.

At the end of the night he took me back to the building where I was staying. We sat on the stoop for a long time, watching people as they walked down the block, listening to cars passing on the street, alternating between conversation and silence. He gave me a hug, holding me in his arms for a long time, longer than necessary. It felt good and relaxing but also twisted my mind. "It's great to see you," he said, his voice so soft I had to lean in to hear him. "I think you're great." I nodded, unsure of what was going on and what I was feeling in response.

Hugh talked for a while about love: how much he loved to love, and how amazing love was. I nodded again in silence as he continued to hold me close. After a long pause he squeezed me harder. "I wish I were ten years younger," he said. Again I nodded in quiet response. It was all I could do. Hugh kissed me goodbye. On the cheek but still a kiss. I had never been so physically close to him. "I don't know which one of us is more nervous," he said, and he left.

I also surrounded myself with Notre Dame boys for the few days I was in London. Notre Dame had an international program running as well, and they housed their students in a building a few doors down from us. We hung out at the neighborhood pub, Prince Alfred, each night.

I don't think they'd ever met, nor seen, anyone like me before, good Midwestern boys that they were. They joked awkwardly about punk styles and stud bracelets. I wore one. I showed up in my inside-out, ripped sweatshirts, and they commented on the *Flashdance* look and how much I resembled Jennifer Beals. I know that was a stretch. She was half–African American and beautiful, but they were reacting to my clothes and wild long brown hair. I pointed out that my sweatshirts were torn and inside out well before the movie was released.

I began to feel strong, desirable, and in control again. Even though I hadn't come abroad to meet guys from Notre Dame, they were fun. There were two in particular that I was drawn to, Michael and Steve, although I most likely flirted with many as was my way.

On my last night in London, my friends threw me an early birthday party. It was two days before my twentieth birthday. We were at the Prince Alfred that night and headed back to my room for wine and conversation—and cake, candles, and a card! I ended up lying on my bed between Michael and Steve. As the night wore down I walked Steve the few doors down to his building, and we hung out in the lounge talking. I suddenly realized I didn't know what should happen next.

I was in the midst of a sentence when he leaned over to kiss me. *What if he doesn't mean this? What if he doesn't really like me?* My heart pounded. That I could be two days away from twenty years old and freaked out by a kiss. Unsure of how to respond, I started joking about everything.

Steve looked at me. "I'm being serious. Real serious. Why do you keep playing around?"

I searched for the right thing to say in return. "Yeah, right. You just like to tease me."

He kissed me again. And again. And again. I remained half-frozen, hesitant and longing for directions on how I should behave.

"You're different from any girl I've ever known," he said, studying me. "That's why I had to talk to you when I first saw you."

I said nothing.

As he leaned in to kiss me again, he paused and stared at me. "Am I still obnoxious?" he asked. I had teasingly called him obnoxious at some point.

"Yes, very," I obnoxiously replied. It was the wrong thing to say. He took me home.

I ached. Not because of a huge loss. I had just met him and knew it didn't matter. But I liked him, and I didn't know what to do about it. I was inexperienced and unable to figure out how to act around a guy, and acutely aware of my stunted upbringing and greenness around dating and kissing and fooling around. I doubted that guys had a real interest in me. I couldn't shake the sense that there was nothing in me to like.

I spent four months in Stirling missing Adam.

I had a great time, made life-long friends, and learned new languages. (I swear, Scottish and Irish, especially from Northern Ireland, are new languages; to this day I translate when my friends come to visit.) I explored three of the four British countries (never made it to Wales). I learned to love warm beer, bought my first pair of fingerless Fagan gloves, began to speak with an accent, called potato chips "crisps" and french fries "chips" and said "ta" instead of "thank you," bought new clothes to look more British, and turned away from anything and everything American (including the other Americans at Stirling). I began to find something in myself, deep in myself, that I could hold on to and see as good. But I missed Adam, and that permeated everything.

I was friendly with guys but stayed away from getting involved. Besides, the ones who liked me were American. I wanted nothing to do with them, and the Brit I was interested in had no interest in me. It was easy to stay unattached.

I ate, albeit barely. Not enough to get my period. I went to talk to someone at the university when my limited meals began to worry even me. They told me to keep eating. I clung to the guidelines Mrs. Bonde had given me and stayed thin and yet alive.

I counted down the days until I was on my way home, back to Adam. Now that I was far from him, he realized he loved me. When I thought of staying for a second semester, or for the holidays through New Year's, he begged me not to. I planned my trip home.

In the middle of the semester, Mother decided to fly over to London, take the train up to Stirling, rent a car, drive me back down to the airport in London, and fly home with me. I didn't want to see her.

Our last time together, before I had left at the end of the summer, had been tough. It was obvious that she wanted me back in the Church and that my breakup with Adam had given her hope that I'd return and no longer stray. I didn't want to go back to the Church, that much I knew.

Even if I did, I don't think I could have. I couldn't imagine facing people who knew I had fallen and been with a boy. Seeing Hugh had been hard enough. I didn't want to subject myself to judgment and condemnation from any other member for even a few moments, much less by returning to the fold.

Mother, however, was determined to come. We'd arrange times when she would call me, and I'd sit in the lobby of the dorm, waiting for the pay phone to ring. With the help of my friend Martin, a first-year Irish student from a farm just outside of Belfast who spent hours teaching me how to say *terrible* with an authentic Northern Ireland accent, I'd prepare a litany of reasons why she shouldn't come, how it made no sense, how unnecessary it was. I never out and out told her I didn't want to see her, but I listed every other excuse I could think of to keep her away. It didn't work. After each conversation I'd crawl back up the stairs to my floor and find Martin. "She's still coming," I'd cry. "She's still coming."

The thought of spending so much time with her slightly sickened me. How weird to remember that when I was young, I camped outside the bathroom door waiting for her, determined to never let her out of my sight. Now I wanted to be with her as little as possible. If she came to Scotland to get me, we'd be shut up in a car for hours and have an entire cross-Atlantic flight. We'd land at Newark, and while she would have to make a connecting flight to get home, Adam would be there meeting me. I didn't want the two of them together, and I didn't want my first minutes with Adam to be shared with her. She hated Adam. Or she hated my being with him.

Our drive and flight were better than I expected. I watched everything I said—wanting to make things okay between us, wanting to be free to be myself, and wanting to spend my time imagining the instant I'd see Adam. But still, Mother was trying. Maybe she was trying to get me back to believing, but she definitely was trying to rebuild a relationship with me as well. She asked me if I thought I might marry Adam, and when I answered yes, she offered to get to know him and to try to like him. I don't know why. Maybe she realized that by pushing me back into the Church she was pushing me away. Maybe she realized that I was on a path that wasn't going to change and wasn't going to turn around. Maybe she missed me. Maybe she was my mother and wanted to be close. I don't know, but whatever it was, it made things easier. She went out of her way for me during our trip together. And most importantly, when we landed in Newark behind schedule, she ran to make her connecting flight and left me alone to greet Adam.

Finding myself in Adam's arms after clearing customs with my many duffle bags stuffed to bursting felt safe—and right.

He drove me back into Manhattan and joined Danny, Robbie, and me for dinner—sesame noodles at my favorite Chinese restaurant followed by ice cream (because I never found any good ice cream in Scotland). I was home, I was loved, and I was eating. We went out that night with a bunch of Stuy friends, and as I complained that the beer was bad and too cold, they complained about my new accent and attitude. I was most certainly back, and Adam and I were unquestionably back together.

During break, before I headed up to school, I heard from Brian. He was in town, home from Alaska, and asked if I wanted to drive with him down to Washington, D.C., to see Reggie and other Church friends.

I hadn't seen or talked to Brian since his phone calls over the summer professing his desire for me and telling me to stay away from him. Months had passed, and I was entangled with Adam again. Yet, as always, I was drawn to Brian. Sickeningly nervous and desperately excited, I said yes.

After an easy day in D.C.—Adam wasn't mentioned and nobody asked me about my Church involvement—Brian and I drove back to New York, enjoying each other's company. I hadn't spent so much time with him since our days at Belvedere. As we neared my apartment, he pulled his pickup truck up to the curb and parked.

"Lisa," he said, turning toward me. He looked good. He leaned over. "Lisa," he said again, reaching out to stroke my face. I was silent. I could feel my heart beating and tried to catch my breath. He kissed me, pushing me back against the passenger door. *Wow. I'm kissing Brian. Finally. Wow.* I didn't resist.

He talked to me. He told me that he had been involved with Jae Eun and that their affair had been the reason he was banished to Alaska. He talked of his Korean wife—they were still married—and what a bad husband he was. At the same time, he professed his love for me, declaring how much he craved me and wanted to be with just me. How he'd always wanted to be with just me.

Shock and confusion don't begin to describe the feelings that coursed through me. In some ways it was like pieces of a puzzle were falling into place, and things were beginning to make sense. *Jae Eun. Alaska. No wonder.* In some ways it was like reality was cracking. Like nothing would ever make sense again. *Jae Eun. He was involved with Jae Eun. He wants me!* I listened, in silence, trying to take it all in.

"Can we go upstairs?" he asked, leaning in even closer.

"Uh, sure," I stammered. "Come on."

By the time we reached my apartment and made it to my room, I was at a loss. I had wanted Brian for so many years, and now he was here and at least somewhat mine, yet all that he had said churned inside me. *Jae Eun. He seduced Jae Eun. He's still married to his wife. He slept with Jae Eun!* We sat on opposite sides of my bed, making small talk, until Brian reached over and took my hand.

"Those eyes," he said, as he stared into my face and began to inch closer. "Those are the eyes that kill me." Despite everything, I felt myself dissolve, responding to him as I always had and felt I always would. He put his arms around me, holding me closer still, and then, as if out of nowhere, something inside of me snapped. I was pulled toward Brian as much as ever and wanted only to give in, but somehow it didn't feel right. I didn't feel right. I sat back, away from him. Putting distance where I needed it.

"Uh, Brian...I think you should go."

"What?" He wasn't hearing me.

"I have to get up early tomorrow. I think you should go."

"You don't mean it." He laughed. "I know you, and you don't mean it."

"Yeah, I do. I think I do." I paused. "I need you to go."

"Are you sure, Lisa?" he asked. His question couldn't have been slower, as if he was giving me plenty of space to change my mind. "After all this time, are you really, really sure?"

My voice lowered to a whisper. Part of me *wasn't* sure. "You should go." I looked away. I wouldn't be able to keep saying no if I didn't look away. Seeing him, having him this close to me, was too much. Too much after all this time, after all that had occurred.

"Okay, I'll go, but first—" He pulled me back to him and kissed me in a way that I'd never forget—as if he finally meant it, as if he'd been wanting to for years. "You know," he declared, staring at me as he let me go, "I could sleep with you if I wanted to. I could make you if I tried."

I looked at him, stunned. Danny was bartending at Raoul's, and Robbie was back at school. Brian and I were alone in the apartment. I was at his mercy and for the first time ever while with him, uncomfortable and afraid.

With that he left.

While I was in Stirling, Adam started doing coke. He eagerly introduced me to his new pastime, and I plunged in. What more magnificent drug could there be? It was so much better than getting high on weed, which left me paranoid and curled up in an incoherent ball. Cocaine made me feel in control and sure of myself. I understood what Danny had meant all those years ago when he said that a one-and-one made him feel like a new man. With coke I was strong and powerful. It killed my appetite and kept me from eating. I had found my drug of choice.

It was easy for us to get. Adam had a friend who was dealing. Danny was also a great connection. In fact, the best coke I ever had was from one of Danny's friends, Hector the judge.

Hector was the judge of a small town in Pennsylvania. One night Adam and I were hanging out in the apartment as Danny got ready to go out with Hector and Hector's girlfriend. "You guys staying in?" Hector questioned, looking over at us across the living room.

"Yeah," I replied. "We're just hanging out tonight."

"You want something to do?" With that he reached into his pocket and pulled out a huge bag of white powder. "Dan," he called to the front of the apartment, where Danny was waiting to leave. "I'm going to give some to the kids." He opened the plastic bag, grabbed a tablespoon that was lying on the table, and scooped two heaping spoonfuls onto the stone that was always out, readily available, hungry for blow waiting to be chopped up. Adam and I stared in amazement.

"Have fun," Hector announced as he put the bag away. He smiled and walked down the hallway and out of the apartment. Adam and I tried to finish all of it that night. We couldn't.

We dove into cocaine whenever we were together through the end of our junior year. Adam was still at Binghamton, and when he'd visit me, he had a supply. When I went to visit him, we turned his friends on. A drug that gave you energy, made you funny, and made you thin. I was in love.

My love affair continued when I came home for the summer. Cocaine was not only a lot of fun, it was something Danny and I could share. Hector would show up with his girlfriend, and Danny and I would join them for the night—doing as much coke as we could and then heading out to go clubbing or to eat dinner. The dinner part never went over well because Danny was still concerned about my eating.

One night Hector had come with tons of blow. We coked up and went across town to try a new French restaurant. All I ordered was an asparagus appetizer, but I couldn't eat it. I struggled to swallow an asparagus head and stopped.

"Lisa, eat," Danny instructed from across the table. I looked at him in amazement, then down at the asparagus in disgust.

"I can't."

"You have to eat," he insisted, his voice getting tighter.

"I'm full."

"Fucking eat." His teeth clenched, and he had that look on his face. The one that scared me.

"Danny, you did this," I whispered. I took a few more bites.

Danny and I shared cocaine at odd hours as well. I had stumbled back into my job at The Cupping Room, starting with the lowliest shifts and working my way up to the ones that offered the opportunity to make the most money. I opened the restaurant four mornings a week, heading downtown to SoHo by seven a.m.

I would wake up to shower and get ready. Danny would still be going from the night before. As I stumbled into the living room to say good morning, he'd look up from the coffee table—his pot box, cigarettes, and papers strewn around in a general mess, and his stone with lines of cocaine laid out. "Want a line before you go," he'd ask, "to get you started?" I nearly always said yes.

By the time I got to work I was flying, but the crash came early and hit hard. I now also knew what Danny had meant when he'd said that the one problem with cocaine was that the new man then wanted a one-and-one. I needed more.

I would ask around at work. I knew who was into coke and who usually had some. While the summer before I hid in the waitress station, stuffing tarragon chicken salad shamefully into my mouth, this summer I hid in the bathroom, snorting cocaine desperately up my nose.

Luckily something clicked, and voices inside me started screaming. It became clear to me that wanting cocaine—looking for it, asking for it, and basing my day around it—was not good. It was pulling me in, and I had been, up until then, willingly and enthusiastically going. Now, thank goodness, a survival instinct kicked in to push me in a different direction. Maybe it was the same instinct that got me across the Stewart Avenue Bridge.

I weaned myself from my daily cocaine use. It was hard. I avoided it at work, turned it down when I got an offer, and said no to Danny on those early mornings and late nights when he laid out a line for me. That was the toughest to give up. Somehow, through our cocaine use, I had imagined for the first time that Danny loved me, that I mattered to him, and that he liked being with me.

It may sound surprising, but I never knew Danny loved me. Not until many years later when I was planning my wedding and even I could see his care in how he showed up for me. Back then, it wasn't something I saw, felt, or believed. When he was drunk and he'd lock himself out of the apartment and wake me up in the middle of the night to let him in, he'd tell me over and over again. Actually, he'd sit at the kitchen table for what felt like hours, repeating his favorite refrain. "I'm your father," he'd say. "I have to love you, so that doesn't count. What matters is that I like you, which I do." I'd leave the room, and when I'd return, he'd still be explaining it to me. It meant nothing, and I felt nothing from him. I don't remember him ever saying "I love you."

20 · diving for the bottom

The guy was sitting in a comfortable chair, holding court with a group of girls gathered at his feet, telling them about his summer in Chile. He wore mirrored sunglasses, even though we were inside at a party and it was nighttime. He was not too tall and had a stocky build, with dirty-blond hair that fell to his ears. He was goddamn gorgeous.

His name was Scott. He had my attention—and as I soon found out, a girlfriend named Jill. She was a long-distance girlfriend who was farther away this semester, in Dublin. Perfect. I had Adam.

I began to go out of my way to run into Scott. I timed my walks from class to class across the Arts Quad so that I happened to see him. If I slowly passed Olin Library at just the right pace, I nearly always had an excuse to say hello. "Oh, hi," I'd mumble, as if surprised. It never dawned on me that he went out of his way to run into me as well.

Within a few months we were together, or sort of. I wanted to wrap myself around Scott, to be a couple, a public couple. I'd never had that at Cornell. He, however, wanted to keep our relationship secret—no one should know (as if they didn't) that I ended up in his room at the end of the night. He wouldn't be affectionate in public. He had a girlfriend.

His girlfriend. I was cool with that. I had Adam and was just playing around. I was so cool with it that when Scott headed over to Ireland to visit Jill for a long weekend and he didn't have the cash to buy himself a ticket, I bought it for him. And kept the receipt in a scrapbook to prove how strong and unemotionally attached I was. I was in this for fun.

This was the first time I could remember liking someone and

going after him—and getting him. I'd always been the responsive one. "Oh, you like me? Okay, I'll like you." A kiss at a party and I was yours. Or I would want to be with someone but torture myself by keeping distant for my myriad reasons: the Church, Adam, my insecurity, whatever. This time I went for it, without hesitation or fear. Other women wanted him, but I picked him and he picked me in return. Even if we both had someone else.

Just how much we had someone else became clear over Christmas break. Scott and I had gotten closer during the semester, and I had spent the last night before break with him. It was the first time we ever made love. I knew he was going home for Christmas and that he was then heading to visit Jill, but I didn't care. I wanted to be with him, figuring I wouldn't see him again for over a month.

Wrong. Scott's roommate, Keith, was coming to New York City for a job interview, and he had asked my roommate Abby to meet him in the city. She didn't want to go alone, so she asked me.

We were sitting in the enormous lobby of the Essex House on Central Park South, perched on a plush cushioned bench waiting for Keith and passing the time talking about the boys, until I looked up and saw Keith approaching. He was not alone; he was with Scott. Scott was not alone either; he was with Jill.

I may have been cool about Jill, but I had no desire to spend the evening with the two of them. Being a third wheel to Abby and Keith would have been fun, but being a fifth wheel to Abby and Keith and the guy I was seeing and his not-so-long-distance girlfriend was not as enticing. But there was no escape. I watched them approach and registered the shock that hit Scott as he saw me. *Shit, last time I saw him I slept with him—and double shit, I'm somehow wearing the same clothes I wore that night.*

We went to a comedy club on the Upper East Side, and each time I looked up and caught Scott's eye I had to turn away. Did he think I'd done this on purpose? Why ever would I? I was awash with guilt toward Jill, longing for Scott, embarrassment with Keith, and a desire to run out of the bar. I hated seeing the two of them together, more than I'd hated anything in a long time.

The night finally came to an end. The contrast between the awkward goodbye I shared with Scott on the street corner and the passion he had expressed the last time I had seen him shook me. I was unquestionably the other woman.

I realized that I wanted to be with Scott, not Adam. Even after seeing Scott with Jill. But breaking up with Adam was hard. We had so much history. We'd been through so much, good and bad. He wanted to stay together, and I didn't know how to not be part of us, even if I wanted to be part of something else. I suggested we take a break and left it somewhat unclear. In retrospect, a bitchy thing to do. Scott, however, stayed with Jill. With me as well, but also with Jill.

For the rest of senior year we had an official unofficial relationship. He continued to insist that nobody knew about us and that nobody should, and I wanted him for my own. I longed for everyone to know how great I felt—when it felt good—but Scott wanted us to remain a secret. A secret our friends and roommates knew about but a secret nonetheless.

Late one night as he was about to leave my apartment, I decided it was time to force the issue. "Scott, you need to choose," I said as he got up to go. I needed to be wanted fully and singularly. For him to be free and totally mine, as I felt myself becoming totally his.

"What do you mean? Everything is fine." He smiled. I loved that smile.

"No," I insisted. "You have to choose."

He looked at me, and I felt my insides melt all over again. "Do I really have to?" he asked, keeping his eyes locked on me. "I love you both." With that he kissed me and left.

My fears snuck up on me in the strangest way.

I was alone in the apartment eating a salad with small, cut-up pieces of carrot in it. I felt one of those pieces of carrot stick in my throat, and I freaked.

My roommate Gemma came home at that minute. "I'm choking!" I said, gasping as she walked in the door. "Help!" I didn't realize I couldn't be choking if I could talk, or gasp.

She grabbed me, and we ran downstairs and next door to the fire department, where they seized me from behind to perform the Heimlich maneuver. Needless to say, nothing came flying out.

"You're fine," they insisted. I wasn't convinced. An ambulance was called to take me to the nearest emergency room. There was nothing wrong, except that I was terrified.

A few weeks later I had the same problem. I felt something stuck in my throat, thought I couldn't breathe, and begged Gemma and her boyfriend to take me back to the hospital to be checked out yet again. I was still fine.

The reassurance from the medical staff did nothing to comfort me. I was certain I was going to die. Back at our apartment, I'd lie in bed at night and wonder if my heart was beating correctly. Or if I was swallowing right. I'd think about swallowing until it felt as if I no longer knew how. I couldn't trust my body to do what it had always done.

I also couldn't eat again, but this time it was from fear. Convinced I would choke, even chocolate chip ice cream frightened me. I could feel the chips going down. Seriously. I was home for break one night, trying to eat ice cream, and I had to call Abby, who was home in Bronxville, for reassurance. The chips were too big, and I was sure I would choke on them and die. I subsisted on smooth ice cream and beer. I was malnourished but lost no weight.

Senior year was like this. A mixture of the best times, memories, and friends—my roommates Abby, Gemma, Susan, Linda, and Karen became steadfast friends for life. Beyond friends to pseudo-family, the group that I'd spend time with every year well into our fifties (and hopefully beyond). And a mixture of the worst times, because of Scott.

Scott and I talked of our future, daydreamed about where we'd go and what we'd do, and spent all our time together through the rest of senior year. Except for graduation day, when, of course, Jill came to celebrate and I was forgotten.

Graduation was momentous. Saying goodbye to my friends, to the home I'd known for the past four years—perhaps the only home I'd ever loved. I'd had so many memories, experienced so many firsts and so many changes. I was, in many ways, entirely different from when I came to Cornell, and now I was heading back to New York City. Back to life with Danny and working at The Cupping Room as I figured out what to do with my psychology degree, still not getting the irony that was pointed out to me years later—that I had grown up in a cult, suffered from an eating disorder and a mild cocaine addiction, jumped from dysfunctional relationship to dysfunctional relationship, and was the victim of abuse from both my parents—and majored in psychology.

Living with Danny was tough, especially after being away from him for four years, and the grossness of Danny's apartment was more than I could take. Linda offered to move in with me in the city for the summer, even though she was leaving for graduate school in the fall.

But I stayed home until I got my first job—at a direct-mail company in SoHo—and my first paycheck, then found a place with Abby. We lived in a one-bedroom apartment on the corner of Twenty-Third Street and Lexington Avenue. It was modern and clean and had a bathroom with a door that closed. I had a loft bed in an alcove above the living room. It felt like heaven.

I also stayed with Scott. I loathed being the other woman but loved him. I detested the lying yet couldn't walk away. I resented Scott for how he treated me, but as he pointed out, I had entered the relationship with my eyes wide open and had chosen it and him.

He moved to Alabama for graduate school. When I went to visit him it was as if we were in our own world, like nothing could ever come between us, like our future was sure. When he came to stay with me it would be nearly as sweet—except that Jill was also now in the New York area, and after our few days hidden away he'd head off to see her. I hated that and tried to ignore it, and kept hoping it would somehow, sooner or later, be different. I kept hoping he'd choose me. Is that what every "other woman" hopes? I don't know. I guess I thought, perhaps mistakenly, that Jill and I were on equal footing and that I could, and would, win out at the end.

I stayed with Scott, the part of him I had, until I found someone else. Someone with whom I could further punish myself for leaving God and Father and the Church. Someone with whom I could take my descent into self-destruction even deeper. Someone with whom I could hit my bottom.

21 · hooked on abuse

I met Will when he got off work. This was Danny's friend Will, who was now the daytime chef at L'Acajou, the French restaurant Danny opened the summer after my college graduation. It was our first date, and Will was making me dinner at his apartment. We walked down Sixth Avenue to Balducci's, where I watched him finger the produce and talk with the butcher, and carefully select two pigeons, baby potatoes, and fiddlehead ferns. I was out of my league.

After a meal that was too amazing for words, Will pulled out a packet of coke. I watched him cut it up on a small stone, and I dove into the lines he set out for me. It had been ages since I'd done blow, not since I'd broken up with Adam, and I was eager for the rush of clarity and self-confidence it would bring.

We did tons, perhaps more than I ever did except for the time Hector gave Adam and me more than we could finish. Now our conversation flowed. (Coke makes you think you're a great conversationalist, whether or not you are.) We finished the blow in front of us. "Let's get out of here," Will suggested. "I can't sit still any longer. Let's go for a walk."

We walked for hours, all night in fact. There was too much going on inside our bodies for us to sleep. We talked about meaningless things, but somewhere around three or four o'clock in the morning we sat to rest on a stoop up the block from his apartment on Seventy-Third Street. Even at that hour, cars—cabs mostly—worked their way up Central Park West.

"Do I have to sleep with you before I want to?" I asked out of nowhere. Will looked at me. "I'm only twenty-two," I continued. "I'm thinking you might be ready to move more quickly than I am."

He didn't answer, and the conversation drifted back to things of no consequence. I didn't know how to get the response I needed. Eventually I went home to shower and change. I was leaving for Philadelphia later in the morning—Linda was at graduate school there, and Susan, Abby, and I were heading down for the weekend. I kissed Will goodbye, feeling the early morning sun on my face, still anxious and uneasy.

I had stopped by L'acajou on my way home from my last day at my first job. After six months at the direct-mail company, I was leaving to join an advertising agency and had celebrated all day long at work—margaritas at my going-away lunch, beers on the way back to the office with friends, and a joint in the stairwell. By the end of the day I was trashed and plodded my way carefully up Sixth Avenue to get home. I decided to drop by to say hi to Danny—and ended up sitting at the bar next to Will, who was having his end-of-shift drink. Will now worked for Danny, having left Raoul's, and I still had my silly, little girl crush on him. He was so cool—black jeans, black button-down shirt, black boots—a real downtown bar guy. And so aloof. And heartbreakingly cute. And older than me by nearly a decade. He smoked Kools, always with one lit cigarette somewhere near him. And he was still Danny's friend, as well as his employee. They hung out and partied together. I thought of the times when he had been to our apartment over the years and how he barely ever said hi to me. I remembered him passing me in the hallway, unaware that I was there. I assumed he saw me then as a little kid and wondered if he did now as well.

Emboldened by the substances running through me, I started talking to him. To my surprise he started talking back, and when he got up to go, he asked me out. I was almost too shocked to answer and worried that my hand was shaking as I wrote my phone number on the inside of a L'acajou matchbook.

Our night of pigeons and coke had followed—and then more dates. Two weeks into the relationship, Will took me to a college graduation party for his ex-girlfriend. Turns out she was younger than I was. He'd started seeing her when she was undercrage, causing a scandal.

We both had a lot to drink, and by the time we got back to my apartment and crawled into my loft bed, fueled by seeing him interact with his ex, I was determined to consummate what we had going on. That would tie him to me and keep him.

I did. We did. I convinced him. I woke in the morning to find that he was gone. There was no note. Nothing. I dragged myself to work and called around looking for him. I couldn't believe what had happened—that I'd slept with a guy, someone I knew, and he'd crawled away before I woke up.

I found Will at L'Acajou later that day and confronted him. He had no excuse, no reason. Well, other than Danny. "I just had to go," he said. "And what if your father finds out?"

"Let's get together tonight" was my reply. With that, I dove in deeper.

Will drank—a lot. Most of our dates involved "bar tours," moving from bar to bar in a neighborhood or throughout the city. We'd be up all hours of the night, drinking and partying, scoring cocaine, and I'd rise early in the morning to get to work. Or we'd hang out at my apartment, quietly cooking dinner and watching TV, until Will would say he needed to run out for a pack of cigarettes at the corner bodega. Thirty minutes later I'd realize he was gone far too long for one pack of cigarettes, and I'd either start racing through the bars in the neighborhood, looking for him, or pacing nonstop up and down our tiny living room, desperate for him to come back. "Where were you?" I'd yell when he returned, or "What are you doing here?" I'd demand upon finding him at a bar nearby.

"I just stopped in for a drink and got talking," he always answered. "No big deal."

It was a big deal to me. Everything became a big deal to me. Will's love affair with alcohol was somehow tougher to accept or beat than Scott's love affair with Jill. It split my self-esteem down the middle and left me gasping for sanity and air. Besides, he was mean, at least to me.

Will was a nasty drunk. He called me dumb even though I had a degree from Cornell and he hadn't finished college; he saw himself as an intellectual while I was too pedestrian. He told me I was fat while fully aware of my anorexia and knowing what havoc that label would wreak on me. Although I had a stable, nine-to-five job with a balance in my bank account and he was paid in cash and had only five dollars to his name at the end of each week, he insisted that I was the incompetent one.

I had found someone to point out for me, again and again, all that was wrong with me. All that I'd known was wrong with me for years. I was driven, albeit unconsciously, to prove my worth—to win back the love of my father and mother, to not be abandoned again, to earn a place near friends who were True and Blessed, and to make up for my shame at deserting the Messiah. With my ceaseless quest for perfection and Will's need to insult and degrade me, we were a lethal, combustible combination.

We fought constantly, and I tried to make sense of everything. I'm not sure what we argued about. Maybe his drinking, although he swore it was my problem and not his. Maybe the fact that I got mad when he didn't come home. All I know is that my life was yelling or crying. I heard his relationship with his ex-girlfriend had been violent; she'd come after him. I did the same. I hit him—only twice—but it scared me.

This kept me wanting more. And more. I clung to Will, desperate to make him love me, love me better, make me whole. Even when I found out that he slept with someone else, a waitress from L'acajou, while I was away for a weekend, I begged him not to leave me. I was in love with him, or I thought I was, and I longed for him to feel the same. I revolved around him and only him. It didn't matter that he wanted nothing to do with my life and that he wouldn't spend time with my friends. "They're too young," he'd snipe. "You're too young when you're with them." I blew them off.

We would break up and get back together. And break up. And get back together. When things were feeling good, or we were pretending that they were, Will would propose. But only if he was drunk. "Lisa, marry me," he'd beg over a Scotch, late at night at the neighborhood bar.

"Ask me when you're sober," I'd say.

I flew out to Illinois for Christmas to meet his family, and as we cooked dinner for everyone, he cornered me in the kitchen and asked once more. But again, he'd been drinking. "When you're sober," I answered, fighting hard not to accept. "Ask me when you're sober so I know you mean it."

Finally, he asked me while sober. We were sitting at a Chinese restaurant on Columbus Avenue, just down from his apartment. As the bill came and I went to pay (I almost always was the one who paid), he proposed again. "You're amazing, Lisa. Marry me."

He hadn't had even one beer with dinner. Without much hesitation, I said yes.

"What?" he asked, as if surprised to hear the response he claimed to have wanted. "Really?"

"Yes," I whispered, almost sure I was giving the right answer and completely sure I wanted to sound like I was giving the right answer. "Yes, I'll marry you."

Danny, to his credit, had stayed out of my relationship with Will. Years later he told me that that was as hard to do as not bad-mouthing the Church or my mother in front of us when we were little. But when I called him to tell him I was engaged, that changed, at least for a few minutes.

"Are you sure, Twink?" was his response. When I said yes, he asked me again. "Are you really sure?" And, "Are you happy?" Again I answered yes. With that he invited Mother to come up to New York City for a celebratory dinner. She was living in D.C. at the time, running a preschool for the Church and trying to start her life with Phil.

The four of us went to Cucina di Pesce. I look back now and wonder if Danny had doubts about the engagement because the restaurant of choice was less than his usual high standard. At the time I could only think how weird it was to be out to dinner with both my parents and Will—and that Will was there because of me, not Danny. I also noticed that Danny and Mother had trouble reading the menu. They were both forty-four to my nearly twenty-four. I laughed at their squinting.

Danny now tells me that he never understood why I was with Will. He says he saw Will as self-absorbed and a mean drunk but decided that if I was happy, he wasn't going to argue with me. Perhaps I was with Will because he worked with, was friends with, and drank with Danny. Even if his drunk was crueler than Danny's. I also probably was with him because it's what I thought I deserved, though I never would have been able to acknowledge that then. My friends—the friends I was ignoring on Will's demand—also thought less of my relationship and engagement than I did. One by one I told them I was engaged, and one by one their responses were supportive but not enthusiastic.

As if on cue, my relationship with Will went from bad to worse. Danny moved him to working nights, and his drinking increased exponentially. He'd get off at eleven, and it would be hours before he showed up at my apartment. He almost always showed up belligerent and drunk.

Then Bobby, my cousin who had sat next to me all those years ago at the Madison Square Garden wedding extravaganza and who was now married to a recovering alcoholic, took me to lunch and asked me a few pointed questions. As I answered him and described my life with Will—our fights, the craziness, the nights he didn't come home, how I was starting to slip at work, the insults he threw at me—Bobby talked about his wife, before she entered recovery. It amazed me that our experiences were so alike, as I felt isolated in my daily insanity and abuse.

"Go to the support group I told you about, Lisa," Bobby offered. "Just go."

I glanced up from my sushi. "Why should I go there? What will it do?"

"It's for people who are involved with alcoholics," he answered.

I would never be with an alcoholic. I went back to my lunch.

Four months later, in November 1987, Will asked if I wanted to get an apartment with him. Our wedding was set for May, so I jumped at the chance to be together sooner. Besides, living with Abby was getting tough. She didn't like Will or how he treated me, and I didn't like her for saying that.

We found an unbelievable little one-bedroom on the Upper West

Side, with a fireplace and a huge balcony—every New Yorker's dream and the beginning of our next nightmare.

Just after Thanksgiving, Will's younger sister came to town to visit him and his older sister for the holiday. The two of them were at our apartment for dinner, and as soon as Will ran to the store for one last ingredient, they pounced on me.

"Lisa," Molly, his older sister, began. "We're so glad you're with Will."

"Yes," Sharon, his younger sister, agreed. "So, so glad."

"But Lisa," Mollly continued. She paused. Both of them stared at me.

"What?"

"Lisa, you have to help him," Sharon started again. "He's an alcoholic."

"Yes, he's an alcoholic," Molly persisted. "You have to get him sober. He needs you. We need you to do it."

I thought of Bobby's comments about the support group and considered the sisters' insistence that I help Will, that I sober him up. I reflected more on the insanity of my life—the drunken fights, the insults, the crying, the nights he didn't come home. I decided to give the group a try.

In New York City support-group meetings are plentiful and almost always in churches. The next Wednesday night I found myself in a church on the corner of Eighty-Sixth Street and Amsterdam Avenue, my heart beating and my mind full of reasons to leave. This felt like an irreversible step, a step I didn't want to take. Like I was somehow declaring Will an alcoholic and myself pathetic.

The meeting was in a small, jam-packed room on the second floor of the church. Nearly twenty people sat on chairs—about a dozen folding metal ones jammed in around numerous soft armchairs. Other people perched on windowsills or stood leaning against the walls.

I glanced around. Everyone seemed normal. They started to talk, and I sank deeper into my seat, hoping no one would recognize me or call on me. My mind echoed with one main refrain: *Tell me if he's an alcoholic.*

I wanted the rule book, the guidelines, the checklist that would make this clear to me. *There's no way I would ever be with an alcoholic. No way I would ever stumble that far down. Just tell me how to tell.* I didn't realize that Danny drank and drugged practically every day, his father had been in a support group for drinking for the last five years of his life, and his mother had been addicted to various prescription drugs over the years. In short, I would come to learn, there were numerous reasons why I would end up with an alcoholic.

The question was, Would I stay with him?

They didn't tell me if Will was an alcoholic during my first meeting. In fact, they didn't really tell me anything. I went back the next week, and they still didn't tell me anything. But I kept going. It felt better to be there somehow. Comforting. Enveloping. Soothing.

One night, by mistake, I went to a meeting specifically offered for adult children of alcoholics. I listened in horror as someone read the list of characteristics: we are frightened by anger and any personal criticism; we judge ourselves harshly and have low self-esteem; we get guilt feelings if we stand up for ourselves instead of giving in to others. They went on and on. Virtually all of them rang true. Frozen in my chair, feeling the freedom of understanding and the terror of realization hit me, I began to silently cry. Still, it was weeks before I could open my mouth at a meeting.

At first I listened to people talking—they called it sharing—and looked at them with pity. They spoke of having low or no self-esteem. *How awful that must feel.* I was unaware of my own unceasing self-beatings; they were so constant and familiar, I didn't recognize them. I was convinced I was holding it together much better than the other people in the room.

Only I wasn't. Will's drinking was increasing, or it was increasingly bothering me. Our new apartment was on the fourth floor of a gorgeous brownstone on West Ninetieth Street. The nights he worked I'd lie in bed listening for the building door to open and close, four flights down, and footsteps on the stairs, my body rigid as I tried to relax and sleep, my mind racing. He was coming home later and later, and I was more and more incapable of handling it.

Finally hearing the sounds I was waiting for, I'd feign sleep. Will would creep into the apartment, slip into our bedroom, and, "wake" me so that we could talk. The few times I was sleeping he did wake me. Night after night, he needed to discuss our future.

"Lisa, wake up."

"Will, I'm sleeping."

"Wake up. They asked me again at work when our wedding was."

I had postponed our wedding. I hated parts of our relationship. I hated his chosen drinks—the Scotch that oozed from his pores, the red wine that stained his teeth, and most of all the martinis that made him cruel. I hated his delusions; with enough alcohol in him, he would tell me he was God. Or God's chosen one.

"Will, not now. Not again. It's late. You've been drinking."

"My drinking has nothing to do with this! Are we getting married?"

"Where were you? What time is it? Why didn't you come home?"

"Are we getting married? When are we getting married?"

"Will, it's late. I'm tired."

"We need to talk about this. I need to know when we're getting married!"

"Where were you? I have to work in the morning."

"This is important. You're so young and childish."

The arguments would circle like this for hours. The nights he didn't come home, I'd go out looking for him and find him in the neighborhood dive bars. (Ninetieth Street was a bit too far uptown in the late '80s to be gentrified.)

"Lisa, have a drink," he'd say when he saw me.

"Will, come home!"

"Nah, have a drink," and he'd call to the bartender to bring me one of whatever he was having.

"It's two a.m. Come home."

"Loosen up. I'm allowed to have a drink when I get off work."

"I have to get up in the morning."

"Leave me alone, Lisa. God has ordained me…"

In retrospect, even I have to admit that it was way beyond weird that I found someone who believed that he was holy or Godlike—or God. Kind of full circle. My first amazing therapist, many years later, would say to me, "How do a sadist and masochist find each other at a party? They just do."

Sitting in the support-group meetings, listening to people share their experiences with alcoholics, I heard not to engage with an active drunk. "Talking to an alcoholic is like trying to blow out a light bulb," they would say. I tried to detach from Will and the situation. But when he argued with me at one or two o'clock in the morning, engaging seemed to be my only option. I'd self-righteously harangue him about the drinking, the coming home late, and the not coming home at all, blaming him for all the wrongs in our relationship. I'd cry—I cried a lot—and get up the next morning to go to work.

I now had a job in advertising that mattered to me, and, for the first time, I was finding myself unable to function. Up to this point, no matter what I'd done or what had happened to me, I'd been able to look good on the outside. I had excelled at both Stuyvesant and Cornell, always had friends, and had managed to succeed at work. Now things were falling apart. My life was becoming unmanageable. Still, I kept on as if everything was okay.

Until I started going numb. Literally. Over a period of days, I felt like I was losing strength in one side of my body. My reflexes were not what I thought they should be. I freaked and went to the doctor, certain she would tell me not to worry and send me on my way.

She didn't. She tested my arm strength, having me squeeze her fingers with each hand, one at a time. She checked my leg strength, having me push up with my knees as she pushed hard against them. She instructed me to stay in the waiting room until further notice. Sitting there for over an hour, alone with my thoughts, trying to calm down, my mind raced. *Why won't she let me leave? What is going on?* I had been certain this whole thing was in my head and had gone to the doctor for confirmation. Whenever I got sick, Danny called me a hypochondriac.

My doctor, however, didn't think I was making this up. She kept me under observation and, late in the afternoon, sent me across town to a neurologist, who told me they were afraid I'd had a stroke. I was only twenty-four, but I was on the pill, so it was possible.

They couldn't explain the failing of half my body any other way. The neurologist ordered as many tests as he could but didn't find anything conclusive. Telling me to take it easy, he scheduled me for an MRI a few days later and sent me home to rest.

It was a nerve-racking few days. I spent most of the time in bed, trying not to be consumed with fear. Robbie and my friends from work visited. Will was barely around. My mother sent me a book to keep me busy: Jill Ireland's *Life Wish*, the story of her battle with cancer. Lying in bed reading, thinking that I, too, had a life wish, my mind kept jumping to the worst possible outcomes. *What if I really did have a stroke? What if something is wrong?*

I remembered the times I had done coke—too much coke—with Will. He had a love of the drug, and while my own cravings for it had not returned, I went along. Even with the hours I spent in church basements complaining of his alcohol and drug use, I did lines with Will to keep us closer. I also continued my destructive pattern of matching the consumption of those around me, and the last few times we'd done coke, on his birthday and then on New Year's Eve, I'd snorted so much that I went to bed feeling my heart hammering in my chest, afraid I would die. I was terrified the coke had affected my brain and caused a stroke.

It turned out my fears were unfounded. The MRI results were negative, and the doctors concluded that I had some sort of viral infection in my nervous system. I was okay this time, but I was also aware that my body was desperate to get my attention. It was trying to tell me something it needed me to hear. I could not go on like this. The obsession, the lack of sleep, the fighting, the verbal abuse—these were taking their toll. I learned one other important thing through this experience: I wanted to live, and I wanted to be okay.

Things with Will continued to get worse and to get more bizarre. He wouldn't sleep with me. Maybe that was what I wanted, a life with someone who didn't want to have sex. It allowed me to pretend that my old demons from the Church were gone, while it ate away at my self-esteem. Especially when he talked to me of his sexual escapades with other women.

After weeks of no sex, not sure what to do, I'd try to bring up the subject. "Will, we need to talk."

"What sweetie?" His reply was innocent and dismissive.

"You know what." I'd fight not to get upset. "It feels like you don't love me..."

"You know I love you."

"No, I don't. When you don't want to have sex with me, I don't."

"Lisa, let's not go there," he'd snap. "We've talked about this before. Yeah, you're a little overweight—but it's got nothing to do with you."

"It's not right." The crying would start. "Especially since we're getting married."

He'd glare at me. "When *are* we getting married? You keep putting off the wedding, and I don't know that you'll go through with it."

With this we'd be off on a tangential argument, and he'd be off the hook, but I always brought it back. I wanted him to want me. I wanted to feel wanted. I never got the answer I craved. His final solution was that I should find someone else.

"Have an affair. Find someone who thinks you're hot. It'll be fine. I'll understand, and you can have fun."

He said this to me so often that I began to think it was an okay idea.

I called Dean, someone who used to work for me, who I knew had a crush on me. Our attraction was mutual, immediate, and extreme. I started seeing him, sneaking off while Will was working. At first guilt consumed me. We fooled around and I kept my shoes on as some sort of weird protection, as if that made the situation less shameful. Soon I got over that and began to enjoy myself. Except I wished Dean was Will, that I was with the man I planned to marry.

The absurdity of the situation hit a peak in the spring. I spent Friday night with Dean and picked Will up at work after his shift. We went out drinking and went home fighting. In the morning I met Julie for wedding dress shopping at Saks Fifth Avenue. As we rode the escalator to the bridal floor, I talked about Dean, with whom I'd been the night before.

"Maybe you should see a therapist or something, someone to talk to," Julie responded.

"Nah, I'm okay," I answered. "It's fine. Marriage is supposed to be tough."

Julie shook her head. "Not before it starts. I don't think it's supposed to be tough, this tough, before it starts."

It got tougher. Our fights worsened, and with my lack of sleep and the chaos in my life, I became more and more lost. Still, I was determined to go through with my marriage, reasoning my way through (and into) it. *I can do this. I can marry him and be okay. I know how to detach and take care of myself. I'll be fine. It'll be fine.*

Only it wasn't fine. I attended as many support-group meetings as possible and cried my way through most of them. I recounted my stories of his abuse and cruel treatment: how he wouldn't let me sleep, how he never came home, how he insulted me whenever he could.

I was at a lunchtime meeting at St. Patrick's Cathedral. It was close to my office, and I found refuge there many a noontime in one of the small meeting rooms downstairs. I again shared my story of life with Will, then sat and listened, sniffling and gathering up my strength to head back to work.

When the meeting ended, a man approached me from the other side of the room. I'd seen him before but didn't know him. "I heard what you said and wanted to share one thing with you." He paused. "There are no victims, only volunteers." He gave me a hug, turned, and walked away.

Somehow, I heard what he said. I really heard it. I'm not sure why or how, but something kicked in—my steel rod backbone, by guardian angel(s)—and it became apparent that I had options. While I could spend the rest of my life with Will and survive, it wasn't my only choice. I didn't have to stay with him to prove I was tough enough. I no longer had to suffer or pay indemnity to prove anything. I had allowed myself, once again, to be influenced and controlled by something—or someone or my false beliefs—but I didn't have to. I didn't have to be a strong warrior. I didn't have to withstand everything. I was only twenty-four. I could opt out.

My involvement in the support group gave me many different things. It gave me a way to believe in God again—or some sort of higher power or spirituality. Since leaving the Church I hadn't been able to contemplate God without drowning in my horror at having let Him down. The group's insistence of sobriety based on belief in a power greater than oneself, as well as the beginnings of self-love and acceptance I found there, allowed me to ease the concept of God back into my life. It was soothing to have a sense of spirituality and wonder in the world.

The support group also gave me the confidence to stand up to Danny. I asked him to stop calling me "slut." Each time I heard that word from him I couldn't help but flash back to Father's decree against me. To the shame I felt back then for being bad, even though I didn't know what I had done that was sinful. To the shame I still felt at times. Danny seemed to take great pleasure in saying it though. He had a small smile on his face when he did.

I practiced with fellow group members and had a script written out for the phone call. I was scared of his reaction. "Danny," I began, "I love you, and it hurts when you call me 'slut.' I'm your daughter. It's not okay with me that you do that."

"But it's a term of endearment."

"Please stop," was all I could say.

I got off the phone with Danny and got on the phone with a support-group friend. "Can 'slut' ever be a term of endearment?" I asked.

"No," she responded. "Never. Not ever. Especially not toward your daughter."

Danny never called me "slut" again.

I decided to leave Will. One Friday night when he got home from work, I told him I was moving out. I had been warned not to give him too much notice and to have a phone nearby in case he got violent. I explained to him that the next morning Robbie and some of my work friends would show up to help me and that I was going to Robbie's to figure out what to do. Will yelled. He pulled the phone cord out of the wall. He went out to drink.

He came back late that night and slept on the couch. In the morning he was civil yet distant. "Goodbye," he said as he left early, hungover and reeking of alcohol. I had no idea where he was going and couldn't ask. I knew I had to do what I was doing, but the arguments inside me were loud. *I love him. I need him. I'm quitting and giving up. I'm weak. This isn't okay.* It required all my strength to keep going.

I took the subway down to the car rental place only to find that even though I had reserved a van, there were none to be had. At a loss, I called my boss, Ken, who was coming to my apartment in an hour to help me move. "Ken," I stammered on the pay phone. "Ken, they have no vans. What do I do?"

"What?"

"They have no vans. They're out of vans. What do I do?"

"Get a car, Lisa," he calmly replied. "Just get a car."

I got a car and headed back uptown to my apartment. Soon everyone showed up to get me out of there. They all but picked me up and moved me. I was useless, huddled in a corner. My friends took turns selecting objects dropped randomly around the apartment, asking, "Lisa is this yours? Is this coming?" As I nodded yes or no, trying to focus on what was going on, my things made their way down the stairs and into the car or ended up in a pile on the table. I sat watching, stunned and unable to help.

Within a few hours, most of what I had was packed. I turned for one last look, one last chance to hold on to Will and our life together. I walked down the stairs to find a way back to me and to start anew.

in-between

"There is no such thing as a problem
without a gift for you in its hands."
—Richard Bach

"Sometimes I go about pitying myself, and
all the while I am being carried across
the sky by beautiful clouds."
—Ojibway saying

22 · choosing true love

After breaking up with Will in May, I moved in with Robbie for about three months. He and I had gotten even closer over the years. He left the Church after his senior year of college. I may have had CARP at Cornell, but Robbie had real live Moonies whom we knew attending the divinity school on Drew University's tiny campus in New Jersey. His spiritual life was "protected" by their mere presence. He was watched, and he knew it. Once he was free from their scrutiny, he chose to leave—and his decision really was exactly that, not a day-by-day "running away and disappearing," as he's described my process. When I asked him about his decision to leave, his reasons were similar to mine. "I thought about it. A lot," he said. "And decided I just couldn't do it." I guess it just wasn't right for him either, although he was able to figure that out himself, and he actually sat down with Mother and told her he was leaving. I still haven't done that.

Robbie and I tried to make sense of all we'd been through. He had been the constant in my childhood and became even more of a best friend in my adulthood. It was great to spend so much time with him. I relished letting him take care of me and cook me dinner.

His job as a computer programmer was three blocks from mine, and we walked to work together in the morning. I would insist we take specific streets and cross at certain intersections—I needed something to control—and he put up with me, teasing me but allowing my quirks. To this day, my refusal to walk down Twenty-Fourth Street is one of his favorite things to rag on me about. And rightly so.

At the end of the summer, I tired of sleeping on the futon in his living room and found my own apartment, a small studio back in the East Village on Fifth Street between Avenues A and B. (When directing people to my apartment I used to say "right between the two abandoned, burned-out buildings.") For the first time, I lived on my own—and loved it.

I started to rebuild myself—physically, emotionally, and spiritually—and rededicated myself to my job. I worked at a small division of Grey Advertising, helping to run the ABC-TV account, and adored what I did, savoring the fact that I got paid to have so much fun. I revived my discarded friendships. No one was too young and immature now.

At the same time, I threw myself into my church basement support groups. Once I started talking I couldn't stop. It's as if I'd opened a spigot to dump out a bottomless pit of gunk inside me. "Garbage in. Garbage out," someone explained. I shared endlessly about my tortured upbringing, the experiences and resulting scars that made me who I was. My mother leaving. The Church. Danny. The drugs. The drinking. My lack of self-esteem.

I let my place in the rooms, as was the saying in meetings, define me and began to change my life by changing my choices, by learning to believe that I was worth more and deserved better. I learned to choose thoughts and behaviors that were gentle and loving. To choose people who were gentle and loving. That's when I started dating Bruce—in the summer of 1989—someone I would never have dated before.

Bruce was tall, taller than any guy I'd ever dated. I'd always sworn I wouldn't go out with someone who had to bend down so that I could kiss him. But I did. He was handsome, with laughing, bright blue eyes. And he was nice. So nice, in fact, that when I was first introduced to him by Pete right after college, I would have nothing to do with him. It took me four years to go out with him. He was not my type.

Bruce was too normal, too straight. Not someone who would supposedly love me but be involved with someone else. Not dressed in black—his leather jacket was brown, and he wore a gold chain that his parents had given him. Not an alcoholic brooding alone at the end of the bar. Not an alcoholic at all—although in the beginning of our relationship, if he'd have even one Scotch, I'd tense up. After one of our first dates, he called to thank me and tell me what a wonderful time he'd had with me. I told him I needed a break soon after that. He was too nice.

I started seeing him again because I enjoyed being with him. I was learning to live "one day at a time." I took our budding relationship "one date at a time," and each date was fun. Bruce would bring me flowers. Big, ornate, formal flowers. Not ones I would have chosen myself; I'm more of a wildflower kind of person. To this day we joke as he tells me I don't like the best flowers. He brought me flowers nonetheless. And he went out of his way to make me laugh. I had never been with someone who treated me with such appreciation and kindness. I hadn't known that something—someone—that wonderful existed.

I dipped myself into this relationship one toe at a time, rather than diving in headfirst as I had in the past. I began to open up a bit more and let myself love him—and him love me. I held back my story at first. I'm proud that we had dated on and off for a few months, and he referred to me as mysterious. "Tell me," Bruce said over dinner one night as we celebrated his new job, "tell me something easy, and more about you. Like...did your mother ever remarry?" I loved that I hadn't divulged everything all at once.

I began to share my demons and pain and was certain I'd scare him away when he saw how damaged I was, but Bruce stuck around. I stayed immersed in the support groups and dove into therapy—pulling apart my past and trying to relearn who I was, develop new truths, and incorporate new coping skills—so that I could feel healthier and could continue to show up in this thriving partnership. Nearly every man I'd been involved with had been unavailable or mean or both, or the relationship had been tormented by confusion and anguish. This new relationship was a constant stream of mutual exploration and enjoyment, a slow deepening of mutual love and respect.

I met his family—a normal Jewish suburban family from New Jersey. He met mine—anything but. We got closer and closer and spent more and more time together, counting our nights apart, which soon became fewer than our nights together. I learned to trust and discovered how to be with someone in a caring, committed way. I began to see more good in myself and in life. Or, perhaps, I'd already learned to see more good in myself and in life, which is why I could date him in the first place.

We moved in together—first into an apartment in Queens that he had shared with Pete, and then into a co-op in Larchmont, a bedroom suburb in Westchester County about twenty-five miles north of Manhattan. We talked about getting married; we fought about getting married; we even looked at rings. I knew that for him, I had to wait for him to ask me, and he was at times hesitant because of what he saw as my demons.

One warm spring Sunday evening in 1992 Bruce asked me to walk into town with him for dinner. At that point I was enrolled in an executive MBA program at Columbia University. My time was spent studying, but he insisted, and I gave in. As we rounded the corner to pass the Larchmont movie theater, he said, "I wonder if *Basic Instinct* is still playing."

I looked up at the marquee to check the title of the movie and saw big black letters across a white background spelling out "LISA WILL YOU MARRY ME BRUCE." I read it, but it didn't sink in. *What a weird name for a movie! That's so strange. Those are our names.*

When I realized the marquee was intended for me, I said yes. Well, technically I managed to nod my head, dumbstruck.

Over the years we've had our tough times and our misunderstandings. Bruce has traits that drive me crazy. I know some of my reactions because of my past drive him crazy. I'm sure other things do as well. But it is functional. It is good. We've learned to put up with each other's quirks and have a relationship that works, even if it takes effort. That is, as Bruce says, NBB—Nothing But Bliss. He became the partner on my journey, on my path to happiness.

But in order to truly be happy I had to find the strength to come to terms with, or possibly repair, my most fundamental relationships— with my mother and father. Could I?

23 · scars

I was sitting in a hot tub with Abby, Susan, Linda and Gemma, the warm water frothing and swirling around us, listening as they discussed sex with their husbands. I froze. The thought of sex terrified me at times, and that embarrassed me.

"Lisa, you're awfully quiet," Linda said.

"Uh," I stammered. "Well. I don't know."

"What?" she continued.

"My therapist thinks I was sexually abused," I spit out, looking down at the bubbling water, wanting only to slink away.

They stared at me, disbelief and concern etched on their faces. "Wow," a few said.

"Do you want to talk about it?" Susan asked.

"No. Sorry, but no, I don't." I sank farther into the tub.

I learned on my journey through self-help programs that I had experienced covert abuse. Too much had happened to me and around me, and much of it had been off-kilter. My relationships with Brian, with Reggie, and perhaps with many of the brothers in the Church who were much older were inappropriate, though I didn't know it at the time. So, too, was my contact with my mother's boyfriends, some of whom, like Larry, petrified me. And then of course there was Danny's open sexuality; the way he loved to discuss my sexuality and virginity—or lack thereof—in front of me; the drugs and alcohol that flowed through the apartment; Danny's friend Tony who asked to buy me, to take me home with him. These things I could recognize and admit—and also discredit as not causing me any real harm. They were no big deal, a classic "*Whatever.*" What haunted me was that there might be something else, some actual sexual abuse that I refused to remember.

Sometimes I was filled with such guilt and shame that I thought I'd rather die. That I deserved to die. There were times I was consumed with the need to fight and scream and push someone away, to defend myself at all costs. I was in a loving marriage, with a husband who adored me, and still I had voices in my head. *Slut!* they yelled, echoing Danny's term of endearment. I hated being reminded of that. *Scum!* Or no words at all, just a sense of being wrong, tainted, repulsive... sinful.

As I became more and more in tune to my reactions and responses, I noticed one that stretched further into my life. When someone came at me quickly, especially toward my face, my visceral reaction was uncontrollable. I was filled with the irrepressible necessity to yell and fight back. To swing my arms madly, while jumping away. To protect myself.

Even my young son was aware of this. He knew that if he flew his hand, his arm, or anything within five inches of my face, I would most likely scream, and most likely at him. I was out of control.

Then there was the retching. At odd times I'd suddenly convulse, losing sense of where and who I was. My body would shake and spasm. It felt like I had dry heaves, like I was trying to vomit something up even though there was nothing there. It always passed. Bruce would hold me and call me back to the present, and we'd try to find a way to laugh about it, to joke and let it pull us closer together rather than further apart.

Over the years I have come to accept these reactions as scars of the traumas of my past. I may never know what happened to me or if anything really did. But by letting my physical responses be okay—by trusting myself, believing in myself, and allowing that this is where I am—I've freed myself in many ways, taking away their power to limit and rule my life.

It makes it okay that I sometimes have challenges. It makes it okay that I have to tell my seven-year-old not to get too close to my face or I will yell for no apparent, explicable, rational reason. It makes it okay that I occasionally retch.

I had learned some truly nasty things about love, intimacy, and trust. Things that I no longer believe are true. I've now chosen to believe in goodness and in compassion and in god with a small *g*—with an intentionally lowercased *g*, to differentiate the god I know and believe in now from the God with a capital *G* with whom I was raised, who rules and judges, decrees and demands. My god with a lowercased *g* is love, life, and goodness and flows in me and through me. God with a capital *G* has too many hang-ups, or causes too many hang-ups, for me to allow deep in my heart.

I've also come to realize that, in some ways, all that happened to me—all I know and those things I don't yet know and may never know—has given me good as well. Or at least the ability to appreciate good. Perhaps more than I would have if it hadn't happened.

I was in the car one morning a few years ago, driving with Bruce on the way back from a night out in New York City with Pete, Adam, Georgi (another friend of ours from high school), and their significant others. (Yes, I'm still friends with Adam.) I turned to Bruce as he drove and said, "Don't you sometimes just look at your life in awe and stop and realize how amazing it is and how lucky you are?"

"No," he replied.

I didn't take that personally. I still don't. But it made me realize that I'm glad for my appreciation of life, even if it came as a result of having gone through some things I wish I hadn't. I now think that all I went through, and the work I've done on myself to recover from it, prepared me to be even more whole and happy and better able to live my life, thrive in my marriage, parent my children, and love.

But I couldn't explain any of this to my roommates that day. That day in the hot tub I was ashamed of where, how, and who I was.

24 · reconciliation

I liken my path with both my parents, and especially my mother, to the SARAH process for dealing with loss or death. As people grieve, they pass through five distinct, predictable stages: Shock, Anger, Rejection, Acceptance, and Hope, or what I like to call "Hello, World!" I shifted among these, back and forth and sideways at times, as I yearned for a better, other way.

Shock—this stage is described as numbness, confusion, or disorientation. The classic joke about the river in Egypt: denial. I lived there for an unbelievably long time. Over the years my mother and I engaged in a dance of getting to re-know and re-love each other on new terms. She had slowly accepted my departure from Principle and gradually seemed to accept me as I was. I thought I was fine—fine with me and fine with her. But I was wrong. Even though she sometimes went out of her way to earn my love and trust, it was never enough. Never, ever enough. The gaping hole inside of me was too big, but I was floating too obliviously down that Nile to ever realize it.

Anger—that was a long, drawn-out stage. I liked that stage. I found it when I first stepped into the support group for children of alcoholics and wanted to stay there forever. To jump up from my seat at a meeting and throw chairs into the middle of the room, screaming. After never being angry, not ever, at anything, it was deliriously empowering to be filled with righteous anger. Ecstatic anger. It was an internal energy source I had never known, and I loved it. My education in anger had been extreme—I had learned it at Danny's knees—and I apparently had Danny-like rage buried deep inside me that I could detonate, obliterating all in my path. I got in touch with the "my mother can never do enough to make up for what she did" part of me and fed it power drinks and protein bars so it would grow.

The Anger stage hit hard whenever my mother would pull an "I'm your mother, so listen to me" move. Or when she'd equate the rough spots in our relationship to those in normal mother-daughter relationships. Every cell within me screamed in protest; every hair on my body stood up; every ounce of my spirit resisted and armed itself for battle. There was nothing normal about our challenges. They were, in my mind at the time, all her fault. All a direct result of her leaving me.

Yet even with all this anger, I longed for a way to reunite and wanted to have her in my life, so we continued our dance, a slow two steps forward and one step back. She was living for a while in Washington (again), working at the Church's magazine, *The World and I*. Whenever Bruce and I would visit friends in D.C., we'd arrange to meet her for dinner. Sometimes I was able to keep the commitment, and we forced ourselves through awkward evenings. Other times I'd call at the last minute and tell her I couldn't see her.

I wanted a relationship, and yet I was scared of what might happen if I let her get close. I was afraid I would continue to feel left, like I was less than a priority. I always came after so many other things in her life. And so many other people. I'd start to feel more comfortable and safe, and I'd open up and ask something of her or tell her how I felt. It would be too much for her, and she'd disappear. She'd pull back and stop calling me. Each time she did that I felt abandoned yet again.

Then my first child, Sam, was born. Up until then, although I was at times consumed with rage, the concept of my mother leaving me had been a concept. Something I talked endlessly about in therapy and shared incessantly about in meetings. Something I felt but never at the deepest level. When I became a mother, I saw *my* mother through new eyes.

It was a rude awakening. I'd look down at Sam nursing at my breast and wonder: *How could my mom have left me?* As Sam grew and became the focus of my life, the refrain continued to play in my mind. *How could she have left me? How could she have left me?*

How could she have left me?

My mother would come to visit, and it was all I could do to not ask her, "How could you have left?" With Danny I could look to his upbringing—to his uninvolved, addicted, unhappy parents—and see the cause of his limitations. I could therefore, to some extent, understand and forgive him. Besides, *he* had shown up for us. He may have been caustic, undemonstrative, and full of rage, but he took us in. I may not have known that he loved me, but he was there. My mother, on the other hand, said the right things and told me she loved me, but she abandoned us. Again and again she chose the Church and its members over me. She was never around. This was the ultimate mind-bend. Plus I could find no explanations for her behavior, no sickness or dysfunction I could see that harmed her when she was little, no reason why she could or should walk away from her children. Away from me.

It didn't matter that my mother had finally left the Church—something I thought would never happen. I suppose that over the years she'd become less wrapped up in it. I know that she'd broken off her arranged marriage with Phil and, after Sam's birth, moved back north from D.C. to attend graduate school at NYU, studying for a master's degree in early childhood special education. Again she was going to take care of other people's children like she couldn't—and didn't—take care of us. She claimed that the Church lifestyle didn't make sense to her anymore and made seemingly as quick and random a decision to leave it as she had to leave us all those years prior. "I couldn't even be a good Moonie," she would come to say. "I couldn't even do that well."

This led me to Rejection, which also was a great place to stay. When I'd left the Church I'd been tormented, wracked with anguish and shame, doubt and guilt. My mother, on the other hand, was fine when she left. Or, it seemed, unwilling to look deeper to see if she was fine. This pissed me off. It felt like one more way she wasn't taking responsibility for her choices and actions, and their repercussions. I pushed as hard as I could against almost everything about her and refused to see any good. I wanted her to pay, to be punished and tormented for what she'd done. I needed to, for once, come first in her life and resented any time she thought of herself before me, or instead of me, or even in addition to me. No matter what she did, it was never, ever enough.

I spent years in Anger and Rejection and thought I'd never leave. Until I found out what was under the anger. It was pain. Anguish. Torment. While Anger had been empowering and the rage had fueled me, when I touched the agony hidden beneath it I thought I would die. In my search to become more whole I had learned that if it didn't kill me to go through something then it couldn't kill me to feel it, but when I hit the depths of what was inside me, I was certain that that concept was wrong. Entirely wrong. Perhaps it was true for everyone else, but I was the exception to the rule.

It was Thanksgiving 2000, and we were at my sister-in-law's house, about fifteen minutes from where my mother then lived. I had asked her to come to the holiday celebration, to go out of her way to see me. She had said maybe, but she didn't come. Just like Christmas when we were kids, she didn't come. She chose to spend the holiday with a friend who lived on the same street as my sister-in-law, about ten blocks away.

I called her one last time to beg her to join us, but she refused. "It's too hard to spend Thanksgiving with you," she said. "It's always been tough to spend holidays with you. I don't want to go through that."

My insides cracked open. I threw my head into Bruce's lap and sobbed, crying as I had never cried before, the emotional poison that had festered inside me pouring out. My body was heaving and shaking as I gasped for air, wondering if I'd ever be able to stop, to focus, to function. I distanced myself from my mother. I needed protection, to never let myself be hurt like that again.

Years later I asked my mother why it was difficult for her. I had heard her say that all holidays, always, had been too tough. That I'd been too much. She explained that she had meant that holidays with Bruce's family were tough. There were too many people—she was never good at fitting in at large gatherings—and she never felt secure enough with me to be comfortable there. Her refusal was all about *her*.

I stayed in that distance for a long time, and then one day, as if out of nowhere, I began a journey toward Acceptance—of me, of her, of life, of all that had happened—and felt the vice grip inside me lessen and loosen. Again, I'm not sure why or how. I know I worked hard—extremely hard—to purge my pain, heal my wounds, and change my thought patterns. I began to live by the mantras "You're exactly where you're supposed to be" and "Things are okay just as they are." And somehow, the more I accepted, the less there was in my relationship with my mother to painfully, painstakingly accept and the more there was to enjoy. I began to need her less and to need her to be different less. It was a miracle.

This acceptance made room inside my heart and soul for tranquility, peace, and love. When I could calmly breathe and know that all was well—or manageable, or, if I could get no further, that it would pass—the love that would permeate my being was intoxicating, overwhelming, and comforting. Not love from my mother but love that, in my belief, envelops the universe. Love I didn't have to earn and couldn't lose. I became addicted to this love and wanted nothing more than to accept. I somehow no longer needed my mother to apologize, to admit she'd made a mistake, to say she shouldn't have left.

However, one day she did. We'd gone out for a walk and the conversation turned to the past. We'd talked about her leaving before, and she'd said that she was sorry for what had happened. Those apologies never seemed heartfelt. I always sensed a "Yes, but" from her. A reason that explained her thinking. An impression that she would, again, make that same choice. That she thought it was the right thing for her to have done.

"Ma," I started that day as we walked, and then I paused, too nervous to continue. (I started calling her Ma years after I left the Church. The formality of Mother no longer worked for me.) "Ma," I launched in again, summoning my courage and looking as far away from her as I could, although she was right next to me. "Do you ever wish it had been different? Your leaving us and all?"

The silence before her answer was endless. I could hear my heart beating, my breath passing in and out, the leaves crunching beneath our feet. I was keenly aware of where I was at that exact moment and of what I was waiting for, frantically trying not to need her, or even very much want her, to say what I so yearned to hear. "Do you mean do I wish I hadn't left?" she asked.

"Yes," I answered, my breathing so shallow I was nearly holding it in. "Do you ever regret leaving?"

After a pause, she replied. "Yes," she said, so quietly I almost couldn't hear her. "Every day. It may have been what I knew I had to do at the time, but I wish I had been there for you. I missed so much. And I wish I hadn't caused you all that pain."

Hearing that freed me, or at least it freed me to finally, fully liberate myself. I was ready to let it go, to decide to no longer be angry. Instead I filled myself with compassion—for the little girl I was then, for the little girl I could sometimes be now, and for my mother, both then and now. I was ready to choose a life of love, peace, and joy. I walked into Hope.

I opened my arms and heart to embrace hope and was embraced in return. And not just by my mother. If you'll forgive my grandiosity, I exposed myself to All That Is and was caught and held in a caring caress—like during Camel Pose in my yoga practice when I kneel with my thighs perpendicular to the floor and lean my body back toward my heels, opening my chest, heart, and throat to the Universe, my arms out to the side as if I'm flying, trusting that I'll be safe. And I am.

This hope somehow allowed me to heal my relationship with Danny as well. Perhaps feeling more at peace with my mother opened me to finding a better peace with my father. Perhaps I was ready. In some ways there didn't seem to be as much to heal. For whatever reason my cuts and pain from him weren't as deep. And in some ways it was harder. I've come to learn that Danny is a mush of love and softness deep, deep, deep inside him. But the outside is crusty and prickly and, for me, dangerous.

Over the years I've told him that his drinking scares me. (One time he said, "Thank you for your concern" in response.) I have limited the time I've spent with him, I've chosen never to drink around him, and I've done my best to protect my children from his rage (which they've never seen) while welcoming him in as their grandfather.

He has been a much better grandfather than he was a father. Or perhaps he has fathered me through grandfathering my children. When my second child, Max, was born and needed constant care and carrying, Danny came to visit me every week on his one day off—to hold Max so I could sleep. He was the only person to do that.

I've come to believe that he made the choices he made when we were growing up with what he saw as our best interests in mind, even if I would never make those same decisions myself. Even if they were poor parenting choices. I've come to acknowledge that I've gotten good from him—my love of good food, my willingness to open my house to others. I've come to accept him, I suppose.

Which is important and useful, because nearly seven years ago he suffered a stroke. When the doctor at Beth Israel Hospital asked him what had happened, Danny replied, "I partied too much." Too many drugs for too many years brought his brain to an abrupt stop for a few minutes. The stroke left him disabled—he lost sight in his right eye and use of the left side of his body. He uses a cane to walk and is scary to watch, especially after a few drinks. He can't use his left arm at all. The stroke left me as his primary caregiver.

When we realized he could no longer live on his own, Robbie and I moved him to an assisted living facility near Princeton, New Jersey. Now I handle his money and pay his bills. I got him set up on Medicare and Medicaid. I'm the one the facility calls to try to convince him to shower. (He claims that showers are no longer fun— which I get—and not necessary.) I'm the one they called, at quarter to one in the morning, when he set a fire in the facility from smoking in his room. I'm the one he calls when he runs out of Kosciusko mustard, or fruit, or peppercorns, or anything.

After the move I went to see him once or twice a month, kept his refrigerator stocked with food, and sprung him from his self-described jail for decent meals and a martini or a bottle of wine. And I felt guilty that it wasn't enough—enough to lessen his misery and his need. Once I was about to leave his room, to set off on my hour-long drive home to pick up my kids. I bent to kiss him goodbye, once on each cheek, the French way, to honor L'acajou, which he'd owned for nearly twenty years. He looked up at me from his bed, where he spent most of his time. "Sometimes I remember you have someone else to look after," he said. "And sometimes I don't mind." He was talking about his grandchildren.

That's Danny.

But with my newfound hope, I have somehow been able to let the Danny-isms roll off me. To stay in peace and love and compassion. To care for him and to remember that somewhere under his depression and anger—at this point he blames me for moving him into the facility—he cares for me. I've learned to trust that I am safe. And I am.

Hope somehow transformed into a stage of Hello, World! My sense of peace was accompanied by wonder and awe. Albert Einstein once said that you can look at life as if nothing is a miracle or as if everything is a miracle. In this stage nearly everything I saw was miraculous to me, or I found a way to find the miraculousness in nearly everything I saw. And, at times, in everyone around me.

They say that forgiveness is giving up all hope of a different past. This is where I got within Hello World! By walking through these stages as I evolved my relationship with my mother, and then with my father, I discovered a place where I could dwell with no regrets, no intense desire for it to have been different, no need to fix what was broken in me and in my childhood. I discovered a peace, calm, and delight that I never thought possible; learned to believe in magic and miracles; and decided to do my best to give up my ways of thinking—and viewing others—that caused me pain. I determined that I would rather be happy than right (well, *usually...*) and began to live as best I could from a place of compassion and love.

25 · learning to mother

When I got pregnant with Sam in 1995, my therapist was worried. She didn't seem anxious—as I was—about my ability to mother despite my own childhood scars. But because of my anorexia in college and the resulting food and body-image issues, she was concerned about my eating and my ability to gain enough weight to sustain the pregnancy and nourish the baby.

I proved her wrong. I ate for two and put almost fifty additional pounds on my one-hundred-pound body. I pleased myself and my therapist, and then I had Sam.

I gave birth without drugs. I was determined to parent in every best way possible, and I figured a drug-free beginning would be safest. That went well. I also planned to breastfeed. That didn't go as well. Sam did not latch on to my breast, and I was so inexperienced I didn't realize it.

We were doing the best we could, Sam and I, and then came the seven-day checkup back at the maternity ward. The nurses freaked because Sam had not gained enough weight and had in fact been losing weight, going well below birth weight. I saw this as my first failure as a mother. I should have realized how thin Sam was. Just skin and bones. The nurses scolded me, pressuring me to get help right away and to put Sam on a bottle, on the dreaded formula. Bruce asked for the name and number of a lactation consultant. He called from a pay phone as I collapsed against the wall of the hallway, sobbing, certain I was defective as a mother. This was, to me, clearly all my fault.

Over the next few days we had numerous sessions with the lactation consultant, and in desperation I tried to get nutrition and liquid into my dehydrated child. I spent hours struggling to nurse and pumping milk into a container so that we could attach a tube to my breast that dripped milk into Sam's mouth. We saw a pediatrician, who put Sam on an IV for rehydration. Sam never made a sound when the needle was stuck in, but as I put my newborn to my breast for a feeding, I heard nothing but screaming. I screamed inside.

"I quit," I said to Bruce in desperation. He suggested we give it a few more days, just through the weekend. Weeping, I agreed. I was more than willing to continue my crazy schedule of nursing for an hour, sleeping for an hour, pumping for an hour, nursing for an hour, sleeping for an hour, pumping for an hour, and on and on if it was best for Sam.

And then it happened! One minute Sam was licking at the tube, and the next minute nursing had begun. We were through this first hurdle, but I was traumatized.

From there my resolve to keep Sam safe grew—exponentially at times. I couldn't fathom letting Sam out of my sight or my care. I spent the first year and a half with no childcare and a full-time business. I would work during nap times and while Sam played on the floor. I'd take my baby to client meetings, nursing when necessary. I became all work and no play and just like Jack I became a very dull boy. A bitch actually. But I knew I was doing what was necessary.

We became closer and closer, and it became harder and harder for Sam when I left, even for a few minutes. That was okay with me. I was determined to never allow my child to feel abandoned or disregarded. Eventually, though, I realized that for Sam's sake (and mine), I had to pull away. I had to learn not to need Sam to need me so much and not to let myself feel guilty or selfish for doing something just for me. ("Put your own oxygen mask on first" comes to mind.) I worked to lessen my obsession to make things better or different through my parenting, stepping away from my fear of getting everything wrong, my fear of repeating my past.

We had Max almost six years later, and my abandonment issues that had calmed a bit as Sam grew older reemerged. I was, once again, determined to fill all of Max's needs, to leave him wanting for nothing, to never, ever let him feel deserted. I jumped into this second chance at parenthood, even more inspired at the thought of attachment parenting and doing all I could to be available—emotionally and physically—for him at *all* times. It backfired.

My final breakthrough came some years later when Max, then three and a half, was still having trouble sleeping. In desperation I turned to someone I considered a spiritual leader for advice. "He barely sleeps," I shared, "and when he does, he wakes up screaming. He leaps out of bed wailing and runs through the house looking for me. Have I done this?" I asked. "How can I undo it? Is it related to my issues? How do I get over those?"

"You'll be mad at your mother until you're ready not to be," I was told. "You'll be in anguish over what happened until you're ready to let it go. You'll cling to the pain until you no longer think it serves you. And your child? Well, he may or may not get over where he is, but that's got very little to do with you. You need to let go and move on for you."

At the time, I found that to be mystifying. Over time, I found that to be true.

now

"Love yourself first, and everything else
falls into line. You really have to love yourself
to get anything done in this world."
—Lucille Ball

26 · becoming whole

I was in the car with Bruce, our two children in the backseat, winding through the roads of upstate New York, heading home from a weekend away. The four of us had spent the morning apple picking, running from tree to tree to find our favorites, sampling them as we went along. It was one of those glorious, sunny fall days—the fall of 2006 to be precise—when the air is so crisp you can almost taste its freshness. One of those days when there can be no bad.

As we drove, I began to recognize the area. *We're near Barrytown!* I hadn't been there in over twenty-five years.

"Stop," I said to Bruce. "Stop. Turn here."

"Why?"

"We're near Barrytown. I have to go there."

"Are you sure?" For years I had talked about my desire to someday visit a Church property, but I'd never been able to take that step.

"Yes. Yes, I need to see it." I had to see it. I wanted to look at the buildings and walk the grounds. With an urgency that surprised me, I craved reconnecting and remembering, touching what at times felt so distant and foreign.

We followed the signs. My stomach churned. I held my breath, and my heart sped. I could feel myself squirming, unable to sit still, staring out the window. I wanted to pull my gaze from the road, focus only on my hands clasping and unclasping in my lap, and tell Bruce to turn the car around and drive away. We went around a bend and drove up to the entrance gate of what is now the Church's seminary. "Oh my God," I whispered as we sat there. Bruce said nothing.

A memory. Robbie and I running through the passages of the

building with True Children. Another flash. Eating Big Macs and kimchi with Hyo Jin and In Jin in the special dining room, with Father at the head of the table. And another: the Japanese sisters who had trouble pronouncing my name showing me shark cartilage and octopus tentacles while they cooked.

I sat in the car as this washed over me. The people, the beliefs, the friendships, and the Church teachings that had been seared on my brain—all that had been my life and had been lost to me—came back in a rush.

I began to cry. The pain I'd felt before the Church, in the Church, and especially in leaving the Church, welled up inside me. At the same time, I was overcome with appreciation and amazement that it was no longer my life.

"Are you ready to go?" Bruce asked after a few more minutes.

"Yeah." I paused, taking one last look. "We can go."

We drove down the road as tears streamed down my face. Oblivious, my kids chattered away. They, like so many people around me today, are unaware of my past. No one who meets me now has any idea how convoluted and bizarre my life was growing up. When they hear my story, their disbelief is palpable.

Years ago a therapist advised me to integrate my past into my present. We were talking about my time in the Church, and she looked at me and said, "You'll never heal if you don't incorporate that part of you into the whole of you."

I looked back at her in disbelief. "Never," I declared. My life since leaving the Church and up until that point had been defined by distancing myself as much as possible, but sitting at the Barrytown guard booth, it felt as if something inside me cracked open and that part of me that had seemed far away and perhaps nonexistent was once again real.

Three years after seeing Barrytown I decided to reach out to Hugh. He was easy to find. A Google search and call to directory assistance was all it took. I sat with his phone number for months.

When I finally had the guts to call, I still didn't have the guts to call. His son answered (he had a grown son!), and when I explained that I was a friend from a long time ago, he shared Hugh's cell number with me. I dialed, fearing that if I didn't call then, I never would.

With my heart pounding, I waited as the phone rang and rang. He answered. "Hello?" His mild English accent had grown milder over the years.

"Hugh?"

"Yes. Who is this?"

"Hugh, it's Lisa," I murmured.

"What?"

"Lisa. It's Lisa. Lisa Kohn."

"Oh my God." Then silence.

I filled the silence. "I got your number from one of your kids. So, how are you?"

"Lisa, wow…"

"So, how are you?" I asked again. "How have you been? It's been a while."

"Yeah it has. Lisa, wow. I can't believe you called."

We spoke for a few more minutes. My heart continued racing, and my palms were sweaty through the entire conversation. It felt strange to talk with him after so many years. I needed to get off the phone, to digest what we'd said. To process that I'd called him at all. I shared my phone numbers and email, promised to get in touch with him when I was next in New York, and hung up, eager to quell the queasiness in my stomach.

I sat, taking in the gravity of what I'd done. Hugh's last words rang over and over in my mind. "I'm so glad you called, Lisa. It's so good to talk with you, and it's been so long. I can't wait to see you."

The next time I was heading into the city I sent Hugh an email, letting him know I'd be there. Would he like to get together for a cup of coffee? His reply shook me. "In Jin wants to see you."

I wasn't prepared for that. I had decided to contact *him,* to reconnect with *him.* He had meant so much to me, and I was determined to begin to own all that had happened to and around me, to claim what was mine. Seeing Hugh was the first step. But I wasn't ready to see In Jin. "Really?" was my response. "Really?"

"Oh yes," came his email. "I told her I spoke with you, that you were coming up to New York. She wants to see you."

All I could answer was, "Okay." With that my fate was sealed.

I finished my client business and headed over to the New Yorker. Hugh not only still lived there, but he worked at the Manhattan Center, reporting directly to In Jin, who now ran the Center and the New York Church movement.

With shaking hands I reached for my cell phone to let him know I was in the Manhattan Center lobby, where we were to meet. Part of me questioned what I was doing, and part of me was the most certain I'd ever been.

"Great," he answered, when my call came through. "Wait where you are. No, go outside and up the block to the parking garage. I'll meet you there. She's on her way in from Boston and wants to see you."

"She wants to see me? She knows I'm here?"

"Oh, of course she does, silly."

I followed his instructions. I had listened to Hugh for so many years, doing whatever he told me to do, that I never questioned him for a second. I entered the parking garage and saw him. He'd aged. We'd both aged. He rushed forward and gave me the biggest hug. I returned it, awash in a jumble of emotions—glad to see him, bizarre to see him, and mildly nauseated that In Jin was on her way. I hadn't seen her since we were teenagers, since I'd been forbidden to be around her. What would I say? How should I act?

Within minutes she pulled up in her car, hopped out, gave Hugh her bag, and saw me. "Hey," I said, self-conscious and somehow shy. "It's been forever."

In Jin's smile was huge. "Lisa!"

We awkwardly hugged hello. We had never hugged when we were kids.

I pulled back from her and took a good look. "Wow! It's great to see you. You look great!"

"So do you. Let's go upstairs." She turned and walked into the building. As always, I followed.

We worked our way into the Manhattan Center and through the hallways that connected with the New Yorker. It was familiar—like coming home—and yet unknown. It even smelled the same. Was I imagining that? The wallpaper along the hallways looked even more faded. The carpet more frayed. Had the New Yorker always been this run-down and I'd never noticed, enamored and perhaps brainwashed, or had it, like the rest of us, aged? I could feel myself vacillating between the kid I had been—reverent, supplicant, in awe—and the adult I was now, with years of support groups and therapy behind me. I wasn't sure which was dominant. I hoped it was the adult.

We ended up in the small suite of unassuming rooms she shared with her husband, Se Jun, someone I had also known when I was a kid. He had been Hyo Jin's best friend. The tension in the air was palpable as Se Jun and I were reintroduced. I thought of one of the last times I had seen him, when we'd been at Belvedere for a holiday. It must have been God's Day, because there was snow on the ground and the little pond behind the artist's cottage (one of the small buildings on the estate) was frozen. I either imagined or felt from him the judgment and critical eye I feared—the "Why did you leave, and why are you here now?" unspoken question. In Jin and I caught up for a few minutes before Se Jun announced that she had work to do and I had to go.

I followed Hugh—as I always had—back out of the suite and around the twisting halls of the New Yorker, looking for exact floors, rooms, and hallways I recognized. We ended up at a nearby coffee shop and caught up after all the years—his marriage, his kids, his life; my marriage, my kids, my life. My heart warmed as I felt joy and acceptance from him. There was no judgment, no questions, no lectures. Only rejoicing at having me back.

I realized the time, gave him a quick hug, and ran for my train. I promised to be in touch again, to let him know when I was coming to the city so that we could have more time together. I needed space, to step back into my reality and life that were separate from what it had been (and what it would have been if I had stayed). In my brief time at the New Yorker I had seen names of members I recognized and full-grown adults who had been little kids when I was last around. It was a peculiar combination of deeply unsettling and unbelievably healing.

I reached out to Hugh again before my next trip back to New York. His reply shook me further. "I'd love to see you," he wrote, "but In Jin made me promise that she could have time with you this visit. She wants you to meet her for dinner."

"Tell her I said yes." There was no question in my mind I was now on a full-blown journey. A chance to see how deep I could dig and how much I could investigate, both inside of me and out.

We sat at the little table set in a corner of her suite and ordered in from the local diner. As the night wore on, we talked about things I never thought we would. She apologized, all these years later, for how we were torn apart and that there was nothing either of us could do about it. She told me stories of all that had happened to her in the over thirty years since we'd seen each other, and of her plans for the Church and how she was trying to transform things to make it better, easier to be in, and kinder to families and children.

I told her stories of my childhood, stories of my life with Danny and things that happened outside the Church. In all our years of friendship, I never shared any of these; I was embarrassed back then and didn't want anyone to know. I explained how and why I left— left her, left the Church, left her father the Messiah—and all that I'd been through since.

If anyone had ever suggested that I would have that conversation with In Jin, I would have told them they were insane. There was no way I was ever going to share the story of my leaving—of my falling, of my choosing not to follow Father—with anyone in the Church, especially her, Father's daughter. But I did. When I finished, In Jin looked at me with tears in her eyes. "Wow," she said. "I'm so glad you're here. I had no idea."

"I know," I answered. "I never told you. I never wanted anyone to know."

"Wow," she said again. "I'm so sorry all that happened. I don't care if you're Jewish now, or Hare Krishna, or whatever. You're Lisa, my best friend, my true friend. I'm so glad to have you back."

We talked about how in some ways our lives ended up alike. She, as a Church leader and pastor, gave motivational speeches for a living and taught others her best practices for a better life. I, a coach and leadership consultant, did as well. She raised her kids with an awareness of wine and a leniency she never had so that they would feel less need to rebel. I did the same. We reminisced and remembered funny stories and felt like friends again, only I was now aware that we were equals. For the first time I welcomed, treated, and viewed In Jin as a peer. I was myself with her and in awe that I was in the place I was.

I left her room that evening feeling calmer, more vulnerable, and more complete than I could have imagined. Before departing, we promised to keep in touch, and she invited me to come hear her speak at a Sunday service. I said yes.

27 · reunion

I was out one Friday evening in November 2009 with Abby, Susan, Linda, and Gemma. Gemma, who now lived in Minnesota, had come east for business and, as always, we used it as an excuse to get together.

I looked around the table at the four women who had known me nearly thirty years. With our fruit-flavored margaritas and beers in front of us, guacamole on the table, and the family-like acceptance and love that had grown over the many years since college enveloping me, I decided to break my news. I could no longer hold it in. I picked up my Corona and took a large, bracing sip.

"Guess what I'm doing Sunday?"

"What?" they asked, stopping their various conversations and looking over at me.

"I'm going to services at the Church. The Unification Church."

Silence. A long silence. Finally the chorus of "Wows!" "Reallys!" and "Whys?" erupted around me.

The "Whys" surprised me. I'd forgotten that they might not understand. By the time I'd gotten close to most of them, near the end of college, the Church was no longer my life. They didn't know that part of me and might not appreciate my need to unearth it so that the bogeymen could be chased away. I looked around at all of them and smiled. "It's time," I said. "It's time to look at it and remember. To face it."

"Wow!" a few of them repeated. They wished me luck and asked me to let them know how it went. I took another sip of my beer and relished that I was doing this.

The next night I happened to be out again, only this time included in the crowd were Pete and Georgi. People who knew me when I was in the Church and who had seen me through leaving. I told them of my plans for the following morning.

"Rock on, rock star!" Pete said.

"Amazing," Georgi said with a gasp and a huge smile. She then asked if I wanted her to come along for support. I didn't.

I knew the services were in one of the ballrooms at the Manhattan Center. I knew In Jin would be speaking, as she was now the pastor of the New York Church. I knew Hugh would be playing in the band onstage. I knew Bruce was coming with me. That's all I knew.

I woke on Sunday with excitement, a bit nauseated and uneasy. In all our years together, as wonderful as they'd been, Bruce had kept his distance from the Church and its teachings. When he'd first learned my stories, and after we decided to get married, he'd been worried that I might one day leave as my mother had. Perhaps the Church threatened him, but he'd never wanted to hear about it. It was amazing that he was joining me, and also somewhat scary. I was glad to have him with me and anxious that he'd freak out. I wanted to share this with him but wondered if I'd be best off alone to deal with whatever came up. I was about to see the Church worship. I had the potential to run into people who knew me "when." Who knew me as a child, as a member. Who knew I failed, and left, and fell. Who might judge me. What if I couldn't handle the judgment?

In Jin had asked me to let her know when we got close. Standing on the corner of Thirty-Fourth Street and Eighth Avenue, the cars passing by, people walking down the street as if it was a day like any other, I called her. I held Bruce's hand and wondered what the morning would hold for us, for me. "Oh great," was her reply. "My hubby greets people at the door. He'll show you where to sit."

We entered the building and walked up the familiar stairs into the large lobby. It was dilapidated, paint peeling, rug fraying. *Was it always like this and I never noticed? Or is it old age?* Suddenly a group of grinning teenagers surrounded us, coming close and beaming deep connection and love. "Welcome to Lovin' Life Ministries," they announced, smiles on their faces. I had forgotten about the Moonie smile, the enveloping welcomes in the Church. We piled into the elevator with a large group of other worshippers.

I could feel my heart beating and glanced up to see Bruce looking at me through the throng of strangers. Strangers, but not quite. These were Church members, of many races and ages. That felt familiar, but so far I hadn't seen anyone I knew.

As we moved with the crowd out of the elevator and poured into the large ballroom, I looked around, taking in the room, the stage, the art on the walls. All of it. Memories rushed at me— of Church holidays and events. Sitting with In Jin and Un Jin. Sunburst performing. Following Hugh everywhere. More smiling greeters surrounded us. "Welcome to Lovin' Life Ministries," they proclaimed. "Great to see you!" I smiled back. My heart recognized and embraced the unconditional love they were expressing—the "love-bombing"—the welcome to all brothers and sisters of God (and especially to anyone who wasn't yet a member, which presented a chance to recruit and save another person). The realization of how intoxicating and comforting this must have been when I was young crept up my body like a flush of embarrassment, warming me and making me uncomfortable at the same time.

I saw Se Jun across the crowd and walked up to him, not sure if he was glad I was there. I didn't know what he thought of my reawakened friendship with In Jin. I awkwardly introduced him to Bruce and asked him where we should sit. "Take a seat in the front row," he answered. "That's where our family sits and where In Jin wants you to be."

We worked our way up front and took our seats. The room was familiar; I felt at home. And also disconcerting. I felt ill at ease. I alternated between looking around the crowd to see if there was anyone I recognized or knew and sinking farther into my chair hoping to run into no one.

Bruce sat next to me, taking in the surroundings and the people. "Brother, great to see you!" I noticed a large man in African dress approaching him. "Stand up and give us a hug!" Bruce had no choice but to comply. He shot me a look, letting me know how weird he thought this person was.

It was time for the band to come on. I saw Hugh take the stage, along with other musicians and singers. I hadn't seen or heard him play in years. So many years. *They're all in jeans, not conservatively dressed. Their hair is long, not cropped short. They look normal and cool.* It was strange.

The band and chorus broke into song: holy songs, Church songs. The lyrics appeared on two large screens hanging on either side of the stage, but I didn't need to read along. To my amazement I remembered them—the tune, the words, the way they used to make me feel.

The crowd sang the words to "Song of the Banquet"

Hushed we stand in awe before you, ready now to give our pledge,
To attend and serve completely with an unchanging eternal love.
Glorious King, mighty God, fill with your blessed grace,
This dearest one; holy banquet of our love.
Hallelujah, Glorious Day of Joy!

Overflowing with your love as dawn proclaims eternal life,
Earth and Heaven come surround the glorious Parents
*   of mankind,*
Gather around, sing the song, fragrant the love of the Lord;
Tell all the world, Spring has come eternally!
Hallelujah, Glorious Day of Joy!

I sang the words, heard the tune, and felt the surety and power I had known in the Church course through me again.

The crowd sang "Day of Glory," and I felt the strength and conviction that had fueled me all those years ago.

Sunrise and morning comes, we rise up in its light,
Spread forth the word of good, giving all your strength.

All holy children come, new days have dawned at last,
March forward one and all, quickly now unite.

"March forward one and all, quickly now unite," reverberated inside my brain. *How could I not have felt myself chosen and determined to do all I could for God?* I had a greater understanding of what my life had been and why the Church had been so all encompassing.

The band broke into other songs—popular songs. I listened to them play "What a Wonderful World" and "Bridge Over Troubled Water." A smile crept onto my face. What a different Church this was from the one I experienced. Regular songs, rock music, musicians in jeans and long hair. What a changed Church In Jin was creating. How much easier it must be to be a member and grow up in it now. How much more assimilated and accepting.

In Jin walked up to the pulpit to speak, and the crowd went wild. They adored her, the daughter of the Messiah. I listened, watching her, taking it in. Here was my childhood friend, all grown up, leading a religious movement. I saw resemblances to her father but also her own approach and manner. Doing my best to pay attention to what she was sharing, I found myself wholeheartedly agreeing with some points and firmly disagreeing with others. I, too, taught that "happiness is an inside job" and "our life is ours to make through our choices." But I no longer believed in a God who needed me to suffer, who taught me through pain, who wanted me to sacrifice.

I was thrilled to realize that I was content with what I now knew and believed. That I no longer saw Principle as absolute truth. That I didn't have to give up everything and follow it again. It still had an influence over me. It most likely always would. But its absolute hold on me had been broken. I had been pretty certain I'd feel this way, but it was reassuring to know for sure.

After her sermon, the band played more—"Mint Car" and "Everlasting Love." I couldn't believe what I was seeing and hearing. I could feel pieces of my life and mind falling together in a way that made such sense, sense that I had desired for so long. The puzzle of who I had been, who I was, what I'd gone through, what I'd experienced, what I'd chosen—it clicked into place. My mind felt clear, totally clear. My heart felt surer and lighter than it ever had before. The essence of free—appreciating and understanding what had been, what was, and what is: free.

When the service ended Bruce and I got up to say goodbye. Hugh jumped off the stage, grabbed me, and swirled me around and around. He put me down and reached over to grab Bruce's hand to shake it.

"So great to meet you. I'm so glad to meet you!"

"That was wild, Hugh," I said breathlessly, shaking my head. "That was wild."

He looked over at me. "We'll talk. I've got to go break down, but we'll talk."

"Okay. I'll be in touch when I'm back in New York."

I turned to look for In Jin so I could say goodbye. Bruce and I had a train to make to pick up our children, who were staying with my mother. There was a long line of people waiting to speak with her, to shake her hand and feel as if they knew her. I walked to the front, explained to the members guarding the line that I was her guest, and cut in, while apologizing to the woman behind me.

In Jin turned to me. "Lisa, my sweet Lisa."

"Wow. You are amazing. That was amazing."

"Thanks for coming. Where's your hubby?"

I called him over and introduced him. She gave him a hug and then hugged me. "I'm so glad you're here," she said. "I'm so, so glad."

There was a brother taking pictures of her with the guests lined up to meet her. I looked over at him and nudged her to see if we could take a picture together. *I'd love to have one after all these years.* He asked us to smile, and I realized that I recognized him. In Jin saw it on my face. "Lisa, do you remember Jim?"

"Oh yeah," I answered, smiling. He had been one of her bodyguards when we were kids. "That's right."

Jim took the shot, and I gave In Jin one last hug goodbye, grabbed Bruce, and got ready to leave. Jim looked at me, his eyes focusing and then pulling back as thoughts ran through his mind. "Who are you again?" he asked.

"Lisa." He still had a questioning look on his face. "Lisa. Lisa Kohn. Robbie and Lisa—that Lisa."

I watched as shock crept over him. "Lisa? Little Lisa?" he whispered as he raised his hand to about chest height to comment on how young I was when he last saw me.

"Yeah," I answered, smiling. "That's me. It's great to see you again."

With that Bruce and I grabbed our bags and moved toward the elevator and down the stairs, out through the familiarity that echoed around me. We crossed the street and headed to Penn Station to start our journey home. I looked back one last time, taking it all in—the love, the people, the good, the bad, the experiences that gave me me—owning fully and wholly that I had found my way back.

acknowledgements

It's as if the people I have to thank for getting me—and this book —here are too many to count. Or thank. But I will try. To any of you whom I somehow forget to mention, please forgive me.

I have been blessed with innumerable "book fairies" through the years who have kept me going each and every time I was ready to quit. Thank you all. Rebecca Holland, for being one of the first people who believed in me. Holley Bishop, for taking what I had and making it stronger. Paul Golob, for opening your contact list for me and referring me to numerous agents. And all the agents who, while rejecting me, wrote me the kindest, most complimentary rejections that got pasted on my office wall and gave me hope.

David Naggar, for re-friending me and always offering encouragement and suggestions. Laura Nolan, for convincing me to write a memoir. I have been edited—and edited well—a number of times. Thank you Steve Fiffer, Alice Peck, and Lisa Kaitz. Laurie Harper, for knowing that we could make the book better and for doula-ing its birth. Your belief in me and in the book were the push I needed. Daralyse Lyons, for letting me pick you up at the Writer's Conference and becoming my author-friend, confidante, and cheerleader.

Catherine Murdock, your friendship, guidance, love, insight, and endless coffee meetings—there are no words to fully express my gratitude, but I will try. You allowed me to crawl under your wing, and you befriended and mentored me. You taught me to add a few more details and to edit ruthlessly. Thank you from the bottom of my heart.

Naomi Rosenblatt, for seeing something in me and my story and for taking a risk with me. To my team at Worthy Marketing Group

(Jayme Johnson, Patty Brower, Alexis Bierman, and Leslie Brogdon) and my team at Smith Publicity (Courtney Link, Jane Reilly, and Janet Shapiro)—I have never felt so supported. Clearly without all of you, this wouldn't be here.

And that's just the book.

I would not be whole and happy without so many people's unconditional love and acceptance—even when I was tormented and unwittingly took everyone through it with me. (Sorry!) With all my heart, thank you! I love you all.

At Stuy I was held together by: Jill Rathus, Andrea Weisbrot, Debbie Schwartz, Adam Speregen, Peter Braffman, Rich Stark, Steve Newman, Roxana Chemych, John Kim, Roger Nehrer, Abby Jahiel, Stuart Eisenberg, Gemma Flamberg, Georgie Fsadni, Monica Blum, and many, many more dear, dear friends.

During my years at Cornell I was kept from falling too far apart by: Anne Noble, Dave Friedman, Bruce Rubin, and the Birds of Prey (we know we're cool)—Amy Jones, Karen Polk, Lisa Forbes, Linda Scherr, Susan Flood, and Becca Gomez.

To my "local" friends who have read and reread, cheered me on when I was giving up, celebrated every win, and went so far as to name and help design the book—Andrea Perrone, Liz Egg-Krings, Beth Cohen, Sara Bayla, Peg Heldring, Stevie Boulden, and the South Wayne Book Club.

To my New York City Subway Token sisters—You know who you are, and you know how I love you.

To my brothers and sisters who did love me, thank you. To everyone from Born Under the Moon, and every former and BC/Second Gen who have reached out to me and who haven't, thank you for your courage, truth, and sharing.

IJM, YSL, HOC—Finding you all has been a gift. They will never tear us apart again.

To the community I found when I first crawled into the rooms. There are no words. Thank you for showing me a new life.

To Laura V. and Sonja L. who both helped me save myself, my deepest love and gratitude.

To my "moms"—Phyllis Freeman, Jennifer Thompson, Gail

Flanery, Karen Shawn, and Catherine Labeau—your various love and care for me was an anchor.

My first family: Ma and Danny—Thank you. I love you. Robbie—My big brother, best friend, only constant in my childhood, and memory. I lulu. Bobby—Thank you for everything. Jenny, Julie, Lisa, Matt, David (and all)—Thank you for being cousin/siblings. The Kohns and Goldsteins—You are all so cool.

My newer family: Thank you Mom and Dad for loving me as your daughter. Beth and Ronnie (and Lee, Sara, Jules, Ben, Scott, Meredith, Matt...)— I am so lucky. Aunt Sally, Uncle Alvin, Evan, Debbie, Margeaux, Ryan, Royce, Lyndsey, Barbra, John, Michael, and Brian—You are a family that is wonderful to join. Thank you for letting me in.

My CCG family: Robyn McLeod, you are a partner and a best friend. Thank you for your love and support and for thinking I had something to join, always laughing at my jokes, and making our dream come true. Melody Bridgewater and Cheryl Almstrom, without your care, love, and finesse our dream would be stumbling along. Thank you all for giving me a team I am lucky to have and delighted to work with and the chance to do work that I love.

And my forever family: Thank you Bruce for your love, comfort, wisdom, support, humor, insight, and oh-so-many other things. You are my rock and have given me a life I never knew existed. A&F and NBB.

And my kids—Thank you for being my kids. I am the most blessed mom ever. I love you most.

about the author

Lisa Kohn is a writer, teacher, and public speaker who owns a leadership consulting and executive coaching firm. She will always tell you that she is a native New Yorker, but she currently lives in Pennsylvania with her husband and two children, whenever they're around.

You can contact Lisa at **www.lisakohnwrites.com, @lisakohnwrites,** and at **www.chatsworthconsulting.com.**

Lisa Kohn in Fifth Grade

book clubs

Book Club Guide available at www.lisakohnwrites.com.

Author may be available—virtually or in person—to participate in your book club discussion. Contact **events@lisakohnwrites.com**.

CPSIA information can be obtained
at www.ICGtesting.com
Printed in the USA
BVHW03s1129040818
523242BV00003B/15/P